From Conflict
JUSTICE to INTER-ETHNIC MEDIATION

A Reflection on the Possibility of
Ethno-Religious Mediation in Africa

BASIL UGORJI

outskirtspress
DENVER, COLORADO

The opinions expressed in this manuscript are solely the opinions of the author and do not represent the opinions or thoughts of the publisher. The author has represented and warranted full ownership and/or legal right to publish all the materials in this book.

From Cultural Justice to Inter-Ethnic Mediation
A Reflection on the Possibility of Ethno-Religious Mediation in Africa
All Rights Reserved.
Copyright © 2012 Basil Ugorji
v3.0

Cover Photo © 2012 canstock. All rights reserved - used with permission.

This book may not be reproduced, transmitted, or stored in whole or in part by any means, including graphic, electronic, or mechanical without the express written consent of the publisher except in the case of brief quotations embodied in critical articles and reviews.

Outskirts Press, Inc.
http://www.outskirtspress.com

ISBN: 978-1-4327-8835-3

Outskirts Press and the "OP" logo are trademarks belonging to Outskirts Press, Inc.

PRINTED IN THE UNITED STATES OF AMERICA

Abstract

THE STRUGGLE FOR cultural justice is not a question which proves to be problematic only in western countries where the claims of the "polyethnic" groups based on immigration and the "multinational" groups enter into conflict with dominant majorities. A reflection on African history and the events that occur today reveal that not only is there a real struggle for cultural justice in its various forms, but that, in addition, this struggle often leads to tribal violence and clashes, or even massacres, ethnic and religious wars, genocides.

Inspired by ethno-religious conflicts which occur in a frequent, incessant and violent manner in the contemporary Nigerian society, Basil Ugorji, the author of this book, examines the relevance of certain measures, judicial and coercive, used to resolve ethno-religious conflicts in Africa. The thesis defended is that ethno-religious conflicts in Africa require a shift at the level of research for peaceful resolution: first, from retributive justice to restorative justice, and second, from coercive method to ethno-religious mediation.

Based on the historical and political contexts (pre-colonialism, colonialism, post-independence), the author examines ethno-religious conflicts in Nigeria, with a focus on ethnic, tribal and religious groups involved in conflicts, the origins, causes, consequences, actors involved, forms and places of occurrence of ethno-religious conflicts.

Finally, he conceives, develops and creates a peace education program.

Dedication

THIS BOOK IS DEDICATED
TO THE MEMORY OF ALL THE
CHILDREN KILLED DURING THE
NIGERIA - BIAFRA CIVIL WAR (1967-1970)

Contents

Introduction 1

Part I
TOWARDS AN UNDERSTANDING OF CULTURAL JUSTICE

CHAPTER 1 Culture 11
    Cultural Diversity 12
    Culture and Language 13
    Intercultural Conflicts 15
        Leitkultur 15
        Melting Pot 16
        Mono-culturalism 16
        Multiculturalism 17
CHAPTER 2 Theories of Justice 19
    Distributive Justice 22
        Strict Egalitarianism 23
        Difference Principle 24
        Resource-based Principle 25
        Welfare Principle 26
        Principles Based on Merit 27
        Libertarian Principles 29
    Retributive Justice 33
    Criminal Justice 35
        Objectives 35
        Criminal Justice System 36
        Police 37

  Courts..38
  Prison 40
  Objectives of Prison...40
  Other Forms of Punishment 41
  Critique of the Notion of Deterrence in the
  Criminal Justice System...42
CHAPTER 3 Cultural Justice: A Reflection on the
Rights of Minorities...45
  Understanding Multiculturalism..48
  Justification of Minority Rights 50
  National Minority Rights...51
  Concept of a "Societal Culture" 51
  Ethnic Minority Rights 54
  Individualism and Collective Rights.....................................55
  Two Types of Group Rights 56
    "Internal Restrictions" 57
    "External Protections" 57

PART II
ETHNIC CONFLICTS IN AFRICA AND THEIR HISTORICAL
MANIFESTATIONS

CHAPTER 4 Ethnic Conflicts in Africa..63
  Analysis Hypothesis...64
  General Overview of Ethnic Conflicts in Contemporary Africa65
  Causes of Ethnic Conflicts in Africa......................................71
    Economic Causes..71
    Historical and Psychological Causes..............................72
    Causes Linked to Preferential Treatment........................72
CHAPTER 5 Nigeria and its Situations of Conflicts......................75
  Methodology Adopted to Understand the Dynamics of Ethno-
  Religious Conflicts in Nigeria 76
  Contextual Clarification of the Choice of Nigeria
  as a Case Study..77

General Presentation of Nigeria 78
Ethnic Groups in Nigeria 81
CHAPTER 6 Historical Manifestations of Ethno-Religious
Conflicts in Nigeria... 85
   Ethnic Conflicts in the Northern Region............................... 87
      Kano Massacres.. 87
      Zango – Kataf Crises in Kaduna State 89
      Hausa - Igbo Combat in Sabon Gari Market 90
      Kaduna – Enugu Riots 91
   Ethnic Conflicts in the Southwestern Zone........................... 92
      Conflict between the People of Ife and the
      Modakeke People 92
      Violent Clashes between the Yoruba and the Hausa in
      Shagamu, Ogun State 95
      Clashes between the Ijaw People and the Ilaje in
      Ondo State 96
      Idi-Araba / Oko-Oba Crisis in Lagos State and the
      Reprisals in Kano 97
   Ethnic Conflicts in the Southeast.. 97
      The Nigeria – Biafra Civil War.. 97
      Aguleri – Umuleri Conflict... 103
   Ethnic Conflicts in the Niger Delta Region.......................... 108
      Ogoni Crisis.. 110
      Ijaw Unrest 113
      Ijaw-Itsekiri Conflict... 115
   Ethnic Conflicts in the North Central Zone......................... 118
      Tiv- Jukun Conflicts in Wukari, Taraba State 118
      Ethnic Conflict between the Jukun / Chamba and the People
      of Kuteb in Taraba State... 121
      The Massacres of Jos in Plateau State 128
   Religious Conflicts in Nigeria 131
      Intra-Religious Conflicts... 132
      Inter-Religious Conflicts... 137

CHAPTER 7 Causes of Ethno-Religious Conflicts in Nigeria and Preventive Measures Already Taken 143
    Causes of Ethno-Religious Conflicts in Nigeria Re-examined 143
    Preventive Measures Already Taken and their Limitations 148
        Federalism and its Secular Character 149
        Creation of New States and the Resource Allocation System 150
        National Reconciliation 151
        Creation of the Institute for Peace and Conflict Resolution (IPCR) 152
        Coercive Method 152
        Judicial Method 154

PART III
INTER-ETHNIC MEDIATION

CHAPTER 8 Transition towards Inter-Ethnic Mediation 159
    The First Shift: From Retributive Justice to Restorative Justice 160
    The Second Shift: From Coercive Method to Inter-Ethnic Mediation 164
        Inter-Ethnic Mediation and the Reduction of Social Distance 164
CHAPTER 9 Forms of Inter-Ethnic Mediation 169
    Mediation Channeled Towards the Largest Ethnic Groups in the Society 170
    Mediation Directed Toward the Re-establishment of Dialogue and Cultural Exchange at a Time when Ethnic Ties are Broken 170
    Mediation Directed Toward the Dissipation of Ethno-Religious Prejudice 171
    The Therapeutic Aspect of Inter-Ethnic Mediation 171
    Workshops and Inter-Ethnic Confrontation 172
    Mediation Channeled Towards the Minority Groups with Specific Identities 173

Mediation Organized for Ethno-Religious Groups
Geographically Marginalized or Isolated 173
Mediation Aimed at Strengthening the Capacity of Communities
in Conflict to "Live Together" 174
Mediation Oriented Towards Sustainable Peace 174
Access to the Community and Civic Enrichment of Students
through Peace Education 176
    Workshop on Attachment 177
    Creative Patriotism Workshop 179
    National Flag of Nigeria 182
    Emblem: Coat of Arms 183
    National Flower 183
    National Anthem 183
    National Pledge 184
    National Motto 184
    The Voice of the Soul Workshop 185
    The Signs of the Time Workshop 190
    Workshop on Diversity and the Core Values of Faith 193
    The Magnetic Force of Attraction Workshop 193
    The "I am" Workshop 194
    Network of Peace Advocates 195
    Effective and Efficient Peacemakers through Self-
    improvement 195
    Multiplying Effect of the Peace Education Program 195
    Inter-Ethnic Mediation through Writing and Music 195
    Spreading Ethno-Religious Mediation Gains through
    Creative Activities 196
    Formation of Organizations that Promote Inter-Ethnic
    and Inter-Religious Dialogues 196
    Community Volunteering Program or Community Service 196
CHAPTER 10 Ethno-Religious Mediation as a Device for
Building Democracy in Africa 197
Acknowledgements 199
Bibliography 201

Introduction

THE STRUGGLE FOR cultural justice is not a question which proves to be problematic only in Western countries where the claims of the "polyethnic" groups based on immigration and the "multinational" groups enter into conflict with dominant majorities. A reflection on African history and the events that occur today reveal that not only is there a real struggle for cultural justice in its various forms, but that, in addition, this struggle often leads to tribal violence and clashes, or even massacres, ethnic and religious wars, genocides.

It is true that in Africa, these claims are based on the necessity to grant specific rights to minority groups, namely, the rights of survival, government representation, cultural freedom and equality in every sense of the term. Nevertheless, one can question the relevance of some established methods used to achieve these ends of cultural justice. Why do the judicial measures or traditional justice not seem to be effective in providing stable solutions to the injustices suffered by minority groups in Africa? What should be done so that children, youths, women and the poor who are always victims of these deadly clashes, as well as the ethnic and religious groups involved in conflict, can throw away their weapons, speak to one another, reach an agreement, understand and forgive one another? The strong desire to find answers to these questions is primarily the driving force behind this theoretical and practical research entitled: "From cultural justice to inter-ethnic mediation: A reflection on the possibility of ethno-religious mediation in Africa".

◀ FROM CULTURAL JUSTICE TO INTER-ETHNIC MEDIATION

This study is mainly devoted to a reflection on the possibility of inter-ethnic mediation in Africa, considered as an alternative method of resolving ethno-religious conflicts. First, and since such claims are made in the name of cultural justice, we will examine in the first part entitled, "Towards an understanding of cultural justice", the concepts of justice and culture, as well as the different rights of the minorities.

To fully understand all the points that will be very useful in the realization of the objective of this book, we will study cultural justice through the liberal theory of minority rights proposed by Will Kymlicka[1]. In effect, cultural justice revolves around a theory of justice for the cultural rights of minorities, that is to say, the recognition of the rights of minorities in a multicultural society, founded on cultural identity and the fundamental principles of liberalism.

More precisely, we are going to raise questions such as multiculturalism, justification of the rights of the multi-national and multi-ethnic minorities, the notion of a societal culture, internal restrictions, and finally external restrictions. The purpose of such an approach is to highlight the implications of this theory in a multicultural society, if the politics of recognition will be primarily or solely based on the values of liberalism. The choice of the "liberal theory of minority rights" in this study does not mean the abandon of other examined theories of justice which are considered to be equally useful.

But, before that, we examine the concept of justice because the understanding of this concept is a prerequisite and necessary condition for a good resolution of ethno-religious conflicts. People are always reluctant to compromise when the cause of their conflicts is linked to justice. Also, the affirmations of injustice often lead to intractable conflicts. The notion of justice is associated with norms and laws which are normally supposed to be at the origin of a decent treatment of human beings. If there is a perceived gap between what a person obtains, what he or she needs, and what he or she believes to have the right to own, that person may conclude that he or she is

---

1   W. Kymlicka, *Multicultural Citizenship: A Liberal Theory of Minority Rights* (Oxford: Clarendon Press, 1995) [Hereafter, *Multicultural Citizenship*].

INTRODUCTION

deprived of the benefits he or she deserves[2]. This can occur when the procedure used and / or the expected outcomes are considered to be unfair. When people believe they have been treated unfairly, they may try to take revenge or question those who have treated them unfairly.

However, the understanding of justice is different in each culture. Nonetheless, there are also some principles of justice which are common in most societies. We summarize therefore some theories of justice. We examine only the following four theories, namely, distributive justice, retributive justice, criminal justice and restorative justice. For methodological reasons, we examine the latter, that is, restorative justice at the beginning of chapter eight of the third part of this book.

Then, we try in the second part to study ethno-religious conflicts in Africa and their historical manifestations. In Africa, ethnic conflicts have become today a very serious challenge, which explains perhaps why ethnicity is regarded as the concept that predominates in "African Studies" at the moment. Ethnic groups are defined as communities of people who share cultural and linguistic characteristics, including history, tradition, myth, and origin. The ethnic situation in Africa reflects the heterogeneity of ethnic groups in terms of culture and language which are endemic in different origins and histories. Researchers have attempted to develop a theoretical approach of ethnicity and ethnic conflicts over a long period. Some, like Donald Horowitz[3], Ted Gurr[4], Donald Rothschild[5] and Edward Azar[6], are convinced that ethnic conflicts being experienced today by Africa are deeply rooted in religion, language, identity, race, discrimination

---

2   Morton Deutsch, "Justice and Conflict", in The Handbook of Conflict Resolution: Theory and Practice, M. Deutsch and P. Coleman, eds. (San Francisco: Jossey-Bass Publishers, 2000), p. 44.
3   Horowitz, Donald, Ethnic Groups In Conflict, (Berkeley: University of California press, 1985).
4   Gurr,Ted, Why Men Rebel (Princeton: 1970); Gurr, Ted and B. Harff, Ethnic Conflict In World Politics (Sanfrancisco: west View press, 1994).
5   Rothschild, Donald, Managing Ethnic Conflict In Africa: Pressures And Incentives For Cooperation (Brookings Press, 1997).
6   Azar, Edwards, The Management Of Protracted Social Conflict. Theory And Cases, (Dartmouth: Aldershot, 1990).

and poverty. Some ethnic conflicts in Africa occur when the claims of a group for land and territory become incompatible with the desire of others to satisfy their own interests and needs within the same physical territory. Other claims are underpinned by political, socio-economic and psychological motives. Becoming so complex, ethnic conflicts in Africa are difficult to resolve or manage. However, no country can afford the luxury of leaving ethnic conflicts or ignoring them. Each multi-ethnic State is trying to find ways to deal with ethnic conflicts. Failure to resolve them, ethnic conflicts have high potential to degenerate into tribal violence and violent clashes, and even in massacres, ethnic and religious wars, genocides.

The main idea of this part of the book is that ethnic conflicts in Africa have their origin in cultural injustice and inequality. Wherever such injustices and inequalities occur among groups, conflicts are inevitable. Hence the question: how can we effectively resolve ethnic conflicts in Africa in order to prevent further massacres? It is therefore necessary to note that adequate analysis of ethnic conflicts in Africa is very important so as to avoid prescribing wrong remedy for this evil.

To obtain a good result, our analysis will focus on one of the multicultural African countries where ethno-religious conflicts pose lots of problems these days and where the struggle for recognition and respect for the rights of ethnic and religious minorities require our urgent attention and our civic and philosophical reflections. We will therefore undertake a detailed analysis of most of the ethnic conflicts that have recently plagued Nigeria. However, we do not pretend to have the complete solution to the threat posed by ethnic conflicts in Africa. Instead, we try to make a modest contribution to the ongoing discussions. We begin by making a general overview of the ethnic conflicts in contemporary Africa.

In addition, it is imperative to know Nigeria and its historical situations of conflict. Based on the historical and political contexts (pre-colonialism, colonialism, post-independence), we examine ethnic, tribal and religious groups involved in conflicts, their origins, causes, consequences, actors, forms and places of emergence of

INTRODUCTION

ethno-religious conflicts in Nigeria. Since these conflicts occurred due to many factors and with negative devastating consequences which are responsible for the strategic intervention of the government, we also underline the preventive measures already taken by the Federal Government of Nigeria and their limitations.

"The frequency of these conflicts and their impact on the socio-economic life of the peoples of Nigeria have always posed a major challenge to the government, and therefore require proactive strategies for resolution in order to control them. Therefore, the governments of Nigeria (past and present) have long been trying to respond to the challenges posed by the different ethno-religious conflicts in the country"[7] through the development of mechanisms for the resolution of ethno-religious conflicts. However, the various responses of governments to these ethno-religious conflicts have been temporary, inefficient and are not organized. We therefore examine some of the key strategies of managing ethno-religious conflicts frequently employed by the governments in Nigeria. These strategies include federalism and secularism, the creation of new states and the system of resource allocation, national reconciliation, the establishment of the Institute for Peace and Conflict Resolution (IPCR), coercive methods, and lastly, judicial method.

We affirm that ethno-religious conflicts which occur in a frequent, incessant and violent manner in our contemporary societies require a shift at the level of research for peaceful resolution, a shift in two stages: first, from retributive justice to restorative justice, and second, from coercive method to ethno-religious mediation.

The quality of relations between rival ethnic groups, and the preservation of ethnic peace depend on the type and the effectiveness of mechanisms of ethno-religious mediation available and the political choices of the government. In addition, the use of mediation tools to resolve ethno-religious conflicts has the potential of creating lasting peace. This was the case in South Africa, where the government

---

[7] B. Salawu, Ethno-Religious Conflicts in Nigeria: Causal Analysis and Proposals for New Management Strategies, European Journal of Social Sciences – Volume 13, Number 3 (2010).

established the foundations of a civil society, accountability and transparency through mediation.

The inability to find solutions to ethnic problems in Africa will have social and economic consequences on a continent that is already affected by conflicts, poverty and diseases including HIV/AIDS. For this reason, we propose to reflect, in the third part of this book, on the possibility of ethno-religious mediation in Africa. Faced with cultural diversity and religious affiliations in some African countries like Nigeria, mediation could prove to be a unique means for the consolidation of peace, mutual understanding, dialogue, mutual recognition, development and unity in democracy. In this respect, our goal in this part will be to reflect on the conception, creation and development of a peace education program and mechanisms for conflict prevention and resolution through ethno-religious mediation in Nigeria.

Inter-ethnic mediation, conceived as a process, consists of a civic, democratic and constructive method of resolving conflicts linked to ethnic or cultural differences. It is an art of conceiving appropriate institutions to direct inevitable conflicts towards a peaceful resolution. The importance of conflict resolution through mediation cannot be overstated. As we are going to see, it is when the leaders and the states fail to address important issues and the basic needs of citizens that violent conflicts trigger off. The management of conflicts, the peaceful resolution of conflicts and the prevention of ethno-religious conflicts through inter-ethnic mediation are not more important elsewhere than in Africa. This part is therefore a contribution to the ongoing research for new ways to manage ethno-religious conflicts in Nigeria, since the coercive method and the judicial measure or retributive justice employed by the Nigerian government prove to be ineffective for the prevention and resolution of ethno-religious conflicts.

It is therefore time to move from coercive and judicial methods or from retributive justice to inter-ethnic mediation as an alternative method which is more democratic and a form of restorative justice. In this regard, we propose two approaches for resolving ethno-religious

INTRODUCTION

conflicts in Nigeria: first, a shift from the judicial method of resolving ethno-religious conflicts or from retributive justice to restorative justice, and second, a shift from the coercive method of resolving ethno-religious conflicts to inter-ethnic mediation. We propose to examine ten practical forms of ethno-religious mediation that could be implemented in Nigeria or in Africa. These forms of ethno-religious mediation are: mediation oriented towards the largest ethnic groups in the society, mediation directed toward the re-establishment of dialogue and cultural exchange at a time when ethnic ties are broken, mediation directed toward the dissipation of ethno-religious prejudice, the therapeutic aspect of inter-ethnic mediation, workshops and inter-ethnic confrontation, mediation channeled towards the minority groups with specific identities, mediation organized for ethno-religious groups geographically marginalized or isolated, mediation aimed at strengthening the capacity of communities in conflict to "live together", mediation oriented towards sustainable peace, access to the community and civic enrichment of students through peace education.

Finally, the last chapter is a conclusion which will open up another field of research for the future, namely, how ethno-religious mediation could be a valuable tool for the building of democracy in Africa.

Part I
TOWARDS AN UNDERSTANDING OF CULTURAL JUSTICE

CHAPTER 1

Culture

THE TERM "CULTURE" corresponds etymologically to the Latin word "cultura" which means in English the action or way of cultivating, enhancing or improving something. This word also takes on different meanings depending on how it is used. When it refers to an individual, we talk about an individual culture, that is to say, a personal acquisition of knowledge. When used to characterize a community, or a particular ethnic group, we speak of a collective culture that forms the basis of a cultural identity of this community or people. Whereas individual culture has a dimension of development, evaluation, and therefore by definition evolutionary, collective culture is rigid and tied to a history that could sometimes be opposed to the development of individual cultures. Thus culture is presented as both a set of general knowledge (intellectual or artistic) of an individual and a set of social or religious structures that characterize a particular group.

From a global perspective, however, culture encompasses the specific features (behaviors, beliefs and symbols) that characterize an individual or a particular group and distinguish that person or group from others. "In its widest sense," says UNESCO, «culture may now be said to be the whole complex of distinctive spiritual, material, intellectual and emotional features that characterize a society or social group. It includes not only the arts and letters, but also modes of life, the fundamental rights of the human being, value systems, traditions and beliefs"[1]. This set of features that characterize one cultural or ethnic group did not fall from heaven; on the contrary, it is gradually developed by the people and transferred in a historical process. It is in this sense that McGrew[2] suggests that culture is a process. He enumerates six steps in this process by which a culture is formed. First, a new model of behavior is invented (invention), or an existing behavior is modified (innovation). The innovator transmits this model to another person. The motivating factor behind this new model of behavior is homogeneous within this group and among those who interpret it, perhaps in terms of recognizable stylistic features. Whoever acquires the model retains the capacity to execute it after acquiring it. The model spreads in all social units of a population. These social units may be families, clans, ethnic groups (...) etc. The model continues through generations[3].

In a specific manner, the culture of a particular people could be nuanced by the term "patrimonium" which originally means in Latin, « inheritance of the father ». According to this historical process of development of a culture, the distinctive features and the set of properties which characterize a people, give them their identity and distinguish them from others, are acquired by inheritance and can be modified. When several ethnic groups living together within a nation-State inherit or modify differently their cultures, we say that this nation-State is culturally diverse.

Cultural Diversity

We speak therefore of cultural diversity when there is a plurality of cultures within a society, each linked to its people, its history, its language, its territory and its heritage. According to the Universal Declaration of UNESCO on Cultural Diversity (2001), cultural diversity

---

[1] UNESCO's definition of culture, Mexico City Declaration on Cultural Policies World Conference on Cultural Policies, Mexico City, 26 July - 6 August 1982.

[2] William Clement McGREW is Professor of Biological Anthropology and of "Leverhulme Centre for Human Evolutionary Studies » at the University of Cambridge. He is also the author of "Chimpanzee Material Culture: Implications for Human Evolution". Cambridge University Press, 1992, p.277.

[3] W.C. McGrew, «Culture in Nonhuman Primates?" Annual Review of Anthropology 27, 1998, p.323

is a "common heritage of humanity". That is why UNESCO considers its preservation to be a concrete and ethical imperative inseparable from the respect of human dignity[4]. Cultural diversity thus appears as a determining factor of culture and cultural heritage. "This intangible cultural heritage, transmitted from generation to generation, says UNESCO, is constantly recreated by communities and groups in response to their environment, their interaction with nature and their history, and gives them a sense of identity and continuity, thus helping to promote respect for cultural diversity and human creativity»[5].

However, we add that a nation-State such as Canada or Nigeria, in any case, is not culturally diverse only because within this State there is a plurality of cultural or ethnic groups. There is cultural diversity in a society because within that same society, there are several cultural or ethnic groups with different values, norms, institutions, and artifacts. Value systems include ideas and materials that appear to be important in life. They guide the beliefs that partly make up the culture. The norms consist of expectations regarding how people should behave in various situations. Every culture has methods called "sanctions" to impose its norms. Sanctions vary according to the importance of the norms. The norms which a society imposes officially have the status of laws. Institutions are the structures of society in and by which values and norms are transmitted. Artifacts are things or material aspects of culture. They describe the values and norms of a culture. These four elements are "transmitted from generation to generation"[6] through the use of written and / or oral languages or by the use of other symbolic means, thus constituting the quiddity of the culture of a particular group.

Culture and Language

The link between culture and language cannot be ignored. Language is seen not only as a cultural trait among many others, but

---

4   Refer to the website of Unesco at http://www.unesco.org/new/en/culture/themes/cultural-diversity/cultural-expressions/the-convention/l
5   For detailed information, see the Convention for the Safeguarding of the Intangible Cultural Heritage 2003, Paris, 17 October 2003.
6   Hoult, T. F, ed. Dictionary of Modern Sociology, 1969, p. 93.

essentially as a direct expression of cultural character of a people, and as a culture in a condensed form. Herder, for instance, points it out saying, «Denn jedes Volk ist Volk; es hat seine National Bildung wie seine Sprache», which means "since every people is a people, every people has its own national culture expressed through its own language." The common language of a people is the most important carrier of their common culture. According to Franz Boas[7], the founder of American anthropology, it is unimaginable to study the culture of a foreign people without also becoming familiar with their language. For Boas, the fact that the intellectual culture of a people was largely constructed, shared and nurtured by the use of language implied that the understanding of the language of a cultural group was the key to understanding their culture. The manner in which people of a particular community express themselves forms part of the culture of this community, just like other shared practices. The use of languages is a way to signal identity with a cultural group and to differentiate it from others.

Nevertheless, Boas and his students knew that culture and language are not directly dependent on each other. In other words, groups of vastly different cultures can share a common language.

However, the moment when members of a particular cultural group do not understand the verbal or symbolic expressions of another cultural group, what Paul Ricoeur calls the "conflict of interpretations"[8] can appear. This conflict is due to the inability of members of a particular cultural group to decipher the meanings embedded in the language or symbols of the other groups. This problem is evident in multicultural societies.

---

7   Having studied the Native American languages, Boas emphasized the importance of analyzing internal linguistic structure, and noted that language is a fundamental aspect of culture. His insistence on a rigorous methodology helped to establish the scientific value of his contributions and methods, and his conclusions are still widely influential. See G. W. Stocking, Jr.'s Franz Boas Reader: Shaping of American Anthropology, 1883–1911 (1982); biography by M. J. Herskovits (1953, repr. 1973) in The Columbia Electronic Encyclopedia, 6th ed. Copyright © 2007, Columbia University Press.
8   Paul Ricœur, Le conflit des interprétations, Editions du Seuil, Paris, 1969, pp. 10-12.

Intercultural Conflicts

Today, almost in all multicultural societies, there are conflicts linked to cultural domination, that is to say, when a culture is hegemonic and imposes itself voluntarily or involuntarily on another or on the entire society. These conflicts are sometimes connected to the system of values, as when a cultural minority group rejects the system of values of the dominant culture. To describe this situation of conflict in relation to cultural differences, some scholars use the terms "dominant culture" and "dominated culture." An important type of dominated culture is the one formed by a community of immigrants or a minority group. In order to resolve these conflicts, many philosophers and other thinkers have established various theoretical models to follow. In a schematic way, we outline some of them.

Leitkultur

The German term "Leitkultur"[9] can refer to a "dominant or leading culture" in English. It is a model developed in Germany by Bassam Tibi. The idea is that the minorities can have their own identity, but they should at least support the cultural values on which modern societies are founded such as those "of modernity, democracy, secularism, Enlightenment, human rights and civil society»[10].

---

9   This term is better understood as « guiding culture », « leading culture » or « core culture ».
10 Bassam Tibi was born in 1944 in Damascus, lived in Germany since 1962 and since 1976 he is a German citizen. As a political scientist and professor of International Relations, Bassam is perhaps best known for introducing the controversial concept of European Leitkultur and the concept of Euroislam for the integration of Muslim immigrants in Europe. The German term Leitkultur is a political controversial concept, first introduced in 1998 by Bassam Tibi . It can be translated as "guiding culture" or "dominant culture", less literally as the «leading culture" or "common culture". Tibi himself sees it as a form of multiculturalism, but from 2000 the term has figured prominently in the national political debate in Germany on national identity and immigration. The word becomes associated with a mono-cultural vision of German society, with European ideas of cultural superiority, and with the politics of cultural assimilation. Bassam Tibi first proposed a "Leitkultur" in his 1998 thesis, "Europa ohne Identität", p.154 (meaning, "Europe without identity"). He defines it in terms of what is commonly called Western values, and spoke of a European rather than German Leitkultur.

◄ FROM CULTURAL JUSTICE TO INTER-ETHNIC MEDIATION

Melting Pot[11]

The English verb "to melt" can also designate "to blend" or "to dissolve". The main idea defended here is that in a multicultural society, all the cultures of immigrants should be mixed, merged or assimilated into the dominant culture. It is a method of assimilation of immigrant populations of various origins into a homogeneous society. All initial differences in culture disappear, in order to form one and the same whole.

Mono-culturalism

Mono-culturalism is an active practice of preserving a culture to the exclusion of outside influences. It should not be confused with a homogeneous society, which is "one" with racial uniformity. But this theory also leaves room for certain openness to foreign cultures. In some countries, culture is closely linked to nationalism. Government policy is thus to assimilate all the cultures of immigrants, although recent rates of immigration have led many countries to experiment forms of multiculturalism.

---

11   The term "Melting Pot" is particularly used to describe the assimilation of immigrants in the United States. The metaphor of fusion was used in the 1780s. In the eighteenth and nineteenth centuries, the metaphor of a "melting pot" has been used to describe the fusion of different nationalities, ethnicities and cultures. It has been used with concepts of America as an ideal republic and a "city on a hill" or a new promised land. It was a metaphor for the idealized process of immigration and colonization by which different nationalities, cultures and "races" will merge into a new virtuous community and it was connected to the utopian visions of an emerging « new American man ». While the term "assimilation" was in common usage, the term "melting pot" came into general use in 1908 after the play "The Melting Pot" by Israel Zangwill.

The first use of the term "melting pot" in American literature is found in the writings of J. Hector St. John de Crevecoeur. In his "Letters from an American farmer" (1782), Crevecoeur writes, "... where did all these people come from? They are a mixture of English, Scots, Irish, French, Dutch, Germans, Swedes and ... What is therefore American, this new man? He is neither a European nor the descendant of a European, hence from where comes this strange mixture of blood that you will not find in any other country? I could point out a family whose grandfather was English, whose wife was Dutch, whose son married a French woman, and whose four children have now four wives from different nations. He is an American, who, leaving behind all his ancient prejudices and customs, receives new ones from the new mode of life he has adopted, the new government he obeys, and the new rank he holds (...). The Americans were once scattered throughout Europe; (...). Here they are incorporated into one of the best systems of population which has never appeared". - J. Hector St. John de Crevecoeur, "Letters from an American farmer."

Multiculturalism

Multiculturalism is a politico-philosophical theory in which immigrants and other minority groups should preserve their cultures while interacting peacefully with the dominant cultures within a nation-State. This concept will be analyzed in the third chapter of this book in a more detailed way, from the perspective of the theory of minority rights of Will Kymlicka.

The study of cultures within a society is very complex. A thorough search in this field must take into account a multitude of variables. That said, the manner in which a nation-State manages conflicts caused by cultural differences will determine the success or failure of the politics of that State. The type of government policies that is chosen by a nation-State and the effectiveness of these policies will show whether this nation-State acts or not according to the fundamental principles of justice.

CHAPTER 2

Theories of Justice

REFLECTING ON INTERCULTURAL or ethno-religious conflicts in contemporary societies[12], we see the need to reflect also on the concept of justice, because the understanding of this concept is a prerequisite and necessary condition for a good resolution of ethno-religious conflicts. People are always reluctant to compromise when the cause of their conflicts is linked to justice. Also, the affirmations of injustice often lead to intractable conflicts. The notion of justice is associated with norms and laws which are normally supposed to be at the origin of a decent treatment of human beings. If there is a perceived gap between what a person obtains, what he or she needs, and what he or she believes to have the right to own, that person may conclude that he or she is deprived of the benefits he or she deserves[13]. This can occur when the procedure used and / or the expected outcomes are considered to be unfair. When people believe they have been treated unfairly, they may try to take revenge or question those who have treated them unfairly.

12 These conflicts sometimes occur in Western countries where multicultural states such as Canada, the United States or even France, etc.., constantly experience conflicts related to cultural differences due to high rate of immigration. It is also a very serious phenomenon in Africa where ethnic or religious groups compete fiercely among themselves or against the governments for reasons related to justice and the fundamental human rights. These are therefore indications that it is important to study justice in a research on the strategies of ethno-religious conflict resolution.
13 Morton Deutsch, "Justice and Conflict," in The Handbook of Conflict Resolution: Theory and Practice, M. Deutsch and P. Coleman, eds. (San Francisco: Jossey-Bass Publishers, 2000), p. 44.

FROM CULTURAL JUSTICE TO INTER-ETHNIC MEDIATION

In effect, a feeling of injustice often leads to aggression or retaliation. People may see violence as the only way to respond to the injustice they have suffered and ensure that their basic needs are met.

This is particularly probable if no procedure is established to correct the structures of social oppression or bring about retributive or restorative justice. However, the powerful often reacts by attempting to quell the unrest and maintain the status quo[14]. This can lead to violent conflicts and massacres.

In fact, those who feel they have been victims of injustice or unfair treatment may become angry and feel justified by revenge. Or, they can blame the members of the other group and denigrate them as morally inferior, paving the way for dehumanization and violence[15]. This may simply lead to further injustices and make conflict uncontrollable.

Now, one of the questions that arises is to know what justice is? When my neighbor forgives me after I asked for forgiveness for the crimes that I intentionally committed against him, can we talk about justice? Is there a link between justice and forgiveness?

Having exposed the different meanings of culture in the preceding chapter, we therefore examine in this chapter some notions related to the concept of justice and its variations. The global understanding of justice is the key to grasp the idea of cultural justice which is our objective in this part of the book.

In order to answer this question: "what is justice?", it will be necessary to begin with the opposite term, in other words, "what is injustice?". The word "injustice" is designated by a privation of justice or the violation of the rights of the "other". It is synonymous with unfairness or unjust act[16]. Injustice therefore becomes an act which inflicts an undeserved evil. It applies to any act that infringes unfairness to another person or the violation of his rights. According

---

14 Peter Coleman, "Characteristics of Protracted, Intractable Conflict: Towards the Development of a Meta-Framework," – I, Peace and Conflict: Journal of Peace Psychology, 2003, 9(1), 1-37, p. 16.
15 Morton Deutsch, op cit., p. 55.
16 Merriam Webster, Encyclopedia Britannica Company, http://www.merriam-webster.com/dictionary/injustice

THEORIES OF JUSTICE

to Aristotle, "what is right (fair or just) is the proportional. What is wrong, on the contrary, is what is disproportional. It therefore occurs when there is too much on one side and on the other too little, as it happens exactly in practice. The author of injustice, in effect, holds a very large share and the victim, too little, when it comes to sharing what is "good". And if it is to share that which is "bad" the reverse is the case, as the lesser evil is preferable when compared to greater evil. The lesser evil is preferable to the greater evil, and so, the preferable constitutes the good and the more it is preferable, the more this good is big[17]. For Aristotle, injustice is a moral vice. Injustice as a moral vice includes unlawfulness and unfairness. It may be classified as inadvertent or accidental (when it is not expected to be a consequence of an action), incidental (to an action which was not intended to cause any injustice), or intentional (when it is an intended consequence of an action). On the contrary, as a moral virtue (arete), justice includes lawfulness (universal justice) and fairness (particular justice). Fairness requires that the privileges and responsibilities of persons in a given situation be distributed proportionally and equally (distributive justice). Fairness also requires that an unfair inequality or disproportion in the privileges and responsibilities of persons in a given situation be rectified (rectificatory justice). Rectificatory justice may restore equality, or may reallocate privileges and responsibilities to persons in a given situation, or may prescribe some form of penalty for persons who have been unjust, or may award some form of compensation to those persons who have been treated unfairly[18].

According to most theories of justice, it is extremely important to note here the conception of justice according to John Rawls, "Justice is the first virtue of social institutions, as truth is of systems of thought."[19]

However, the understanding of justice is different in each culture. Nonetheless, there are also some principles of justice which are

---
17 Aristote, l'Ethique à Nicomaque, Mémoire V, §15, 20, trad. Richard Bodéüs, Flammarion, 2004
18 Aristotle. Ethica Nicomachea. Translated by W.D. Ross, in The Basic Works of Aristotle. Edited by Richard McKeon. New York: Random House, 1941.
19 John Rawls. A Theory of Justice (revised edition, Oxford: Oxford University Press, 1999), p. 3.

common in most societies. We summarize therefore some theories of justice. Knowing that there are several theories of justice, we examine only the following four theories, namely, distributive justice, retributive justice, criminal justice and restorative justice. For methodological reasons, we examine the latter, that is, restorative justice at the beginning of chapter eight of the third part of this book.

We therefore affirm that ethno-religious conflicts which occur in a frequent, incessant and violent manner in our contemporary societies require a shift at the level of research for peaceful resolution, a shift in two stages: first, from retributive justice to restorative justice, and second, from coercive method to ethno-religious mediation.

But before reaching this level, we need to understand the other theories of justice, beginning with distributive justice.

Distributive Justice

Distributive justice includes normative principles intended to guide the equitable distribution of resources between the different members of a community. Equitable distribution generally takes into account some important elements. First, it takes into account the total amount of goods and services to be distributed, second, the object of distribution (revenues, wealth, opportunities, jobs, welfare, utility, etc.), and third, beneficiaries of the distribution (individuals, groups of people, etc.). Subsequently, the distribution of resources among different members of a community must be realized following certain principles or models. These principles to follow include: strict egalitarianism which advocates equal distribution of material goods to all members of the society, the difference principle of John Rawls which allows the distribution that is not consistent with strict equality as long as inequality has the effect of ensuring that the most disadvantaged in the society are materially better than they would be under strict equality, the resource-based principle, the welfare principle which states that material goods and services have no intrinsic value and are valuable only insofar as they increase welfare. Also, according to them, the principles of distribution should be designed and evaluated according to their impact on well-being. Other principles to be examined include the principle based on what people deserve because of their work (the merit principle), the libertarian principle which critiques the other distribution models, arguing that they are in conflict with the most important moral demands such as those of freedom or self-ownership.

Since societies have a limited amount of wealth and resources, the question which arises is to know how these goods should be distributed or which model will be the most effective for the distribution of goods and services. The common answer is that public goods should be distributed in a reasonable manner so that each person receives a "fair share". But this leaves open the question as to know what constitutes a "fair share". Therefore we examine briefly these different principles underlying the theory of distributive justice, starting with strict egalitarianism.

STRICT EGALITARIANISM

One of the simplest principles of distributive justice is that of strict equality. This principle says that every person should have the same level of material goods and services. The principle is most often justified by the fact that we should accord people equal respect, and that equality of material goods and services is the best means to reinforce this ideal. However, this principle poses many problems. The two main problems are the construction of suitable indicators to measure goods and services (the index problem), and the specification of deadlines. The index problem arises mainly because the goods to be distributed must be measured if they are to be distributed according to a certain model (such as equality). The principle of strict equality indicates that there should be "the same level of material goods and services." The problem is to know how to define and measure "levels". The second problem concerns time. Many principles of distribution identify and require that the distribution of goods and services should be carried out according to a particular model. But they should also specify when this model is necessary.

There are a number of moral criticisms directly made against the principles of strict equality. It is claimed that this principle unduly restrains freedom and that it does not give the best effect to equal respect for people. Critics argue that the principle of strict equality conflicts with what people deserve, and so on. But the most common criticism is the one of welfare which is based on the idea that everyone can be materially better if revenues are not strictly equal[20]. It is this fact that inspired in part the difference principle.

Difference Principle

Economic wealth does not remain a fixed amount from one period to another. More wealth can be produced and in fact this has been the experience of the industrialized countries over the centuries. The most common way to produce more wealth is to have a system where those who are more productive earn more revenues. This has partly inspired the formulation of the difference principle.

The most widely discussed theory of distributive justice in the last three decades has been that proposed by John Rawls in "A Theory of Justice"[21] and "Political Liberalism"[22]. Rawls proposes two principles of justice:

1. The First Principle of Justice (the principle of equal liberty): Each person is to have an equal right to the most extensive total system of equal basic liberties compatible with a similar system of liberty for all.
2. The Second Principle of Justice (the difference principle): Social and economic inequalities are to be arranged so that they are both: (a) to the greatest benefit of the least advantaged, consistent with the just savings principle, and; (b) attached to offices and positions open to all under conditions of fair equality of opportunity[23].

---

20 See Carens, Joseph, 1981, Equality, Moral Incentives and the Market (Chicago: Chicago University Press)
21 For a detailed understanding of distributive justice, please see John Rawls, 1971, A Theory of Justice (Harvard, MA: Harvard University Press)
22 See also John Rawls, 1993, Political Liberalism, (New York: Columbia University Press)
23 Ibid., pp. 5-6

The principal moral motivation for the difference principle is similar to that of strict equality: equal respect for people. Indeed, the difference principle collapses materially to a form of strict equality under empirical conditions where differences in income have no impact on work incentives of individuals. The prevailing opinion is that in the foreseeable future the possibility to earn a higher income will encourage more production effort. This will help boost the total wealth of the economy and, under the difference principle, the wealth of the least advantaged. Opinions are divided on the size of inequalities which, as an empirical fact, are authorized by the difference principle, and on how the least advantaged would become much better under the difference principle than in the principle of strict equality. The principle of Rawls, however, provides sufficient and clear guidelines on this type of arguments that is presented as a justification for inequality. Rawls is not opposed to the principle of strict equality per se; his concern is on the absolute position of the least privileged groups rather than their relative position. If a system of strict equality maximizes the absolute position of the least privileged groups in society, then the difference principle will defend strict equality.

Resource-based Principle

The resource-based principle (or principle based on resources) prescribes equality of resources. Interestingly, the resource-based principle affirms that results are determined by the free use of one's resources. The theorists of this principle argue that the difference principle is not sufficiently "ambition-sensitive" and that people should live with the consequences of their choices. They argue, for example, that people who choose to work hard to earn more revenues should not be forced to contribute for those who freely choose leisure and consequently less income.

The most remarkable theory of principles based on resources, developed by Ronald Dworkin[24], suggests that individuals begin with

---

24 See Dworkin, Ronald, 1981, "What is Equality? Part 1: Equality of Resources", Philosophy and Public Affairs, 10: 185-246; See also, Dworkin, Ronald, 1981, "What is Equality? Part 2: Equality of Welfare", Philosophy and Public Affairs, 10: 283-345.

equal resources, but end with unequal economic benefits because of their own choice. What constitutes a fair material distribution should be determined by the result of an experience of thinking conceived to model a fair distribution of goods and services. Supposing that each person has the same purchasing power and that everyone uses this purchasing power to negotiate in a fair auction sale, for the resources best suited to each person's life projects. Everyone then is entitled to use these resources as he or she wishes. Although people can end up with different economic benefits, none of them receives less consideration than any other in that if they wanted a package of resources from someone else, they could have negotiated for it.

As mentioned above, many theorists of resources, including Dworkin, add to this system of resources and ambition sensitivity, sensitivity to inequalities in natural endowments. They note that natural inequalities are not distributed according to the choices people make; they are not justified by reference to another morally relevant fact on people. Dworkin proposes a hypothetical compensation system.

In contrast to the difference principle, what could constitute the implementation of resource-based theories and their variants in a real economy is not clear at all. It seems impossible to measure differences in natural talents of the people. A system of special assistance to persons with physical and mental disabilities and the sick would be a partial implementation of the system of compensation, but most of the natural inequalities would not be taken care of by this assistance, while the theory requires that such inequalities be compensated. It is simply not clear how to implement equality of resources in a complex economy, and thus, despite its theoretical advantages, it is difficult to see in it a concrete improvement of the difference principle.

Welfare Principle

The principles based on welfare are driven by the idea that what is primarily important in a moral perspective is the level of the well-being of people. The defenders of the welfare principles see the concerns of other theories such as equality, the least privileged, resources, or freedom as derived preoccupations. Resources, equality, or liberty are only valuable insofar as they increase well-being. Therefore, all distribution questions must be resolved such that distribution maximizes welfare. However, "maximize welfare" is vague, and so, the welfare theorists propose functions of particular welfare to maximize. The functions of welfare proposed vary enormously both on what will be regarded as well-being and the level of well-being. In almost any distribution of material goods there is a function of welfare of which its maximization will enhance this distribution.

In addition, most philosophical activities on the principle in question are focused on a variant known as utilitarianism. This theory can be used to illustrate most of the main characteristics of the welfare principle. Historically, Utilitarians have used the term "utility" rather than "welfare", and utility has been defined in various ways such as pleasure, happiness, or satisfaction of preference. For example, the principle of distribution of economic benefits for the utilitarians of "preference" is to distribute them in a manner that maximizes the satisfaction of preferences. The function of welfare for such a principle has a simple theoretical form: it consists in choosing the distribution that maximizes the arithmetic sum of all satisfied preferences (unsatisfied preferences being negative).

Principles Based on Merit

Another criticism against the welfare principle is that it ignores the idea (or the requirement) that people deserve certain economic benefits depending on their actions. This criticism is often driven by the fear that the various forms of welfare treat people as merely beneficiaries of welfare, rather than reflective human beings responsible for their actions and creative in their environments.

The different principles of distribution based on merit differ mainly in terms of what is considered to be the basis for merits. Most contemporary proposals fall under one of the following three broad categories:

- Contribution: People should be rewarded for their professional activity based on the value of their contribution to social product[25].
- Effort: People should be rewarded based on the effort expended in their professional activity[26].
- Compensation: People should be rewarded based on the costs incurred in their professional activity[27].

Aristotle affirms that virtue should be the basis for the distribution of rewards, but most of the contemporary principles could be traced to John Locke. Locke argued that people deserve to have the goods produced by their labor and industry; the products (or the value of the latter) is a reward for their work. His idea was to guarantee individuals the fruits of their own labor. According to contemporary theorists of the merit principle, people freely apply their skills and talents, in varying degrees, to a socially productive work. People come to deserve varying levels of revenues by providing goods and services needed by others[28]. Distribution systems are fair insofar as they distribute revenues according to the different levels earned or deserved by the individuals in society for their contributions, effort, or production cost.

It is important to distinguish merit from authorization. For the theorists of the merit principle, a well-designed institutional structure will make sure that many people who are authorized to do something well deserve the authorization. But, of course, authorizations and merits are not the same. A person may be authorized to a payment

---

25 For an in-depth study on this subject, see Miller, David, 1976, Social Justice (Oxford: Clarendon Press); and, Miller, David, 1989, Market, State, and Community (Oxford: Clarendon Press); See also, Riley, Jonathan, 1989, "Justice Under Capitalism", Markets and Justice, ed. John W. Chapman (New York: New York University Press), 122-162.

26 Milne, Heather, 1986, "Desert, effort and equality", Journal of Applied Philosophy, 3: 235-243; See also, Sadurski, Wojciech, 1985a, Giving Desert Its Due (Dordrecht, Holland: D. Reidel).

27 Dick, James, 1975, "How to Justify a Distribution of Earnings", Philosophy and Public Affairs, 4: 248-72; See also, Lamont, Julian, 1997, "Incentive Income, Deserved Income, and Economic Rents", Journal of Political Philosophy, 5: 26-46.

28 Feinberg, Joel, 1970, "Justice and Personal Desert", Doing and Deserving (Princeton, NJ, Princeton University Press), 55-94.

without deserving it, just as a person may be authorized to assume a presidential function without deserving it[29]. Similarly a person may merit something without being allowed to have it. In sum, payments well deserved refer to what is already accomplished or what will be accomplished. They are justified by reference to the work activities accomplished in the present or in the past.

Libertarian Principles

Most of the contemporary versions of the principles discussed thus far have played some role in the market as a means of achieving the aims of distributive justice. The difference principle uses it as a way to help the least advantaged. The utilitarian principle commonly uses it as a means to achieve the distribution model designed for the maximization of utility. The principle based on what people deserve as a result of their work also uses it in order to distribute goods based on merit. On the other hand, advocates of the libertarian principle rarely see the market as a means of certain desired models, since the principle they advocate does not at all propose ostensibly a "model, but instead it describes the kind of acquisitions or exchanges which are fair. The market will be fair, not as a means of achieving a model, but to the extent the exchanges allowed on the market satisfy the conditions of fair exchange described by the principles. For Libertarians, fair results are those achieved by the actions of different individuals; a particular model of distribution is not necessary for justice. Robert Nozick put forward this version of libertarianism[30], and he is its best-known defender in the contemporary period. His theory of justice that explains how people acquire goods will be understood through his theory called «Entitlement Theory», summarized in the following three points:

a. A person who acquires a property according to the principle of justice in matters of acquisition is entitled to that property.
b. A person who acquires a property according to the principle of

---
29 Ibid., p.86
30 For a global idea of this argument, see Nozick, Robert, 1974, Anarchy, State and Utopia (New York: Basic Books)

justice in matters of transfer from someone else having the right to that property is entitled to the property.

c. No one is entitled to a property, except by the repeated applications of (a) and (b).

The theory of "Entitlement" makes reference to the principles of justice in acquisition and transfer[31]. The principle of justice in transfer is the least controversial and is designed to specify fair contracts while excluding theft, fraud, etc. The principle of justice in acquisition is more complex and controversial. The principle is supposed to govern the obtaining of exclusive property rights over the material world. For the justification of these rights, Nozick takes his inspiration from the idea of John Locke that everyone "owns" himself or herself, and through the introduction of one's work in the world, self-ownership can generate the appropriation of a portion of material world. However, concerning this metaphor of lockean "mixture", Nozick legitimately asks: "... Why is the fact of mixing what I own with what I do not own, not a way of losing what I own rather than a means of getting what I do not have? If I am the owner of a can of tomato juice and pour it into the sea such that it ... mixes regularly with the sea, do I become as well the owner of the sea, or have I foolishly dissipated my tomato juice?[32] Nozick concludes that what is significant about mixing our work with the material world is that in doing so; we tend to increase its value, so that self-ownership can lead to ownership of the outside world in such circumstances[33].

The obvious objection to this assertion is that it is not clear why the first people to acquire a portion of the material world should exclude others (and, for example, be the owners of land while those who come later become wage laborers). In response to this objection, Nozick puts the emphasis on fair acquisition, called "Lockean proviso" according to which an exclusive acquisition of the outside world is right if, after the acquisition, there remains "sufficient common property for others".

---

31 For more details on these principles, see Nozick, ibid., pp.149-182.
32 Ibid., p.174
33 Ibid., pp. 149-182

THEORIES OF JUSTICE

One of the main challenges for Libertarians has been to formulate a morally plausible interpretation of this clause (proviso). According to the interpretation of Nozick, an acquisition is fair if and only if the position of others after the acquisition is not worse than their position was when the acquisition was not owned or 'held in common ".

Will Kymlicka provided a summary of the steps of Nozick's argument on self-ownership:

1. People are owners of themselves.
2. The world was initially not owned.
3. You can acquire absolute rights over a disproportionate part of the world, if you do not aggravate the situation of others.
4. It is relatively easy to acquire absolute rights over a disproportionate part of the world.
5. Therefore once private property is appropriated; a free market in capital and labor is morally required[34].

The evaluation of this argument is quite complex, but the difficulties mentioned above call into question steps (3) and (4). The challenge for libertarians is to find a plausible interpretation of (3) which will give (4).

Of course, many existing properties are the result of acquisitions or transfers that, at one point, did not satisfy principles (a) and (b) above. As a result, Nozick completed those principles with a principle of correction or rectification of past injustices. Although he does not specify this principle, he describes its purpose:

"This principle uses historical data on previous situations and injustices committed ... and information on the real course of events that resulted from these injustices until now, and it provides a description (or descriptions) of property in society. The principle of rectification will no doubt make use of its best estimate of subjective information on what would have happened ... if injustice had not taken place"[35].

---
34 Kymlicka, Will, 1990, Contemporary Political Philosophy (Oxford: Clarendon Press) p.112
35 Robert Nozick 1974, op cit., pp. 152-153

FROM CULTURAL JUSTICE TO INTER-ETHNIC MEDIATION

The practical application of this theory is challenging because the task is, in practical terms, difficult. The number of injustices perpetrated throughout history, both within and between nations, is enormous and the necessary details of the vast majority of injustices are not available. Even if the details of injustices were available, the hypothetical chains of causality could not have been determined with certainty and, as Derek Parfit has pointed out; even people who have been born in a similar context would have been different[36]. Accordingly, Nozick's theory provides no guidance as to what the current distribution of material goods, must be, or what distributions or redistributions are legitimate or illegitimate.

As stated above, Nozick argues that because people are the owners of themselves and hence of their talents, they should own all they can produce with these talents. In addition, it is possible in a free market to sell the products of the activities of one's talents. All taxes on revenues from the sale according to Nozick, transfers one's ownership of property and the products of the activities of one's talents to other people[37]. Individuals, according to this argument, have exclusive rights of ownership. Taxation therefore simply consists in violating these rights and authorizing some people to own (in part) others. In addition, it is stated that any system that does not legally recognize these rights violates Kant's categorical imperative that commands that people be treated always and simultaneously as ends in themselves and not merely as means.

In addition to the arguments of self-ownership and the obligation to always and simultaneously treat each person as ends in themselves, the most common way for other scholars in order to justify exclusive property rights has been to argue that these rights are necessary for the maximization of freedom and the minimization of human rights violations.

---

36 To understand Derek's thoughts on the subject, see Parfit, Derek, 1986, Reasons and Persons (Oxford: Oxford University Press)
37 Robert Nozick, op cit., p.172

In order to protect the fundamental human rights, like self-ownership and rights to property, some libertarian scholars like Friedrich A. Hayek have reflected on the notion of State and the role of the rule of law. For Hayek, "(...) the rule of law means that government must never coerce an individual except in the enforcement of a known rule; it constitutes a limitation on the powers of all government, including the powers of the legislature. It is a doctrine concerning what the law ought to be, concerning the general attributes that particular laws should possess"[38]. But the time when these principles of the rule of law are violated, an appropriate procedure and a well-deserved and proportionate punishment will be applied. It is from this perspective therefore, that some theorists of justice developed the theory of retributive justice.

Retributive Justice

Retributive justice regulates proportionate response to crime through legal evidence, so that punishment is appropriately imposed and considered morally correct and well deserved. It is a theory of justice which considers that punishment, if proportionate, is a morally acceptable response to crime, with an eye to the satisfaction and psychological benefits it can give to the injured party, family and society. "Let the punishment be suitable to the crime committed is the principle which says that the severity of punishment for a crime or wrongdoing is reasonable and proportionate to the gravity of the offense"[39]. The concept is common to most cultures around the world and in all societies where sanctions are given to the one who has done wrong, and rewards to the one who did well. Its presence in the ancient Jewish culture is represented by its inclusion in the Law of Moses[40], which includes the sentences of "life for life, eye for eye, tooth for tooth, hand for hand, foot for foot." Many other documents reflect this value in cultures around the world.

---

38   F. A. Hayek, The Constitution of Liberty, Chicago, The University of Chicago Press, 1960, p.205
39   See Cicero's De Legibus, 106 BC. See also, W. S. Gilbert's The Mikado, 1885.
40   Especially in Deuteronomy 19:17-21, and Exodus 21:23-25

FROM CULTURAL JUSTICE TO INTER-ETHNIC MEDIATION

At the beginning of the period of all systems of law, an approximate idea of justice required the imposition of a sentence commensurate with the aggressor as he or she has inflicted on his victim. In the 19th century, Immanuel Kant, in the "Metaphysical Elements of Justice," wrote about retribution as a legal principle: "The judicial punishment can never be used merely as a means to promote another good for the criminal himself or for the civil society, but we must in all cases, impose it on him only on the grounds that he has committed a crime"[41]. Immanuel Kant sees punishment to be based on justice. He states that if the guilty are not punished, justice is not done"[42].

The theory of retributive justice is therefore concerned with the punishment for crime committed and the need to address three questions:

- Why punish?
- Who should be punished?
- What punishment does the offender deserve?

The retributivists think that the utilitarian argument is disastrously wrong. According to them, if someone commits a crime, we must respond to that crime, and to him (the author) as an individual and not as a part of a calculation of total welfare. To do otherwise is to disrespect him as a human being. If the crime had victims, it also means to disrespect the victims. Criminal acts must be balanced or repaired in some way, and so, the criminal deserves to be punished. Retributive justice stresses the idea of reprisals or recovery rather than the maximization of welfare. As the theory of distributive justice states that we must give to everyone what they deserve (as we saw above), retributive justice asserts that all those who are guilty, and only the guilty deserve appropriate punishment.

The concern associated with this theory is to know how to measure the gravity of the offense against the level of the sentence

---
41 Jacqueline (2005). The English Legal System (4th ed.), London: Hodder Arnold, p. 174.
42 Rachels, James (2007). The Elements of Moral Philosophy.

to be given. For the retributivists, the proportionality requires that the level of the sentence be weighed against the gravity of the offense. However, this does not mean that the sentence must be equivalent to the crime committed. A system of retribution should punish more serious crimes than severely minor ones; however the retributivists differ on how to apply this principle, that is to say, should the system generally apply it in a severe or mild way? But according to retributive justice, punishment is backward-looking, and strictly for punishing crimes according to their gravity[43]. In this respect, the level of severity of the offense may be determined by the amount of damage caused, an unfair advantage or moral disequilibrium caused by the crime. But in order to identify and measure such damages caused and the appropriate sentences to be given, the institutionalization of criminal justice is required.

Criminal Justice

Criminal justice is the system of practices and institutions of the governments aimed at maintaining social control, deterrence and reduction of crimes through the application of criminal sanctions and rehabilitation efforts for those who violate laws.

OBJECTIVES

The Commission of 1969 on law enforcement and the administration of justice in the United States defined the criminal justice system as a means for the society to "enforce standards of conduct necessary to protect individuals and community "[44].

The criminal justice system in England aims to "reduce crime and increase public confidence to the fact that the system is fair and will bring citizens to respect the laws"[45]. In Canada, the criminal justice system aims to balance the objectives of the fight against crimes and

---

[43] Cavadino, M & Dignan, J. (1997). The Penal System: An Introduction (2nd ed.), London: Sage. p. 39.
[44] See President's Commission on Law Enforcement and Administration of Justice (1967). The Challenge of Crime in a Free Society. U.S. Government Printing Office.
[45] Scottish Executive Consultations. Criminal Justice - Aims and Objectives". Disponible à http://www.cjsonline.gov.uk/the_cjs/aims_and_objectives/index.html

justice (fairness and protection of individual rights)[46]. In Sweden, the overall goal for the criminal justice system is to reduce crime and increase public safety[47].

All the principles of criminal justice are based on law. What is law? Law is a system of rules usually applied in all institutions. The purpose of law is to provide an objective set of rules to govern conducts and maintain order in society. These codified laws can coexist or be inconsistent with other forms of social control, such as religious precepts, professional rules and ethics, or cultural mores and customs of a society.

Criminal justice is therefore concerned with actions that are dangerous or harmful to society as a whole, for which prosecutions are pursued not by an individual, but rather by the State. The purpose of the criminal justice system is to provide a precise definition of what constitutes a crime and pronounce sentences for committing such a crime. No criminal law can be valid unless it involves these two factors - the definition of a crime and the pronouncement of a sentence. The goal of criminal justice is primarily concerned with the implementation of criminal law.

CRIMINAL JUSTICE SYSTEM

The criminal justice system consists of three main parts:

- law enforcement or security agents (police);
- arbitration (courts);
- correctional (prisons etc.).

In a criminal justice system, these distinct agencies work together both pursuant to the rule of law and as the primary means of maintaining the rule of law in society. We examine these three main parts of the criminal justice system.

---

46 Scottish Executive Consultations. Criminal Justice - Aims and Objectives". Disponible à http://www.cjsonline.gov.uk/the_cjs/aims_and_objectives/index.html
47 Scottish Executive Consultations, op cit.

POLICE

The first contact of an offender with the criminal justice system is often with the police (or security officers) who investigate a reprehensible act (alleged) and proceed to make an arrest. When justified, security officers or the police are empowered to use force and other forms of legal and effective means to maintain public and social order. The term is most often associated with police headquarters of a State, authorized to exercise the powers of the police of that State in a legally defined area of responsibility. The word "police" is derived from the Latin word, politia (civil administration), which derives from the ancient Greek word, πόλις - polis (city)[48]. The first police comparable to the police of today was created in 1667 under King Louis XIV in France, although modern police force in general traces its origin to 1800: the creation of the Marine Police in London, police of Glasgow, and the police of Napoleon in Paris[49].

The Police are primarily responsible for peacekeeping and the enforcement of criminal law based on their particular mission and jurisdiction. Formed in 1908, the "Federal Bureau of Investigation (FBI)" began in the United States as an entity that could investigate and enforce specific federal laws as a security agency[50]. This, however, constituted only a small part of the general activity of the police[51]. The police include a range of activities in different contexts, but the predominant activity concerns the maintenance of order and the provision of services[52].

---

48 Harper, Douglas. "police". Online Etymology Dictionary. http://www.etymonline.com/index.php?term=police. Retrieved 2007-02-08 .
49 Dinsmor, Alastair (Winter 2003). "Glasgow Police Pioneers". The Scotia News. http://www.scotia-news.com/issue5/ISSUE05a.htm. Et "History". Marine Support Unit. Metropolitan Police. Available at: http://web.archive.org/web/20070716200107/http://www.met.police.uk/msu/history.htm. Retrieved 2007-02-10 et "La Lieutenance Générale de Police". La Préfecture de Police fête ses 200 ans Juillet 1800 - Juillet 2000. La Préfecture de Police au service des Parisiens. http://www.prefecture-policeparis.interieur.gouv.fr/documentation/bicentenaire/theme_expo1.htm.
50 FBI (2009). THE FBI: A Centennial History, 1908-2008. Washington,D.C.: FBI. pp. 138.
51 Walker, Samuel (1977). A Critical History of Police Reform: The Emergence of Professionalism. Lexington, MT: Lexington Books. pp. 143.
52 Neocleous, Mark (2004). Fabricating Social Order: A Critical History of Police Power. London: Pluto Press. pp. 93–94.

Courts

The courts serve as the place where disputes are resolved and justice is administered. With regard to criminal justice, there are a certain number of important figures in any judicial framework. These important figures are referred to as the working group of the courtroom and include both professionals and non professionals. This also includes the judge, prosecutor, and the defense attorney.

The judge or magistrate is a person elected or appointed, who is very familiar with the law, and whose function is to administer objectively the legal procedures and provide final decisions to a case.

In this procedure, culpability (the guilty) or innocence (the not guilty) is decided by the adversarial system. In this system, both parties offer their versions of events and defend their case before the court (sometimes before a judge, sometimes before a jury). The case must be decided in favor of a party that offers the strongest and undeniable arguments founded on the law as applied to the facts of the case.

The Prosecutor is an attorney who lays charges against a person, persons or a corporation. It is the duty of the prosecutor to explain to the court which crime was committed and to specify which elements of evidence were found to incriminate the accused. By having the function of filing a complaint before the court, the prosecutor is a public servant who accuses in the name of the State during criminal proceedings.

A Defense Attorney advises the accused on the judicial process and the most likely outcomes of the case, and then suggests strategies to follow. The accused, not the lawyer, has the right to make final decisions regarding a number of key issues, including the ability to testify, and to accept a plea offer or request a trial before a jury in appropriate cases. It is the duty of the defense attorney to represent the interests of his client, to clarify the questions concerning procedure and evidence. The defense attorney can challenge the evidence presented during the prosecution or present defense evidence and advocate on behalf of his client. At the proceedings, the defense

THEORIES OF JUSTICE

attorney may attempt to offer a rebuttal to the accusations of the prosecutor. The final determination of guilt or innocence is usually done by a third party who is supposed to be disinterested. This function can be performed by a judge, a panel of judges or a jury composed of unbiased citizens. This process varies depending on the laws of specific jurisdiction. In some places, the panel (whether judges or a jury) is required to give a unanimous decision, while in others only a majority vote is required. In America, this process depends on the state, the level of the court, and even agreements between the parties.

Some cases can be resolved without the need for a trial. If the accused confesses to be guilty, a shorter process can be used and a judgment can be passed more quickly. Some countries, like America, allow the plea bargaining process in which the accused pleads guilty or not guilty, and can accept a diversion program or a reduced sentence when the charge is low or in exchange for the cooperation of the accused with other people. This reduction of sentence can be a means of saving the State the cost of a formal trial. Many countries do not allow the use of the plea bargaining process, believing that it forces innocent people to plead guilty in an attempt to avoid severe punishment.

The entire trial process, regardless of the country, is confronted with problems and subject to criticisms. Prejudices and discrimination constitute an ever-present threat to an objective decision. Any prejudice on the part of the lawyers, the judge or jury members threaten to destroy the credibility of the court. Some people argue that the rules that regulate the conduct and proceedings in a courtroom often limit the ability of an ordinary or lay person to participate, thereby reducing judicial proceedings to a battle between lawyers. In this case, the criticism is that decisions are based more and more on the lawyer's eloquence and charisma rather than on a sound justice. The manipulations of the judicial system by the defense attorneys and prosecutors, security officers and the defendants often take place, and there have been cases where justice was denied.

Prison

Offenders are then handed over to the correctional authorities of the judicial system after the accused has been found guilty. Like all other aspects of criminal justice, the administration of sentence has taken many different forms throughout history. From the beginning, when civilizations lacked the resources needed to build and maintain prisons, exile and execution were the primary forms of punishment. Historically, shameful sentences and exile were also used as forms of censorship.

The most visible form of punishment in the modern era is the prison. Prisons can be used as detention centers for prisoners after trial. For the confinement of the accused, prisons are also used. At the beginning, prisons were in most cases used to sequestrate the criminals and little thought was given to their living conditions within their walls. In the United States (specifically in Pennsylvania), the Quaker[53] movement is generally credited to enforce the idea that prisons should be used for the reform of criminals. This can also be seen as a critical moment in the debate on the purpose of sentencing.

Objectives of Prison

Sentences can serve various purposes. First, not only that imprisonment and other forms of punishment remove the criminals from the general population and inhibit their ability to perpetrate further crimes, they also deter others from committing similar crimes in the future. This concept is usually called "general or indirect deterrence," which stresses the prevention of crime by showing the examples of specific deviants. The individual actor is not only the object of the

---

53 The corrections reform agenda in the United States was first initiated by William Penn, at the end of 17th century. For a certain period, the penal code of Pennsylvania was revised to prohibit torture and other cruel forms of punishment in prisons replacing corporal punishments. These reforms were changed after the death of Penn in 1718. Under the pressure of a group called the Quakers, these reforms were revived in Pennsylvania towards the end of the 18th century and led to a sharp decline in crime rates in Pennsylvania. Patrick Colquhoun, Henry Fielding and others spearheaded major reforms in the late eighteenth and early nineteenth centuries. For more details, see Garland, David (2002). "Of Crimes and Criminals." In Maguire, Mike, Rod Morgan, Robert Reiner. The Oxford Handbook of Criminology, 3rd edition. Oxford University Press. pp. 20.

attempt to change behavior, but rather receives a sentence in public in order to deter others from future misconduct. The main idea here is not to ensure that criminals become aware of the consequences of their reprehensible acts and then change their bad behavior, but in order to alert the public by giving them deserved sentences. Many societies also see prison sentences as a form of revenge or reprisals, and any discomfort that prisoners suffer constitute the "retribution" for the harm done to their victims. A new goal of imprisonment is to give criminals the opportunity to be rehabilitated. Many modern prisons offer education or employment trainings to the prisoners as an opportunity to learn a profession and earn a legitimate living when they return to the society. Religious institutions are also present in many prisons, in order to teach ethics to prisoners and to instill in them a sense of morality.

OTHER FORMS OF PUNISHMENT

There are many other forms of punishment that are commonly used in conjunction with or in lieu of imprisonment. The monetary fines are one of the oldest forms of punishment still used today. These fines may be paid to the State or to the victim as a form of reparation. Probation and house arrest are also sanctions that seek to limit the mobility of an offender and his or her possibilities of committing more crimes without being detained in a prison environment. In addition, many jurisdictions may require some form of public or community service as a form of reparation for the offenses committed.

Execution or capital punishment is still used in some countries. Its use is one of the most hotly debated topics of the criminal justice system. Some societies are willing to use death penalty as a form of political control, or for relatively minor offences. Other societies reserve it for only the most sinister and brutal crimes. Others have completely prohibited this practice, believing that the use of capital punishment is too cruel or hypocritical.

◀ FROM CULTURAL JUSTICE TO INTER-ETHNIC MEDIATION

CRITIQUE OF THE NOTION OF DETERRENCE IN THE CRIMINAL JUSTICE SYSTEM

Some have argued that deterrence is ineffective in achieving its ultimate goal. Critics of deterrence argue that offenders do not consider the punishment for a crime they are about to commit, especially in the heat of the moment, and when drugs or alcohol are involved. Some suggest that potential offenders are more likely to be deterred by the threat of being arrested rather than the threat of sanctions. General deterrence has also been heavily criticized for relying on advertising severe penalties, and was described as "the least effective and fair principle of sentencing"[54]. In addition, it is sometimes used by some leaders to induce fear in their country. It is true that this practice will have some effects on the population; however, it could arouse anger from citizens in a situation where the victims were erroneously sentenced to death as occurred in Nigeria in 1995 during the military dictatorship of a Nigerian former military general named, Sani Abacha. On November 10, 1995, the writer Ken Saro-Wiwa and eight other activists and leaders of the Movement for the Survival of the Ogoni People (MOSOP) who were opposed to the oil policy implemented in the region by the military dictator, Sani Abacha and Shell (an oil company operating in the region), were executed by hanging in Port Harcourt by the Nigerian government of General Sani Abacha. Before their execution, Ken Saro-Wiwa was arrested by the Nigerian government back in June 1993, and released a month later. In May 1994 he was arrested the third time and charged with incitement to murder following the death of four Ogoni people. Ken Saro-Wiwa had always rejected the charges brought against him. After a year of imprisonment, he was convicted and sentenced to death by a special tribunal. In his closing remarks to the tribunal, Saro-Wiwa said: "I repeat that we all stand before history. I and my colleagues are not the only ones on trial. Shell is here on trial and it is as well that it is represented by counsel said to be holding a watching brief. The Company has, indeed, ducked this particular trial, but its day will surely come and the lessons learnt here may prove useful to

---

54   Martin, Jacqueline (2005). The English Legal System (4th ed.), London: Hodder Arnold, p. 176.

it for there is no doubt in my mind that the ecological war that the Company has waged in the Delta will be called to question sooner than later and the crimes of that war be duly punished. The crime of the Company's dirty wars against the Ogoni people will also be punished"[55].

"In my innocence of the false charges I face here, in my utter conviction, I call upon the Ogoni people, the peoples of the Niger delta, and the oppressed ethnic minorities of Nigeria to stand up now and fight fearlessly and peacefully for their rights. History is on their side. God is on their side. For the Holy Quran says in Sura 42, verse 41: "All those that fight when oppressed incur no guilt, but Allah shall punish the oppressor. Come the day"[56].

The death sentence of Ken Saro Wiwa and his eight colleagues is one of many examples of the ineffectiveness and weakness of the systems of criminal justice in resolving inter-ethnic or inter-cultural conflicts in a multicultural country where the minorities are constantly fighting for their fundamental human rights and cultural justice.

---

55 Cited in the article of Cindy Baxter and Paul Horsman of Greenpeace International at http://archive.greenpeace.org/comms/ken/murder.html
56 Ibid.

CHAPTER 3

Cultural Justice: A Reflection on the Rights of Minorities

TO UNDERSTAND ALL the points that will be very useful in achieving the goal of this book, we study cultural justice through the liberal theory of minority rights proposed by Will Kymlicka. Indeed, cultural justice revolves around a theory of justice for the cultural rights of the minorities, that is to say, the recognition of minority rights in a multicultural society based on cultural identity and the fundamental principles of liberalism. Specifically, we will raise questions such as multiculturalism, the justification of the rights of the multinational and multiethnic minorities, the notion of a societal culture, internal restrictions, and finally external restrictions. The aim is to highlight the implications of this theory in a multicultural society, if the politics of recognition will be mainly or solely based on liberal values. The choice of the "liberal theory of minority rights" in this study does not mean the abandon of other theories of justice examined which are considered to be equally useful.

In contemporary societies, a reflection on liberal democracies reveals one of the most pressing problems that confront us: how can we manage politically ethno-cultural diversity? Although the League of Nations developed treaties for the protection of cultural minorities after the First World War, the United Nations Charter which was adopted after the Second World War did not have an explicit conception of minority rights[57]. The codification of "human rights" was the central tenet of the UN Charter, and the protection of individual rights was seen as sufficient protection for persons belonging to cultural minorities[58] since these individual rights such as freedom of association, of religion, of speech, of mobility, and of political organization enable individuals to form and maintain groups and associations, and promote their views and interests within the general population.

However, it is increasingly admitted that these common rights of citizenship are not sufficient to accommodate all forms of ethno-cultural diversity. Groups that are marginalized within nation-States, such as, indigenous peoples, national minorities and other minority groups - like immigrant groups - have increasingly advanced claims for rights and equality. They demand in effect, "greater public recognition of their identities, and greater freedom and the possibility to preserve and develop their cultural practices"[59]. These so-called "claims of cultural groups" are diverse and exist on a continuum from general cultural rights (language rights, for example), to territorial claims, equal representation as well as demands for self-determination or autonomy (i.e. the rights of self-government). Although these claims have put pressure against nation-States in which these groups are located, the need to respond to these demands is becoming increasingly important in the world.

In view of these demands, political theorists have stressed the need to theorize the relationship between the identity of a cultural group and the principles of democracy[60]. This chapter discusses some

---

57 Crawford, James and Susan Marks, (1998), The global democratic deficit: An essay in international law and its limits. In Re-imagining political community: Studies in cosmopolitan democracy, ed. D. Archibugi, D. Held, and M. Kohler, (Stanford: Stanford University Press) 72-90.
58 Hannum, Hurst. 1990. Autonomy, sovereignty and self-determination: The accommodation of conflicting rights. Philadelphia, PA: The University of Pennsylvania Press
59 WILL KYMLICKA AND RAPHAEL COHENALMAGOR, Democracy and Multiculturalism in R. Cohen-Almagor, Editor, Challenges to Democracy: Essays in Honour and Memory of Isaiah Berlin (London: Ashgate Publishing Ltd., 2000). Chapter 5, p. 89.
60 Kymlicka, Will and Wayne Norman. 2000. Citizenship in culturally diverse societies: Issues, contexts, concepts. In Citizenship in diverse societies, ed. Will Kymlicka and Wayne Norman, 1-41. Oxford: Oxford University Press.

CULTURAL JUSTICE: A REFLECTION ON THE RIGHTS OF MINORITIES

of the questions, theoretical and practical, raised by these demands, while focusing in particular on the difficulties that may arise in the multicultural countries when the minorities seeking recognition are not themselves liberal. How are these cultural group rights linked to individual rights? What should we do if group rights conflict with individual rights? Can a liberal democracy allow minority groups to restrict individual rights of their own members, or should it insist that all groups respect the principles of liberalism? An attempt to find answers to these questions will form the basis of our reflection on a liberal theory of minority rights proposed by Will Kymlicka.

In "Multicultural Citizenship: A Liberal Theory of Minority Rights", Will Kymlicka defends what he describes as an «impeccably liberal system"[61] of the rights of cultural minorities. This book clarifies a lot of discussion that was developed since the publication of his influential book, "Liberalism, Community and Culture"[62] resulting from the global response to the "challenge of multiculturalism"[63]. Although Kymlicka highlights the most central theoretical and practical problems facing liberal democracies (for example, the politics of representation and the basis for the commitment of liberal democracy itself), the objective of this chapter concerns specifically his defense of minority rights.

Since the members of the minority groups are equally citizens of a given State, it then becomes imperative to clarify the term "citizenship". Kymlicka is concerned about a specific question to which any general theory on citizenship must answer, namely, in what ways are citizens incorporated in a multicultural society? The question that arises here is to know what is meant by the word "citizen". Michael Walzer describes two definitions of citizenship. "The first describes citizenship as an office, a responsibility, a burden proudly assumed; the second describes citizenship as a status, an entitlement, a right or a set of rights passively enjoyed"[64]. In this regard, a citizen

---

61　W. Kymlicka, Multicultural Citizenship, op cit., p.153.
62　W. Kymlicka, Liberalism, Community and Culture (Oxford: Clarendon Press, 1989) [Hereafter, Liberalism, Community and Culture].
63　A. Gutmann, "The Challenge of Multiculturalism in Political Ethics" (1993) 22 Phil. & Pub. Affairs, p.170.
64　"Citizenship" in T. Ball, J. Farr & R.C. Hanson, eds., Political Innovation and Conceptual Change (Cambridge: Cambridge University Press, 1989), p.216

refers to a «member of a political community who is entitled to all the prerogatives and encumbered with all the responsibilities attached to this status»[65]. This means that at least any theory of citizenship must provide an account not only of civic rights and duties of citizens, but also of what or who the citizens are and on what grounds they should be incorporated into the political community. In his defense of the rights of cultural minorities, Kymlicka argues that there are sound principles of justice which require that the rights of citizenship be based on cultural group membership, that is to say, members of certain groups can only be incorporated into the political community, if "the group differentiated rights, powers, status, or immunities, beyond the common right of citizenship are accepted"[66].

Kymlicka's book aims to elucidate the fundamental principles of cultural justice. In addition, these principles are intended to provide the tools with which we can formulate fair and reasonable solutions to racial, ethnic and cultural conflicts present in contemporary societies[67]. By examining the arguments of Kymlicka, we try to show that the various important distinctions he employs have enriched our understanding of these conflicts. Among these distinctions, we will reflect on the distinctions between different types of minority groups in a multicultural society, that is, multinational groups and polyethnic groups and the different kinds of «rights» that these groups are demanding. But before that, it will be very helpful to understand what Kymlicka means by the term «multiculturalism.»

Understanding Multiculturalism

In Multicultural Citizenship, Kymlicka is firmly committed to his longstanding claim that cultural membership should be explained from a perspective of liberal justice. But what is culture according to Kymlicka, and how can we understand multiculturalism? In the first chapter of this book, we analyzed the most interesting notions

---
65 Ibid., p. 211
66 Multicultural Citizenship, op cit., p. 206
67 In Multicultural Citizenship, op cit., P. 1, Kymlicka notes that "since the end of the Cold War, ethno-cultural conflicts have become the most common source of political violence in the world, and they show no signs of decreasing."

CULTURAL JUSTICE: A REFLECTION ON THE RIGHTS OF MINORITIES

of culture. But for Kymlicka, the central concept in the definition of culture is "nation", in other words, "a historical community, more or less institutionally complete, occupying a given territory or homeland, sharing a distinct language and culture"[68]. Thus, a State is "multicultural if its members belong either to different nations (a multinational state), or have emigrated from different nations (a polyethnic state), and if this is an important aspect of personal identity and political life"[69]. Sometimes multiculturalism is used as a topic for the discussion of all historically disadvantaged social groups. While Kymlicka is fully aware of the injustices suffered by women, homosexuals, disabled and the poor - to mention just a few - he considers them as emerging from separate questions as they occur within 'a national society or an ethnic group of the individual"[70].

Multiculturalism is therefore defined in ethno-national sense, characterized by "national minorities" and "ethnic groups"[71]. According to Kymlicka, if a nation is incorporated into a larger state, then this nation becomes what would be called "national minority". National minorities derive from voluntary or involuntary incorporation of a whole nation, whereas ethnic minorities result from individual or family immigration from different nations. As the method of incorporation has a profound influence on the institutions, identity and aspirations of a cultural minority, any response to the politics of multiculturalism must begin by examining which legitimate demands could be made in these situations of cultural diversity. Thus, Kymlicka avoids the non-plausible conclusion that all cultural minorities should be accorded the same treatment, and demonstrates convincingly that what is appropriate for ethnic groups is not necessarily appropriate for national minorities[72]. He also argues that a reflection on the national minorities and ethnic groups can help structure our thinking in regard to groups that do not fall easily

---

[68] Op cit., p. 11
[69] Ibid., p.18
[70] Ibid., p.19
[71] Ibid., p.10
[72] Liberalism, Community and Culture, op cit., p. 2; See also J.R. Danley, "Liberalism, Aboriginal Rights and Cultural Minorities" (1991) 20 Phil. & Pub. Affairs, p.176.

into the two camps (for example, African Americans and refugees) these cases should also be considered on their own merits. But while Kymlicka is keen to stress that there is no "magic formula"[73] to resolve all cultural conflicts, the causes are more historical than theoretical: "difficult cases that exist today have often emerged as a result of past injustices and inconsistencies"[74].

According to the understanding of Kymlicka, the myth of a "culturally homogeneous State"[75], accepted by most of the liberal theorists is unsustainable[76] and, most countries around the world are multinational, polyethnic, or both. Has this hypothesis, however, distorted the liberal practice? Does the existence of multiculturalism have implications on the rights of citizenship? The received ideas of contemporary liberalism "insist that the liberal commitment to individual liberty is opposed to the acceptance of collective rights; and that the liberal commitment to universal rights is opposed to the acceptance of the rights of specific groups "[77]. Kymlicka argues that this politics of "benign neglect" to attempt a strict separation "between the State and ethnicity" is deeply wrong[78].

Justification of Minority Rights

In fact, the central argument of this chapter is that a proactive attitude with regard to cultural membership should be taken. In concrete terms this will mean that at least some minority rights, beyond the common rights of citizenship, are fair in most countries. We therefore examine two minority rights proposed by Kymlicka, namely the rights of national minorities and the rights of ethnic minorities.

---

73 Multicultural Citizenship, op cit., p. 1
74 Ibid., p. 25
75 Ibid., p.9
76 See V. Van Dyke, «The Individual, the State, and Ethnic Communities in Political Theory" (1977) 29 World Pol. 343.
77 Multicultural Citizenship, supra note 1 at 68
78 Ibid., pp. 107-08

National Minority Rights

Although Kymlicka maintains that both the national minorities and ethnic groups make legitimate demands for minority rights, his most interesting argument concerns national minorities. The central justification continues in two stages. First, he argues that individual autonomy "is dependent on the presence of a societal culture, defined by language and history and that most people have a strong bond with their own culture"[79]. Second, liberal justice "is not only compatible with, but even requires, high level of preoccupation with cultural identity[80]. Minority rights may thus be justified to the extent that they ensure that the collective good of cultural membership of the minorities is also protected as it is done for the majority. In this context, Kymlicka proposes political autonomy or territorial jurisdiction to ensure the free and full development of a societal culture of national minorities. For him, the rights of self-government should be granted only to national minorities. Without these rights, national minorities will not have "the same opportunity to live and work in their own culture like members of the majority, and this is unfair according to egalitarian liberalism" of Rawls or Dworkin, who place emphasis on the importance of correcting uncaused inequalities"[81]. Kymlicka's insistence that the protection of societal cultures is important for individual autonomy remains crucial for his intellectual analysis.

Before analyzing the first defense of minority rights for the national minorities, it is very important to note that "all societal cultures are almost always national cultures; thus nations are almost societal cultures"[82]. Understanding the concept of "societal culture" is therefore of crucial importance.

Concept of a "Societal Culture"

For Kymlicka, a societal culture is "a culture which provides its members with appropriate means of life in all range of human

---
79 Ibid., p. 8
80 Ibid., pp. 7-8
81 Multicultural Citizenship, op cit., p.109
82 Multicultural Citizenship, op cit., p. 80

activities, including social, educational, religious, recreational and economic life, encompassing both the public and private spheres"[83]. Like nations, societal cultures are territorially based and founded on a common language. The societal cultures thus provide "the daily vocabulary of social life" which, in the modern world, means that they "must be institutionally incorporated in schools, media, economy, government, etc."[84]. In essence, therefore, societal culture is one that can, in a modern sense, be lived within the community, not in the sense that it is completely independent, but because it provides a full range of options for a fulfilled life.

In "Liberalism, Community and Culture," Kymlicka argued that the importance of cultural communities lies in the fact that it is within these communities that "individuals form and evaluate their goals and ambitions"[85]. Hence, ethnic groups and national minorities are the groups in which people make important choices concerning their lives. There are, however, many other small communities, such as religious groups and subcultures that, at least in some cases, are of great value to the formation of individual goals.

With this clarification, we can now return to the first point of the defense of Kymlicka for minority rights of national groups, which tries to expatiate on the relationship between individual freedom and membership to a societal culture. Starting from the idea that multinational politics is associated with several societal cultures, Kymlicka argues that, in general, immigrants enlarge and enrich the dominant culture, while the national minorities seek to preserve their distinctive societal cultures, which "were already integrated into a complete set of social practices and institutions, covering all aspects of social life"[86]. Although Kymlicka believes that both the national minorities and the ethnic groups have legitimate claims for minority rights, only the former have a claim of justice to maintain their own societal culture.

---
83 Ibid., p.76
84 Ibid.
85 Multicultural Citizenship, op cit., p.135
86 Multicultural Citizenship, op cit., p. 29

CULTURAL JUSTICE: A REFLECTION ON THE RIGHTS OF MINORITIES

But why are societal cultures so important for individual liberty? According to Kymlicka, liberalism promotes individual autonomy by allowing individuals not only to choose their own conception of "good life" but also to review those choices, if and when they deem it necessary to do so"[87]. Fundamentally, our societal cultures do not only provide us with options from which we can choose, but also they make these options meaningful for us. Individual action can be made alive only through shared vocabularies of language and history. Thus, without belonging to a societal culture, we lack the prerequisite criteria for making "intelligent decisions on how to lead our lives"[88]. And, since the differentiated group rights promote access to a societal culture, they «have a legitimate role to play in a liberal theory of justice»[89]. That is to say, access to a societal culture is the «primary good» of Rawls - a «good that people need regardless of their chosen way of life, as it provides the context in which these particular choices are made"[90].

Many critics have been quick to point out that often people successfully pass from one culture to another in the society, and that this cosmopolitan alternative "undermines any claim according to which people should have access to their own societal cultures"[91]. Kymlicka rightly notes that this objection is often exaggerated and argues that it is not all that is due to a person by virtue of his or her right must be guaranteed. More precisely, a right may be renounced, and absolutely, voluntary immigration is a way to give up a specific right to live in one's own societal culture. According to the interpretation of Kymlicka of rawlsian liberalism, it seems fairly accurate. The important point regarding the designation of a good

---

87   Ibid., p.80
88   Ibid., P.83. Compare Liberalism, Community and Culture, op cit., P. 190, "where it is argued that cultural membership is a necessary condition for a meaningful individual choice, "because it is only through a rich and protected cultural structure that people can become aware, in a lively way, of the options available to them, and intelligently examine their value ".
89   Multicultural Citizenship, op cit., p. 84
90   Ibid., P. 214. See also, Liberalism, Community and Culture, op cit., P. 192. Kymlicka defended this idea, arguing that the context of choice is "a precondition for self-respect, (....)". For J. Rawls, A Theory of Justice (Cambridge, Mass..: Harvard University Press, 1971) on page 440, self respect is the greatest important and primary good.
91   See, J. Waldron, "Minority Cultures and the Cosmopolitan Alternative" (1992) 25 U. Mich. J.L. Ref. 751

as a primary "good" is that it is reasonable for people to desire it no matter what other things they want[92]. Kymlicka highlights a variety of plausible explanations to explain why access to one's societal culture is something "that people cannot reasonably be expected to leave behind ... although some people voluntarily choose to do so"[93].

In the modern world, we have access to the cultural meanings coming from various sources, and some theorists have wondered whether it is appropriate to speak of individuated cultures at all. Kymlicka stresses that, while cultures are susceptible to external influence and that cultural identity is dynamic, the incorporation of cultural elements from other nations should take place through the choice of the members of the national minorities themselves. While it is appropriate that cultures change in accordance with the choice of their members, "the decisions made by people outside the culture can threaten the survival of a culture itself"[94]. Thus, modifications in a culture coming from its own members can change its character, but cannot threaten its existence or survival. This thesis, however, seems to be the foundation of cultural change (or perhaps the value of cultural diversity, autonomy or self-determination).

Thus, Kymlicka believes that the various "rights to autonomy" which delegate powers to minority groups, for example, language rights, and rights to certain forms of indigenous lands, are legitimate in that they correct the inequalities in the distribution of the "good of cultural membership"[95]. Because cultural membership is a good thing that people can reasonably be expected to possess, it should be protected in an equal manner for both the members of the majority and the minorities.

Ethnic Minority Rights

According to Kymlicka, polyethnic groups also make a legitimate claim for the rights of minorities. More precisely, they are entitled to

---

92   See also Rawls, op cit., p. 62
93   Multicultural Citizenship, op cit., p. 86
94   Multicultural Citizenship, op cit., p. 105
95   Multicultural Citizenship, op cit., p. 113

"polyethnic rights", which ensure that they are incorporated into the dominant culture in fair conditions, that allow ethnic and religious minorities to "express their cultural particularity and pride"[96] without detriment to their success in the economic and political institutions of the dominant society. Not only that the common rights of citizenship can be more strictly applied to eliminate all forms of discrimination and prejudice, some specific group rights should also be justified. Neutral cultural politics means that the laws, such as the one establishing public holidays or uniforms in public institutions should not discriminate against particular ethnic groups. Multiculturalism for immigrants, therefore, is best understood not as a rejection of linguistic and institutional integration, but as a change in the terms of integration. Immigrants are still expected to learn the language of the majority, and to integrate into the common institutions. Multiculturalism believes that it is neither necessary nor fair to insist that institutional and linguistic integration be accompanied by a broader cultural assimilation. On the contrary, in order for the requirement of the government concerning institutional and linguistic integration to be fair, these common institutions need to be reformed so as to accommodate the identity of immigrant groups.

In order to guarantee the representation of groups with the intention of giving a voice to the minorities and to allow a fair representation of their concerns in decision-making procedures of the State, Will Kymlicka also stresses the importance of giving minority groups the rights of representation. This right seeks to make the political process more representative and respond to some systematic disadvantages or barriers in the political process.

Individualism and Collective Rights

In maintaining that his theory is a liberal theory of minority rights, Kymlicka is unambiguous in his commitment to "moral individualism" - the idea that what matters most, from a moral point of view, is the individual. Perhaps what makes the defense of minority rights of

---

96 Multicultural Citizenship, op cit., p. 31

Kymlicka typically liberal is that these rights are uniquely recognized "to the extent that they are compatible with the respect for freedom and individual autonomy"[97]. It is therefore reasonable that most of the claims for the differentiated group rights be for «external protections» (against the society as a whole), as opposed to «internal restrictions» (which could undermine the fundamental freedom of the members of the group).

However, most of the rights of minorities that Kymlicka defends, such as the rights of language and self-determination protect the interests that the isolated individuals cannot enjoy independently, because they need the collective production in order to make them useful. The value of the right to one's own language or to self-government cannot be fully understood by a simple aggregation of the interests of individuals as individuals. The full value of these rights to an individual is «incomprehensible outside their reference to the enjoyment of others»[98].

The conflict between collective rights and individual rights is possible. Here we are in a relatively familiar territory because individual rights are often in conflict with group rights, and there is no reason to believe that the general strategies developed to address these conflicts cannot be extended to cases where individual rights and collective rights come into conflict. In addressing these questions, Kymlicka's distinction between external protections and internal restrictions significantly enriches our understanding.

Two Types of Group Rights

What then is the relationship between individual rights and the rights of a cultural group? Can one say that they are mutually reinforcing? Or are they always antagonizing each other? In order to answer these questions, Kymlicka identifies two types of rights that a group may claim. The first involves the right of a group against its

---
97 Ibid., p.75
98 J. Waldron, "Can Communal Goods Be Human Rights?" in J. Waldron, Liberal Rights: Collected Papers 1981-199 1(Cambridge: Cambridge University Press, 1993), p.355.

own members. The second is the right of a group against the larger society, that is to say, society as a whole. These two types of rights that a cultural group could claim can be understood as ways of ensuring the stability of national, ethnic, or religious groups. The first type is intended to protect the group from the destabilizing effect of internal dissidence (for example, the decision of individual members not to follow traditional practices and customs); while the second is intended to protect the group from the impact of external pressures (for example, economic or political decisions of the whole society)[99]. To distinguish these two types of group rights, Kymlicka calls the first one "internal restrictions" and the second "external protections".

"Internal Restrictions"

According to Kymlicka, "internal restrictions concern intra-group relationships. In this practice, an ethnic or a national group uses power to restrict the freedom of its members in the name of group solidarity. This indicates the danger of individual oppression"[100]. The majority often takes this kind of action to restrict the freedom of each member in the name of group solidarity. These practices are contrary to liberal ideals.

An example of these practices could be some form of internal restrictions within some cultural minorities in Nigeria. Some ethnic and religious groups demand the right to put an end to proper education of their children (especially girls), so as to reduce the chances of leaving the community or strengthen the obligation to continue with the traditional customs such as mandatory arranged marriages that are common among some of the cultural communities in Nigeria.

"External Protections"

External protections involve inter-group relationships. Indigenous groups, for instance, need protection in order to limit their vulnerability from the decisions of external groups or society. Therefore, they should

99 Multicultural Citizenship, op cit., p. 35
100 Ibid., p.36

have the right to their own taxes, health care, education and governance.

Kymlicka argues therefore that "the Liberals can and should adopt certain external protections, where they promote fairness between groups, but should reject internal restrictions which limit the right of the group members to question and evaluate traditional authorities[101]. For him, the liberal vision requires freedom within the minority groups and equality between minority groups and the majority[102].

This citation shows the commitment of Kymlicka to autonomy. The right to culture is good as long as it does not infringe on the rights of the members of the group as citizens (in fact, as human beings). The essential point about the protection of societal cultures (from outside interference) is that the cultures of a society are important for the freedom and equality of their members. Our freedom consists in our ability to choose from a wide variety of options, and our societal culture constitutes a good number of these possible options. So it would be contradictory for Kymlicka, after arguing that "the right to societal cultures" is necessary for the autonomy of members, to allow culture to limit the autonomy or freedom of members in a way that cannot be impartially justified. If autonomy is a fundamental liberal value, and if "the right to societal cultures" is justified by an appeal to individual autonomy, it would not be logical to allow culture to encroach on the autonomy of the members.

The purpose of Kymlicka's book is the articulation of the principles of justice which should be applied to intercultural conflicts. As he has already affirmed, Kymlicka supports the rights of minorities only to the extent that they do not require "internal restrictions" or establish a system that allows a group to exploit another. In theory, this means that minority rights are justified only insofar as the minorities accept the principles of liberal democracy, autonomy and tolerance, which, for Kymlicka, are "two sides of the same coin "[103].

101 Ibid., p.37
102 Ibid., p.152
103 Multicultural Citizenship, op cit., P. 158. Conflicts between individual rights and collective rights must therefore be resolved by an analysis of their "internal relation", a technique that can also be used to resolve conflicts between individual rights. For more explanations, see, J. Waldron, "Rights in Conflict" in Liberal Rights, Sop cit., P.203.

CULTURAL JUSTICE: A REFLECTION ON THE RIGHTS OF MINORITIES

"Multicultural Citizenship" raises many important and challenging questions. Given the increasing number of intercultural conflicts in North America, the shortcomings that underline the modernization theory are highlighted by Kymlicka. The idea that modernity would be understood by a smooth transition from Gemeinschaft (community) to Gesellschaft (association), with the gradual dissolution of ethnicity, has not yet proven to be a solution to ethno-religious conflicts in the contemporary societies. Ethnicity has persisted in North America, in Africa and elsewhere. This failure simply means that ethnicity will remain, and that the stability of African States, for instance, is threatened not by ethnicity per se as we will see very soon in the next chapter, but by the failure of the institutions of the State to recognize and take into account ethnic differences and diverse interests. According to these arguments, the lesson learned from the examination of ethnic conflicts is that governments should not discriminate against minority groups[104] otherwise they will create more conflicts.

The "liberal theory of minority rights" proposed by Will Kymlicka, though a very efficient tool in re-establishing social equality and promoting cultural justice in the Western multicultural States like Canada, does not seem to be sufficient in resolving ethno-religious conflicts in Africa, and particularly in Nigeria. It needs to be accompanied by other conflict resolution models. As a result, we propose to reflect in this book on the possibility of inter-ethnic mediation in Africa, considered as an alternative method of resolving ethno-religious conflicts, and a valuable tool for peace-building and democracy. One of the reasons for this argument is that Kymlicka's definition of "polyethnic" groups is completely different from the African notion of ethnicity. For him, a multi-ethnic society is based on voluntary or involuntary immigration, while the multi-national groups constitute the indigenes or the autochthones. In Africa, however, it could be argued that the term "ethnicity" encompasses both the "polyethnic" and multinational groups described by Kymlicka. Nevertheless, it has to be admitted

---

104 Since this negates the principle of 'liberal justice' that guarantees the right of some form of 'autonomy' and equality.

◄ FROM CULTURAL JUSTICE TO INTER-ETHNIC MEDIATION

that Kymlicka's liberal theory of minority rights has broadened our knowledge of intercultural and ethnic conflicts, and has proffered valuable tools and guidelines for a democratic and peaceful ethno-religious conflict resolution in Africa.

PART II
ETHNIC CONFLICTS IN AFRICA AND THEIR HISTORICAL MANIFESTATIONS

CHAPTER 4

Ethnic Conflicts in Africa

IN AFRICA, ETHNIC conflicts have become today a very serious challenge, which explains perhaps why ethnicity is regarded as the concept that predominates in "African Studies" at the moment. Unlike Kymlicka's definition of "polyethnic groups" in terms of immigration, ethnic groups from the African perspective are defined as communities of people who share cultural and linguistic characteristics, including history, tradition, myth, and origin. The ethnic situation in Africa reflects the heterogeneity of ethnic groups in terms of culture and language which are endemic in different origins and histories. Researchers have attempted to develop a theoretical approach of ethnicity and ethnic conflicts over a long period. Some, like Donald Horowitz[1], Ted Gurr[2], Donald Rothschild[3] and Edward Azar[4], are convinced that ethnic conflicts being experienced today by Africa are deeply rooted in religion, language, identity, race, discrimination and poverty. Some ethnic conflicts in Africa occur when the claims of a group for land and territory become incompatible with the desire of others to satisfy their own interests and needs within the same

---
1 Horowitz, Donald (1985) Ethnic Groups In Conflict. Berkeley: University of California press.
2 Gurr, Ted (1970). Why Men Rebel (Princeton); Gurr, Ted and B. Harff (1994) Ethnic Conflict In World Politics. (Sanfrancisco: west View press.)
3 Rothschild, Donald (1997), Managing Ethnic Conflict In Africa: Pressures And Incentives For Cooperation. Brookings Press.
4 Azar, Edwards (1990), The Management Of Protracted Social Conflict. Theory And Cases, Dartmouth, Aldershot.

physical territory. Other claims are underpinned by political, socio-economic and psychological motives. Becoming so complex, ethnic conflicts in Africa are difficult to resolve or manage. However, no country can afford the luxury of leaving ethnic conflicts or ignoring them. Each multi-ethnic State is trying to find ways to deal with ethnic conflicts. Failure to resolve them, ethnic conflicts have high potential to degenerate into tribal violence and violent clashes, and even in massacres, ethnic and religious wars, genocides.

The main idea of this part of the book is that ethnic conflicts in Africa have their origin in cultural injustice and inequality. Wherever such injustices and inequalities occur among groups, conflicts are inevitable. Hence the question: how can we effectively resolve ethnic conflicts in Africa in order to prevent further massacres? It is therefore necessary to note that an adequate analysis of ethnic conflicts in Africa is very important so as to avoid prescribing wrong remedy for this evil.

Analysis Hypothesis

This analysis is structured around a central hypothesis. Conflict is inevitable in any society where people are deprived of their fundamental human rights, including the rights of survival, government representation, cultural and religious freedom as well as equality in all its meanings, security, dignity and association. It is also likely to occur when the action of a government is considered to be contrary to the national or ethnic interest of a people and where government policy is biased in favor of a particular ethnic group.

In order to obtain a good result, our analysis will focus on one of the multicultural African countries where ethno-religious conflicts pose lots of problems these days and where the struggle for recognition and respect for the rights of ethnic and religious minorities require our urgent attention and our civic and philosophical reflections. We will therefore undertake a detailed analysis of most of the ethnic conflicts that have recently plagued Nigeria. However, we do not pretend to have the complete solution to the threat posed by ethnic conflicts in Nigeria and Africa in general. Instead, we try to make a modest contribution to the ongoing discussions. We begin by making a general overview of the ethnic conflicts in contemporary Africa.

General Overview of Ethnic Conflicts in Contemporary Africa

For many years, questions related to ethnic identity were ignored in Africa. Recently, accumulated evidence brings to light the negative impacts of violent conflicts between different ethnic groups in the African States as a whole. Today, African countries are confronted with greater challenges to peace, stability, security and development. Despite all the efforts of some African governments, sub-regional, regional and international organizations, such as the United Nations, many African countries suffer every day the harmful effects of ethnic conflicts. The histories of wars and violent conflicts in Rwanda, Somalia, Sudan, Egypt, Democratic Republic of Congo, Burundi, South Africa, Angola, Kenya, Liberia, Sierra Leone, Ivory Coast, Togo, Benin, Senegal, Mali, Niger, Nigeria, and in several other countries of sub-Saharan Africa, from the year 1965 until today, have raised concerns that ethnic divisions, affiliations, discriminations and racism can affect the prospects for economic and political developments in Africa. These countries, like many other countries in Africa, are ethnically diverse, and unfortunately have not yet developed or found adequate and democratic solutions to address the causes and effects of ethnic conflicts.

Ethnic diversity in itself is not a bad thing in that it constitutes part of the wealth of a nation-State. However, it can lead to an increase in civil unrest if the leaders do not find proactive and fair ways for the distribution of resources. This view is supported by both individual scenes of ethnic violence and by their global correlation: Africa does not only have the greatest ethnic diversity, but it has also experienced the highest incidence of civil wars. In traditionally stable countries, inter-ethnic conflicts are now becoming increasingly known. In Kenya, for instance, ethnic tensions linked to multi-party elections resulted in the death of about 1,800 people and at least 350,000 displaced persons following the clashes that took place from November 1992 to July 1995 according to "The Human Rights Watch." The number of people wounded in July 1995 was put to 3000[5]. Other deaths occurred in relation to the elections of 1997 and 2007. According to the statistics of the United Nations Human Rights Council, 21,000 people died in political violence in South Africa during apartheid of which 14,000 people died during the process of transition from 1990 to 1994 when fighting between militarized supporters of the African National Congress (ANC) and the Inkatha movement reached its climax. Political competition between and within the different organizations continues to be a source of violent conflicts in the province, which was responsible for about 200 deaths in the first half of 1998.

Several other conflicts that have affected Africans are remarkable in Sudan. This is a civil conflict which is said to have started four decades ago between the Arab-Muslim region of the North and the non-Arab groups, the Christians and animists of the South. The most recent phase which began in 1993 resulted in the deaths of approximately one million people due to war or starvation caused by war. Specifically, the United Nations says that about 300,000 people have died from the combined effects of war, hunger and disease and that 2.7 million people fled their homes since the outbreak of hostilities in the Western arid region in 2003[6]. In these conflicts, deprivation of food is often used as an instrument of war. Because of media control by the government and the nature of conflict, these conflicts are almost forgotten by the Western society except at the time when the call for a referendum was launched.

In Rwanda, dramatic events had also taken place when the Hutus organized a massacre of the Tutsis causing many casualties in the first half of 1994. The United Nations estimates that some 800,000

---

5   See, John R. Rogge, Draft Report: "The Internal Displaced Population in Western, Nyanza and Rift Valley Provinces: A Needs Assessment and Rehabilitation Programme", April 28, 1993, as report in "the Government of Kenya/UNDP Programme Document: Programme for Displaced Persons, Inter-agency Joint Programming, October 26, 1993 P.8.

6   Q&A: Sudan's Darfur conflict, BBC News, Page last updated at 14:39 GMT, Tuesday, 23 February 2010 à http://news.bbc.co.uk/2/hi/africa/3496731.stm

Rwandans, mostly the Tutsis, were killed during those three months[7] and 20,000 in refugee camps of the neighboring countries, where a total of 1.7 million people had fled. Some of the Hutus who expressed solidarity towards the Tutsis were killed as traitors to the Hutu cause. Over a period of one hundred days, it was the fastest genocide in history and that of a larger scale in terms of deaths per day. The tension between the same ethnic groups in Burundi, the neighboring country, was very high for a large part of the period of independence, causing the death of about 100,000 people in 1972[8]. New ethnic conflicts shook Burundi in 1988; the Tutsi army massacred several tens of thousands of Hutus, while 45, 000 others took refuge in Rwanda. In addition, in 1993, almost 100, 000 people died in combat in Burundi following an attempted coup d'état by the majority of the Tutsi army after the electoral victory of a political party mainly Hutu. Despite the presence of a contingent of the OAU who arrived to offer protection to the government in December 1993, clashes between the army and Hutu militias continued. In 1996 the military overthrew President Sylvestre Ntibantunganya (a Hutu) and replaced him with Pierre Buyoya (Tutsi). In response, the neighboring countries imposed sanctions on the foreign trade of Burundi. In 1997, about 750,000 Burundian refugees were encamped across the borders of the country, mainly in Zaire (Present Democratic Republic of the Congo). A truce agreement in July 1998 ended most hostilities that have caused 200,000 deaths in five years, mostly civilians[9].

In Angola, the peace negotiations between União Nacional para a Independencia Total de Angola (UNITA) and the Angolan government during the 1990s was accompanied by intermittent wars. The rejection of the results of the presidential election in September

---

7   Lettre datée du 15 décembre 1999, adressée au Secrétaire général par les membres de la Commission indépendante d'enquête sur les actions de l'Organisation des Nations Unies lors du génocide de 1994 au Rwanda retrouvable à http://www.un.org/french/documents/view_doc.asp?symbol=S/1999/1257
8   Regarding this information, read Evariste Ngayimpenda, "Histoire du conflit politico-ethnique burundais, les premières marches du calvaire 1960-1973, Bujumbura, Editions de la Renaissance, 2007, p. 501.
9   Tom Lodge, Towards an Understanding of Contemporary Armed Conflicts in Africa, Published in Monograph No 36: Whither Peacekeeping in Africa? April 1999, retrouvable sur : http://www.iss.co.za/pubs/monographs/No36/ArmedConflict.html

◄ FROM CULTURAL JUSTICE TO INTER-ETHNIC MEDIATION

1992 by UNITA was immediately followed by some of the most serious conflicts and extensive experience during the Thirty Year War in Angola. The prolonged nature of the war in Angola can be attributed to the complexity of a liberation struggle that involved three popular movements fighting for supremacy. It is a reflection of a colonial experience and the cultural and historical divisions between the Bakongo elites in the north, a creolized intelligentsia in the Western coastal capital, and the leaders of a relatively prosperous farming community that developed along the railway of Benguela. A massive external military assistance for the main contenders of the war after the collapse of Portuguese domination removed any attempt for compromise or resolution, which accentuated the ideological distinctions between them, and greatly expanded the scope of the war.

In Somalia, since the fall of President Mohamed Siad Barre in 1991, between 300,000 and 500,000 Somali people were killed, of whom the vast majority was civilians, during the fighting between rival militias[10]. Hundreds of thousands of others took the path of exile to neighboring countries or within the country despite the efforts of the Western governments, NGOs and the United Nations.

In West Africa, regional rebellions and ethno-religious conflicts have intensified. The civil war in Nigeria, also known as the Nigeria - Biafra War, lasted about three years. It was a bloody conflict with a very high number of deaths of more than one million people. Seven years after Nigeria's independence from Great Britain, the war started because of the secession attempt of the southeastern region of Nigeria on May 30, 1967, when it declared itself the independent Republic of Biafra. The battles that followed and greatly increased human suffering attracted the indignation and the intervention of the international community. During this civil war, from 3,000 to 5,000 people approximately were dying every day from hunger in Biafra

---

10 See the article titled : «Somalie: un obus de mortier tue 14 personnes à Mogadiscio dans une mosquée publié par Jeune Afrique le 10/05/2009 à 15h:2 disponible à http://www.jeuneafrique.com/actu/20090510T152620Z20090510T141610Z/actualite-afriquesomalie-un-obus-de-mortier-tue-14-personnes-a-mogadiscio-dans-une-mosquee.html

ETHNIC CONFLICTS IN AFRICA

as a result of naval blockade[11]. Today, the hatred implanted by this war has generated painful consequences with increasing massacres during violent clashes between different ethnic groups, especially between the North and South.

The two years of Tuareg uprising in northern Niger with its impacts in Mali, was appeased by a peace treaty in April 1994. Local insurgencies in southern Chad and the secessionist Movement of Casamance in southern Senegal are also examples. The latter has had the most serious consequences in recent times, with the displacement of about 20,000 refugees caused by the rebellion.

In Liberia, Charles Taylor's rebellion was directed against the government of the former army sergeant, Samuel Doe, whose coup d'état of 1980 overthrew the former political regime, the True Whig. The True Whig Party was supported by the descendants of American slaves who were resettled in the 1970s and had built an administration completely around three poles of the dominant family. Doe had fortified his administration after an election of which the opposition parties rejected the results as fraudulent. The rebellion was terminated by the tensions of this period, but also attracted the support of the military that was deeply divided into factions. At this point, the conflict had caused the death of 150,000 people and led to a series of regional maneuvers by warlords according to national predominance.

The war in Liberia was extended to Sierra Leone in 1991 with the creation of the Revolutionary United Front (RUF) by Foday Sankoh, and two allies, Abu Kanu and Rashid Mansaray, and with substantial assistance from Charles Taylor of Liberia[12] who hoped to dissuade the government in Freetown from participating in ECOMOG through his sponsorship of a rebellion in Sierra Leone. The war in Sierra Leone is said to have displaced more than two million people, nearly half of the population of the country.

---

11 For more information on this war, read J. O. G. Achuzia, Requiem Biafra (Enugu: Fourth Dimension Publishing Co., 1986); See also, A. A. Madiebo, The Nigerian Revolution and the Biafra War (Enugu: Fourth Dimension Publishing Co., 1980).

12 David M. Crane, "Indictment proceedings of the special court for Sierra Leone Case No. SCSL - 2004-15-PT", Special Court for Sierra Leone (February 5th, 2004).

◄ FROM CULTURAL JUSTICE TO INTER-ETHNIC MEDIATION

Religious fundamentalists are also contributing to the outbreak of ethno-religious conflicts in Africa. Militarized Islamist movements opposed to Christianity and Occidentalism are really active in several African countries. Consequently, some radical Christians are beginning to take revenge by retaliation in many African countries including Nigeria, Egypt and Libya. In Nigeria, an armed Islamist movement called Boko Haram,[13] active in the north-eastern part of the country, rejects modernity and aims to establish Sharia law in northern states of Nigeria. Boko Haram was founded in 2002 in Maiduguri, the capital of Borno State, by Ustaz Mohammed Yusuf. Yusuf was opposed to democracy and Western secular education system, vowing that «this war which has not yet started will continue for a long time» if the political and educational system is not changed[14]. On July 26, 2009, a series of violence exploded following a simultaneous attack by Islamists in four northern states of Nigeria, known as Bauchi, Borno, Yobe and Kano. These violent clashes were between government forces and members of Boko Haram in Maiduguri and lasted five days. On July 30, 2009, security forces inflicted a serious defeat to the fundamentalists and expelled them from the capital. The number of casualties was over 700 dead including at least 300 Islamist militants. Mohamed Yusuf, captured in Maiduguri, was executed by the security forces according to media reports.

In northern Uganda, for example, the Lord's Resistance Army (LRA), established by the prophetess Alice Lekwana in 1987 aimed at establishing a government in Kampala based on the Ten Commandments, gave rise to violent conflicts. Since 1996, thousands of civilians have been killed or mutilated, and many children were abducted[15].

Alarmingly, most of these countries lack the political will to maintain the previous peace agreements, and are therefore plagued by

[13] A name that comes from the Hausa dialect which means "Western education is a sin" whose ideology was inspired by the Taliban movement in Afghanistan
[14] See Deadly Nigeria clashes spread, Last Modified: 27 Jul 2009 19:47 GMT à http://english.aljazeera.net/news/africa/2009/07/2009727134953755877.html
[15] Tom Lodge, Towards an Understanding of Contemporary Armed Conflicts in Africa, Published in Monograph No 36: Whither Peacekeeping in Africa? April 1999, found on: http://www.iss.co.za/pubs/monographs/No36/ArmedConflict.html

continuous armed ethno-religious conflicts[16]. This is partly due to the inefficient management and resolution of conflicts, and in particular, a lack of a well-developed ethno-religious mediation program.

The conflicts in these countries are mostly between ethnic or religious groups and not between states. If they do not receive special attention, ethnic conflicts which seem to be contagious can spread rapidly across borders like cancer cells. Ted Gurr and Monty Marshall wrote that most of the African conflicts are caused by the combination of poverty and weak states and institutions[17].

Causes of Ethnic Conflicts in Africa

As we demonstrated earlier in this book, specifically in the first part and at the beginning of this chapter, there are several causes of ethnic conflicts in Africa. But central to all these causes remains an objective and transcendental truth: cultural minorities fight for cultural justice. Thus, they demand that the majority should grant them the same rights to survival, government representation, cultural freedom and equality, security, dignity and association that they (the majority) enjoy. However, to achieve the objective of this part of our research, we will not be concerned here with theoretical considerations of these liberal principles as we did in the third chapter with Will Kymlicka. Instead, we reflect on the following causes: economic causes, psychological and historical causes, and finally, causes related to preferential treatment.

Economic Causes

Economic factors have been identified as one of the main causes of conflicts in Africa. Some theorists believe that competition for scarce resources is a common factor in almost all the ethnic conflicts

---

16 Monty G. Marshall and Ted Gurr, (2003) Peace and Conflict 2003: A Global Survey Of Armed Conflicts, Self Determination Movements and Democracy. (Center For International Development and Conflict Management. University of Maryland 2003)
17 Monty G, Marshall, Ted Gurr and Deepla Khosla (eds) Peace and Conflict 2001: A Global Survey of Armed Conflict, Self Determination Movements and Democracy. (Centre For Institutional Development and Conflict Management. University of Maryland, 2001) p. 11-13.

in Africa. In multiethnic societies such as Nigeria, South Africa and other African countries, ethnic groups are fiercely competing for material goods, rights, jobs, education, language, social services and good health care facilities. In his study, Okwudiba Nnoli produced empirical evidence linking socio-economic factors to ethnic conflicts in Nigeria. According to J.S. Furnival, cited in Nnoli, "the functioning of economic forces causes tensions between groups with divergent interests"[18]. According to the instrumentalist argument, in Africa where poverty and deprivation are becoming endemic, mainly because of distributive injustice, ethnicity remains an effective means of survival and mobilization. Ethnic groups mobilizing for economic reasons become peaceful after the realization of their goals[19].

Historical and Psychological Causes

Another major cause of ethnic conflict in Africa is at the psychological level, especially fear and insecurity of ethnic groups during the period of transition. It was stressed that the extremists rely on these fears to polarize the society. In addition, memories of past traumas magnify these concerns. These unpleasant memories produce a toxic mixture of distrust and suspicion that often leads to ethnic violence.

Causes Linked to Preferential Treatment

According to Lakes and Rothschild[20], ethnic conflicts are a sign of a weak state or a state involved in the ancient loyalties. In this case, the states act with bias in favor of a particular ethnic group or region, and behaviors such as preferential treatment fuel ethnic conflicts.

So far, we have established that although ethnicity in Africa is powerful, it is not inherently destructive. People choose to be ethnically inclined when it suits their needs and expectations.

---

18 J.S. Furnival in Nnoli, Okwudiba, (1980) Ethnic Politics In Nigeria. Fourth Dimension Press. Enugu, pp. 72-3.
19 For a detailed study, read Glazer, N, and Moynihan D.P., (1975) eds Ethnicity And Experience. Cambridge. Mass. Harvard University Press. Atlanta Georgia.
20 See Lakes, D. A. and Rothschild, Donald (1996), "Containing Fear: The Origins and Management Of Ethnic Conflict," International Security, vol. 21, no. 2, pp.41-75.

Ethnicity is a support to an individual's identity, which provides him a psychological safety net. But in Africa, it is sometimes a weapon of manipulation by some states, especially in multi-ethnic countries such as Nigeria.

CHAPTER 5

Nigeria and its Situations of Conflicts

THE VIOLENT CONFRONTATIONS between the north and south on the one hand, and between Muslims and Christians on the other, characterize Nigeria as a unique and important case study of ethno-religious conflicts. "With over 250 ethnic groups divided between the two major religions (Christianity and Islam), Nigeria since its independence from British colonial rule, has produced a catalog of ethno-religious conflicts which have resulted in an estimated loss of over three million human lives and an unquantifiable psychological and material damage"[21]. The British colonialists, while pretending to carry out a mission of uniting warring ethnic groups, had systematically separated the different peoples of Nigeria thereby creating an atmosphere of conflict. A survey[22] conducted in 2000

---

21 B. Salawu, Ethno-Religious Conflicts in Nigeria: Causal Analysis and Proposals for New Management Strategies op cit.

22 «International Foundation for Election Systems, Washington, DC 20005, Nigeria: Attitudes Toward Democracy And Markets in Nigeria, Report of a National Opinion Survey », published in April 2000 and found on this website: http://www.ifes.org/~/media/Files/Publications/Survey/2004/248/Nigeria_00_PO.pdf.
In this report, IFES affirms that, in general, membership association appears to be high in Nigeria, 86.2 percent of respondents indicated that they are members of a certain type of association. In addition, the most common form of membership is in religious organizations: nearly four out of five Nigerians belong to religious associations (see p.23). Although most Nigerians show some caution towards strangers, they show higher levels of trust in family, neighbors and members of their ethnic group (p.25). Not surprisingly, members of cultural minorities are more likely to define their ethnic identity. For example, 79.2 percent of the Ijaw, and 71.6 percent of the Igbo and Tiv consider themselves primarily as representatives of cultural diversity. Of the two largest ethnic groups, the Yoruba are much more likely to define themselves ethnically (45.5 percent) than the Hausa-Fulani

by «International Foundation for Election Systems (IFES)» on behalf of the U.S. Agency for International Development[23] revealed that ethnicity is the strongest type of identity among Nigerians. Nearly half of all Nigerians choose to associate with an «ethnic» identity. This survey was focused on the following question: «In addition to being a Nigerian, to which specific group do you feel you belong before all?" The answers to these questions are revealing: almost half of all Nigerians (48.2 percent) chose to associate with an ethnic identity, compared to nearly one third (28.4 percent) who opted for the «class» identity. The second category that has shown to be the most common is religious identity, chosen by 21.0 percent. At least, these figures confirm that group identities are important to Nigerians and that cultural or ethnic affiliation has not been displaced by individualism. At first glance, these figures also suggest that Nigerians have a tendency to regroup more readily around the cultural solidarities of kinship than class solidarities in the workplaces.

Methodology Adopted to Understand the Dynamics of Ethno-Religious Conflicts in Nigeria

In this analysis, two interdisciplinary methods have been chosen to understand the dynamics of ethno-religious conflicts in Nigeria, namely, the comparative method and historical method. First, we believe that the comparison of the various instances of ethno-religious conflicts in Nigeria can provide a better understanding of

---

(29.9 percent), who prefer to opt for a religious identity (i.e., Muslim). On this point, Muslims are much more likely to express a religious identity than Christians. While 35.5 percent of Muslims describe themselves as part of a faith community, less than one in ten Catholics, Protestants and members of African religions and independents do the same thing. Obviously, these group identities are strongly felt. An overwhelming percentage of Nigerians agree that they "feel proud" to belong to their group (96.8 percent) and to say that they "want their children to think like them" with the same identity (89.5 percent). They also believe that their group is the "best" (80.5 percent) and that their links with the group are "stronger than other Nigerians" (88.4 percent). Yet while the potential of group chauvinism is high, it is also compensated by a strong commitment to national identity. Entirely 97.2 percent of respondents agree that they are "proud to be called Nigerians", and they feel equally strong about this national identity as that of their sub-national, or their groups. Nigerians seem to feel no contradiction between the identity of ethnic group and the national identity; they profess firm commitments at a time (p.26-7).

23 United States Agency for International Development (USAID)

NIGERIA AND ITS SITUATIONS OF CONFLICTS

the complexity of the problem and eventually help in developing proactive mechanisms to ensure ethno-religious harmony and peace. A comparative study of the different ethno-religious conflicts in Nigeria focuses on the identification of the zones of ethno-religious conflicts and subsequently helps in the evaluation of the similarities or differences in the conflict resolution approaches and their effectiveness in ensuring inter-ethnic co-existence. Second, the historical method is relevant because ethno-religious conflicts in Nigeria today have a long history. Thus, the contemporary developments of these conflicts need to be examined through the lens of the historical past.

Contextual Clarification of the Choice of Nigeria as a Case Study

There are good reasons why Nigeria is chosen as a case study. Although there are other African multicultural countries, like South Africa, Nigeria is regarded as the giant in the region. It has a great economic, political and military influence in sub-Saharan Africa. Nigeria is among the richest countries on the continent in terms of natural resources. It can boast of its oil, coal, tin, bauxite and gold. But the majority of the population, particularly the inhabitants of the region of the Niger Delta (oil producing region) in the south, unfortunately have not yet felt the impact of oil revenues due to corruption, discrimination and poor economic management. After independence, the Nigerian government strongly interfered in all spheres of economic life. This country is blessed with cultural diversity, an asset for national and economic development. In addition, ethnicity, centralized government and the lives of corrupt elite leaders eclipse Nigeria.

In order to reflect on these problems, this chapter examines Nigeria and its situations of ethno-religious conflicts. Based on historical and political contexts (pre-colonialism, colonialism, post-independence), we examine the ethnic, tribal and religious groups involved in conflicts, the origins, causes, consequences, actors involved, places and forms of occurrence of ethno-religious conflicts in Nigeria. But before analyzing the concrete situations of these ethno-religious conflicts, we undertake from a general perspective, a presentation of Nigeria.

General Presentation of Nigeria

In an area of almost twice of France, Nigeria is about one fifth of the total population of sub-Saharan Africa. With about 140, 431, 790 inhabitants[24], Nigeria is the most populous country in Africa. It has more than 500 language groups (of which the most spoken are Hausa, Yoruba and Igbo), but English is the official and administrative language of the country.

It is a land of ancient civilizations (Tarouga-Nok in the ninth century BC), marked in the twelfth century by the influence of powerful and flourishing kingdoms, such as those of Ife, Oyo and Benin in the Yoruba area, preceded in the ninth and tenth centuries by the Igbo-Ukwu civilization (southeastern Nigeria), and that of Kanem-Bornu, which extended from the Libyan desert to the current north-eastern Nigeria, or even a few centuries later, the Sultanate of Sokoto and the Hausa Emirates.

Nigeria was a British colonial creation. The British imperial administration in Nigeria divided the indigenous ethnic groups and reinforced their identities, their languages and symbols through a strategy known as "divide and rule"[25]. Nigeria was born in January 1914 with the amalgamation of the Lagos colony[26], Southern protectorates (established from 1885 to 1894) and the Northern Protectorate (pacified in 1903). During this time, the merging of the separate colonies into one country called Nigeria was carried out with force without the consent of the entire peoples. It has been a major seed of conflict that has always troubled Nigeria. Until then, the British ruled these colonies as distinct but interrelated territories.

---

24 According to figures from the 2006 population published by « National Population Commission of Nigeria » in the Official Gazette of the Federal Republic of Nigeria, vol. 96, n° 2 of February 2, 2009, retrievable from http://www.population.gov.ng/index.php?id=3. But according to « World FactBook » of « Central Intelligence Agency (CIA), Nigeria has a population of 152, 217,341 inhabitants.
25 This provision resulted in violent conflicts when different ethnic groups were forced to compete for scarce resources.
26 The first annexed in 1861.

NIGERIA AND ITS SITUATIONS OF CONFLICTS

Local participation in government was introduced in 1922 when politicians of the South, Lagos and Calabar took their place in the central Legislative Assembly. Their Northern counterparts had no legislative experience until 1947 when a new constitution introduced the principle of regional representation. The Constitution of 1954 created in its own right, regional governments, and federal elections were held in 1959, the year before independence.

Nigeria gained independence on October 1, 1960. In 1963, Nigeria cut off its direct link with the British Crown, and became a Republic within the Commonwealth. The independence constitution provided for a federation of three autonomous regions - North, East and West - each with extended powers, its own constitution, its official language, its public service and its commercial offices. The federal government had limited powers to national (regional) issues, including control of the police and the military as well as economic planning. The political system was derived from the Westminster model. A fourth region - the Midwest - was created in 1964 to meet the demands of minorities.

In the early 1960s, the inherited regional structure led to a series of crises and conflicts, both within and between the three regions ethnically centered, as competition for control of the federal center had progressed. The elections of 1964 of the federal government were marred by violence. Interethnic tensions and tensions between political parties continued, leading ultimately to a military coup d'état in January 1966, led by some military officers from the southeast.

Subsequently, the post-independence history of Nigeria has been marked by a series of military interventions in politics: coups d'état, backlash, and a civil war (1967-1970) when the Eastern Region attempted to secede and become the Republic of Biafra. Over one million people died in the conflict. On June 12, 1993, Chief Moshood Abiola, a Yoruba of southwestern Nigeria, won the presidential election in Nigeria, but the election was annulled by the military regime, throwing Nigeria into turmoil. In retaliation, southern Nigerians began to form militant organizations to protest against the unfair treatment and ask for a democratically elected government. During the authoritarian regime of General Sani Abacha, a Northern Muslim, Southerners feared more political marginalization and demanded an end to the domination of the Hausa-Fulani from the political arena. This change was an indication to the government's weakness and lack of effective mechanisms to manage ethnic conflicts in Nigeria. In addition to the ethno-religious conflicts in Nigeria, was the boycott of the Yorubas from the 1994 constitutional conference organized by the regime of General Sani Abacha. The conference was intended to address the national debate on ethnicity. Inspired by the pan-Yoruba socio-cultural associations, the Afenifere and the Oodua Peoples Congress (OPC) in southwestern Nigeria threatened the authorities with secession and the intensification of violent protests across the country. As a result, Nigeria has only experienced three short periods of civilian rule: from 1960 to 1965, from 1979 to 1983, and from 1999 until today[27]. Intervention periods, a total of 29 years, saw military governments in power.

In an attempt to reduce the power of the regions and prevent future conflicts, the regional structure was dismantled in 1967 and replaced by 12 states. At the same time, the federal center took over most of the powers for itself, a radical new form of revenue sharing was established which deprived the new states of most of their derivation funds.

Additional states have gradually been established in response to the requests from local groups. In 1976, the number rose to 19; in 1987, it went up to 21; in 1991, it rose to 30; finally in 1996, the number of states became 36. No new states have been created since then, although the pressure for new states is still present. A new federal capital, Abuja in the center of the country, was created in 1976 but was not fully operational until the mid-1990s.

Ethnic conflicts in Nigeria continued up to the democratic transition. Olusegun Obasanjo, a former military, was the democratically elected president for eight years (starting from 1999

---

27 This is the longest period in the history of the democratic transition in Nigeria.

until 2007), succeeded by President Umaru Musa Yar'Adua[28] who was democratically elected in 2007, but unfortunately died on May 5, 2010. His Vice President, President Goodluck Jonathan assumed the presidency on May 5, 2010. However, ethno-religious conflicts continue to escalate, because the various ethnic groups claim a political restructuring. The federal structure has developed deep cracks and requires urgent measures to repair it. But what is more worrisome is the religious dimension of ethnic competition for power and oil wealth in Nigeria. The multiple ethno-religious conflicts in the northern cities of Kano, Kaduna, Jos and Zamfara showed up as a result of the introduction of Muslim Sharia law in the courts and the claims of the South for autonomy. The continuing conflict is an indication that Nigeria has not yet developed effective mechanisms to manage its ethnic conflicts.

Ethnic Groups in Nigeria

The three regions in which Nigeria was divided at independence are each dominated by a majority ethnic group constituting about two-thirds of the regional population. These three main ethnic groups, the Hausa-Fulani in the north (29%), the Yoruba in the southwest (21%) and the Igbo in the southeast (18%), are distinguished not only by region, but also by religion and way of life. The rest of the population in each region consists of a number of minority tribes with their own distinct cultures and languages. The most important among these groups are the people of Ijaw (10%), Kanuri (4%), the Itshekiri, the Edo and the peoples of Ishan in the central western part of the Western Region; the peoples of Ibibio (3.5%), Ogoja, Calabar, and the other peoples of the Niger Delta in the Eastern Region; and the Tiv (2.5%), the Idoma, the Jukun, the Nupe, the Bachama, the Biron Angas, and the other peoples of the Middle Belt in the northern

---

28 Umaru Yar'Adua studied chemistry at the Ahmadu Bello University, Zaria. After graduation, he became a lecturer until he took office as governor of Katsina State, on May 29, 1999. He remained mostly in his state and did not venture into the national political arena. But as the brother of Shehu Musa Yar'Adua, a former general and millionaire and a friend of President Olusegun Obasanjo, Umaru Yar'Adua was chosen as presidential candidate in 2007 of which he became the winner.

region. Despite the fragmentation of the country into thirty-six states today by successive governments in order to ease ethnic tensions and promote the development of the culture of unity in diversity, ethnic rivalry still persists.

There are currently three major religions in Nigeria, namely, Islam, Christianity and African traditional religions. Muslims constitute the majority with 50% of the population. Christians make up 40% and the followers of traditional African religions 10%.

Ethnic conflicts in Nigeria usually occur because of natural resources, political manipulation, injustice towards the minorities, religion, and militarization of ethnicity among others. Over the years, the phenomena of ethnicity and religious intolerance have led to the recurrence of incessant ethno-religious conflicts, which have given rise to the foundation of numerous pan-political, social and cultural associations such as the Arewa Consultative Forum (for leaders in the north), the Afenifere (for the Yoruba people), the Ohaneze Ndi Igbo (for the Igbo people), etc. The incessant nature of these conflicts and the ardent desire to protect the interests of one's ethnic group further inspired the establishment of ethnic militant and / or vigilante groups such as the Arewa People's Congress (APC), the Oodua Peoples Congress (OPC), the Movement for the Actualization of the Sovereign State of Biafra (MASSOB), the Bakassi Boys, the Movement for the Emancipation of the Niger Delta (MEND), the Ijaw Youth Council (IYC), the Egbesu Boys, etc. With the emergence of these ethnic militias and the deep divisions between the different ethnic groups, religious intolerance has become more violent and bloody with more devastating results, while using ethnic militias as the executors of ethno-religious order.

Even though it is not possible to know the exact number of ethno-religious conflicts in Nigeria due to lack of adequate statistical data on this issue, it is interesting to note that nearly forty percent (40%) of ethno religious conflicts are credited to the Fourth Republic of Nigeria. The fact that there is a recent increase in the number of ethno-religious conflicts in the country, is a relevant question in the discussion on contemporary Nigeria and a lesson for other nations of the world that are also multi-ethnic and multi-religious in their composition. Also, the violent nature of ethno-religious conflicts, which often take the form of riots, murder, armed combat, guerrilla, war, and secession in Nigeria, no doubt, have implications for political and economic development in the country. As a result, these conflicts deserve to be thoroughly discussed. The discussion of the historical manifestations of ethno-religious conflicts in any context is all the more necessary given the fact that there is a phenomenal recurrence of ethno-religious conflicts across the country, which of course increases the level of general insecurity, particularly in areas where such conflicts have never occurred before.

CHAPTER 6

Historical Manifestations of Ethno-Religious Conflicts in Nigeria

AS MENTIONED EARLIER, we define ethno-religious conflicts as a situation in which the relationship between members of an ethnic or religious group and members of another group of this type in a multiethnic and multi-religious society is characterized by a lack of cordiality, suspicion and mutual fear as well as a tendency toward violent confrontation. In B. Salawu's view[29], ethnic and religious fanaticism in Nigeria have become a fulcrum of different nations or different ethnic groups, ranging from language affirmation, cultural autonomy and religious superiority to the demands for local political autonomy and self-determination. According to Salawu, all these problems sometimes lead to some form of contextual discrimination of members of ethnic or religious groups against members of another on the basis of differing systems of socio-cultural symbols and religion[30]. The frequent, incessant and violent manifestations of ethno-religious conflicts in Nigeria could therefore be explained from the perspective of this mutual suspicion and lack of cordiality between the different ethnic groups.

However, it is important to note that despite the ethnic lines,

---

29 B. Salawu is a Lecturer at the Department of Sociology, University of Ilorin, Ilorin, Nigeria. For his view as noted, read B. Salawu, Ethno-Religious Conflicts in Nigeria: Causal Analysis and Proposals for New Management Strategies, op cit.
30 Ibid.

◀ FROM CULTURAL JUSTICE TO INTER-ETHNIC MEDIATION

some of the intense fightings have been intra-ethnic battles, that is, between the communities of the same ethnic group, as is the case in the Igbo ethnic communities, between the community of Aguleri and that of Umuleri situated in the southeast of Nigeria on the one hand, and the communities in the Yoruba ethnic group - the Ife and Modakeke on the other.

Among the ethno-religious conflicts examined in this book are those that occurred prior to and even after the transition to the current democratic regime in Nigeria, which started in 1999. These conflicts include: the Nigeria[31] – Biafra[32] war from 1967 to 1970, the religious troubles of Maitatsine in some areas of Kano and Maiduguri in the early 1980s, the religious disturbances of Djimeta and Yola (1984), the crises of Zango - Kataf in Kaduna State (1992), the violent clashes between the Yoruba and the Hausa in Shagamu in Ogun State (1999), Kaduna - Enugu riots (2000), the Idi- Araba / Oko-Oba crisis in Lagos State and that of Kano (2000), the Tiv- Jukun conflicts in Wukari, Taraba State, the violent clashes between the Kuteb and the Jukun / Chamba in Takum, the conflicts between the Ijaw and the Ilaje in Ondo State, the massacres of Jos in Plateau State, the violent conflicts in the south-south geopolitical area, sometimes called the Niger Delta region, which have manifested in several ways of which we mention four: the interstate border dispute between Oku Iboku in the Local Government Area of Itu, Akwa Ibom State and Usung Esuk in Odukpani Local Government Area, Cross River State, then the intercommunity conflict between Eleme and Okrika in Rivers State, and finally inter-ethnic conflicts between the Itsekiri, the Urhobo and the Ijaw in Delta State; and the Ogoni crises in Rivers State. Others are the riots between Christians and Muslims at the School of Education Kafanchan, the clashes between Muslims and Christians in Kaduna Polytechnic School (1981 - 1982), and the conflict between Christians and Muslims on the position or place to build the University Mosque and the Cross of the Chapel of the Resurrection at the University of

---

31 Which included the northern region called the Hausa-Fulani and predominantly Muslim and the southwest, the Yoruba region.
32 The southeastern Nigeria called the Igbo and mainly Christians who wanted secession.

Ibadan in Oyo State (1981-1985). In addition, other ethno-religious conflicts include the Muslim-Christian riots at Bulumkutu (1982), and also at the Usman Danfodio University, Sokoto (1982), the violent confrontation between Muslims and Christians during a Christian Easter procession in Ilorin, Kwara State (1986), the violent confrontation between an armed Islamist movement active in the north-eastern Nigeria called Boko Haram and the law enforcement agencies (2009), and finally the new instances of massacres in Jos due to conflicts between Muslims and Christians that recently occurred.

In order to properly present these conflicts, we examine them according to their zones of occurrence, namely, ethnic conflicts in the northern region, ethnic conflicts in the southwest region, ethnic conflicts in the southeast, ethnic conflicts in the Niger Delta region, and ethnic conflicts in the north central zone. Finally, the religious conflicts in Nigeria will be discussed.

Ethnic Conflicts in the Northern Region

For the ethnic conflicts in the northern region, we examine the massacres in Kano, the Zango - Kataf crises in Kaduna State, the Hausa - Igbo combat at the Sabon Gari market, and the Kaduna - Enugu riots.

KANO MASSACRES

Kano has remained a center of ethno-religious violence since colonial times. Most of the violence places the indigenous Hausa-Fulani Muslims against their Christian counterparts from southern Nigeria. Kano, the largest industrial and commercial city in northern Nigeria has been a center of attraction for immigrants from various ethnic and religious groups since the colonial period. While the immigrants during the pre-colonial period were physically and culturally integrated and assimilated, the immigrants of the twentieth and twenty first centuries find it difficult or impossible to integrate. This situation was encouraged by the political system of British colonial rule that introduced a sense of discrimination, segregation and division[33].

33 Abdu Hussaini (2000) "Religion and the Challenges of Democratization And National Integration in Nigeria. Equal Justice, Kaduna, HRM, p.18.

FROM CULTURAL JUSTICE TO INTER-ETHNIC MEDIATION

Since the colonial period, most of the immigrants in Kano settled at Sabon Gari - created in 1913 under the politics of segregation. Sabon Gari attracted both Christian and Muslim settlers. The district of Sabon Gari was created to ensure that the colonial government directly administers these immigrants, notably, the Yoruba, Igbo, Nupe, Hausa, Chadians and other migrants who settled in Kano during the colonial period. This polarization between immigrants and the natives primarily served the politics of "divide and rule", which was rooted in white racial supremacy[34]. The consequence of this situation is the strengthening of the powers of the traditional leaders (emirs) and traditional institutions. This increase in the influence of traditional leaders led to greater cohesion between the local Indigenous population around the traditional bureaucracy and the authority of the chief, and therefore a much more active orientation towards the colonial power. This helped to reinforce the importance of local ties, norms, values and customs, thus helping to strengthen the sense of exclusivity of indigenous communities. Immigrants find it hard to integrate. As a result, these districts reserved for immigrants and other locations have become areas of crises since the colonial period.

The first crisis in Kano manifested due to the manipulation of ethnic and regional sentiments by the colonial powers in order to suppress anti-colonial forces. In 1953, the Igbo were attacked at Sabon-gari. This crisis was fueled by a political disagreement between the Northern Peoples Congress "NPC" and other political parties in Nigeria, for example, the Action Group (a Yoruba political party).

The consequence of this disagreement was the demonstration of May 15, 1953 in Kano, against the visit of the leaders of the Action Group in Northern Nigeria (Kano in particular). A total of twenty-one southerners were officially declared dead, while about seventy-one wounded. Most of the victims were Igbo according to reports. Southerners also killed and wounded fifteen Hausa-Fulani[35].

---

34   Ibid., p.25
35   Albert, Olawale Isaac (1999). "Ethnic and Religious Conflicts in Kano". In Otite and Albert (eds): Community Conflicts In Nigeria. Spectrum, Ibadan, p.281

HISTORICAL MANIFESTATIONS OF ETHNO-RELIGIOUS CONFLICTS IN NIGERIA

The second crisis was the reaction following the military coup d'état of January 15, 1966 led by Major Chukwuemeka Nzeogwu Kaduna, during which many politicians from the North were killed. There was a demonstration in Kano on March 29, 1966, against the decree of unification of Aguyi Ironsi (the new head of state). Between 100 and 200 Igbo were killed in Sabon Gari. This demonstration was followed by another violence in July of that same year. Since then, there have been series of violent crisis in Kano.

Zango – Kataf Crises in Kaduna State

Zango and Kataf are two villages of the same community in the southeastern part of Kaduna State in Nigeria, located about 230 km from the capital of Kaduna State. This community consists of nearly fifty autonomous villages[36].

The south of Kaduna where the Zango and Kataf communities are located occupied a volatile position in the history of communal conflicts and tensions in northern Nigeria in the twentieth century. This area has experienced complex conflicts, sometimes violent, and especially taking the hypothesis of an ethnic form. Closely related to these points are questions of social equality, citizenship, community rights, and social democracy. All these took place in a rural area and represent global problems experienced in the Nigerian society. Until the 1990s, most of the Christian populations (now constituting the predominant, but minority in the entire Northern Territory) were the adepts of African traditional religion. In this community, the Muslim population, mostly Hausa and Fulani are the minority even though they are the majority at the regional level[37].

The history of Southern Kaduna is the one of struggles between different ethnic groups under the emirate system, which was imposed on the area by the system of British colonial indirect rule.

---

36 Akinteye, O. et al. 1999. "Zangon-Kataf Crisis: A Case Study", (pp 222-245) in O. Otite and I. O. Albert (eds.), Communal Conflict in Nigeria, Management, Resolution and Transformation. Ibadan: Spectrum Books.
37 Kazah-Toure, T. 1995. "Inter-Ethnic Relations, Conflicts and Nationalism in Zangon-Kataf Area of Northern Nigeria: Historical Origins and Contemporary Forms." Paper presented at the 8th CODESRIA General Assembly, Dakar.

FROM CULTURAL JUSTICE TO INTER-ETHNIC MEDIATION

These struggles have continued in various forms, resulting in bloody confrontations between the Zango and Kataf in 1992. The dispute between the Zango (Hausa-Muslims) and the people of Kataf (Christians) is primarily caused by a long-term misunderstanding over land ownership. The Kataf stated that the land where the Hausa-Muslims were living belonged to them; and that they were settlers. They tell their oral tradition dating back to 1967, when a Hausa itinerant merchant, Mele, from Niger received a portion of land in the heart of the city to settle after many years of trade relationships with them. Shortly afterwards, in their view, Mele was joined by members of his family. Thus, the name, Zango-Kataf means a Hausa transit camp in Kataf. But the Hausa-Muslims stated that the claim by the Kataf was unfounded. The Kataf, they believe, came gradually to settle there. For them, the real name of Zango-Kataf was Zango-Katabiri, which means the gradual arrival of the Kataf.

The controversial issue of land ownership is rooted in the emirate system, which was practiced there. In this system, the Christian communities and the chiefdoms in the southern part of Kaduna State, remain under the control of the Emir of Zaria. At present, apart from Jama'a Kagoro, Jabba and Marwa, the other eighteen chiefdoms in southern Kaduna express their loyalty to the Emir. The district chiefs pay homage to their Emir. "The system is very bad,"[38] complained one Kataf, saying that the traditional system of land ownership in this area is in favor of the Hausa-Muslims, and was the cause of the crisis between the Zango (Hausa-Muslims) and Kataf (Christians). The people of Kataf complained of domination by the Hausa-Muslims.

Hausa - Igbo Combat in Sabon Gari Market

In June 1995, another violent crisis erupted at Sabon Gari. The crisis was the product of a fight between an Igbo trader, Mr. Arthor Nwankwo and a Hausa man, Abubakar Abdu along the Hausa / Igbo road (Russed Avenue) near Sabon Gari market[39]. During this time of

---

38 Dent, M. 1995. "Ethnicity and Territorial Politics in Nigeria", (page 129) in Graham Smith (eds.). Federalism: The Multi-Ethnic Challenge, London and New York: Longman.
39 Albert, Olawale Isaac (1999), op cit

fighting, Abubakar Abdu was pushed into a hot pot of vegetable oil, which had compelled others to intervene in the fighting between the two men divided across ethnic and religious lines. This conflict was therefore moved from interpersonal conflict to an interethnic confrontation. The official report mentions five dead, but it is estimated that from 15 to 20 people may have been killed. Eighty-three people were seriously injured[40]. Many Churches and Mosques were burned. The police arrested fifty-four people involved in the violence.

Kaduna – Enugu Riots

Another ethno-religious conflict that left a remarkable footprint in Nigeria was the Kaduna - Enugu riots. The root cause of this series of riots was the introduction of the Islamic law (Sharia) by some state governors in northern Nigeria. Governor Ahmed Yerima of Zamfara State was the first to introduce the Islamic legal code in October 1999, which was greeted with protests. Initially, little damage had occurred as a result of protests against the introduction of the Sharia code. However, the fire was lit when Governor Mohammed Makarfi of Kaduna State tried it in February 2000. Because of the deep hostility between Muslims and Christians all over Kaduna State and in the state capital in particular, coupled with the fact that both religions are nearly equal in population, the two took their swords and a lot of people were massacred in cold blood.

In these Kaduna riots, the Igbo (a predominantly Christian ethnic group) were mainly affected. In retaliation, as expected, Enugu[41] and other Igbo towns exploded into violence when many Igbo people were returned dead and those who were lucky to escape had sad stories to tell, because they also had been targets of attack by the Hausa / Fulani in Kaduna. It is important to note here that the ethno-religious riots in Kaduna and Enugu have certain characteristics that are similar to the scenario characterizing the cause and the beginning of the 1967-1970 civil war in Nigeria. In other words, these riots

---

40   See Hussaini Abdu, Ethnic and Religious Crises in Northern Nigeria, op cit
41   Enugu is the capital and principal city of Enugu State in the southeastern Nigeria. Its name means the city on the hill (Enu gwu in Igbo).

constituted a force sufficient to have caused a second civil war since law and order had collapsed in the two regions.

Ethnic Conflicts in the Southwestern Zone

We choose to examine the four types of conflicts that have occurred in the southwestern zone of Nigeria. These conflicts include: the conflict between the people of Ife and the Modakeke people, the violent clashes between the Yoruba and the Hausa-Fulani in Shagamu in Ogun State, the clashes between the Ijaw and the Ilaje in Ondo State, and the Idi-Araba / Oko-Oba crisis in Lagos State as well as the Kano retaliation.

Conflict between the People of Ife and the Modakeke People

The oldest intra-ethnic conflict in Nigeria is that of the Ife-Modakeke crisis. This crisis has been going on for over a century[42]. As it has been detached from its original cause, this conflict had degenerated with time, into other crises[43]. Although the causes of the crisis are many and varied, we highlight those related to cultural identity, economic and political interests. These causes have been identified in some research works as important elements in ethnic conflicts.

The Ife and the Modakeke come from Osun State in southwestern Nigeria. The southwest area is composed of six States, namely, the states of Ekiti, Lagos, Ogun, Ondo, Osun and Oyo. This area is

---

42 Aguda, A. S. 2001. "The effect of communal conflict and violence on urban residential segregation", A paper presented at the International Conference on Security, Segregation and Social Networks in West African Cities 19th to 20th centuries, Organised by the French Institute for Research in Africa (IFRA) and Institute of African Studies and Centre for Urban and Regional Planning, University of Ibadan, Ibadan Nigeria, 29th to 31st October 2001. See also Albert, I. 1999. Ife – Modakeke Crisis. In Otite, O. and Albert, I. S; Community conflict in Nigeria: Management, Resolution and Transformation. Ibadan: Spectrum Books; Agbe Adetola Gabriel 2001. The Ife – Modakeke crisis: An insider view. Ife Psychologia 9 (3), pp. 14 – 20 ; Toriola Olu Joseph 2001. The Ife – Modakeke crisis: An insider view. Ife Psychologia 9 (3), pp. 21 – 29.
43 Augsburger, D. W. 1992. Conflict mediation across culture: pathway and pattern. Alouisville, Kentucky: Westminster John Knox Press. See also, Omotayo Bukky 2005. "Women and conflict in the new information age: Virtual Libraries to the rescue" A paper presented at the World Library and Information Congress: 71th IFLA General Conference and Council "Library - a voyage of discovery" August 15th – 18th 2005, Oslo, Norway.

HISTORICAL MANIFESTATIONS OF ETHNO-RELIGIOUS CONFLICTS IN NIGERIA

traditionally inhabited by one of the three largest ethnic groups in Nigeria, the Yoruba. Historically, the Ife and the Modakeke are the sons and daughters of the same parents. As Yorubas, their ancestor is attributed to Oduduwa, the ancestor of the Yoruba. It is the collapse of the old Oyo Empire in the 19th century that caused a flow of refugees toward the South. Most of these refugees were directed towards Ile-Ife, the capital city of Ife. They were probably drawn towards Ile-Ife by the historical image of the city as the ancestral home of the Yoruba[44]. The Ooni, that is, the traditional king of Ife had voluntarily accepted the refugees who had moved to Ile-Ife[45] and subsequently formed a community known today as Modakeke on a separate territory created for the refugees. The relationships between the Ife and these refugees from Oyo who came to settle in Modakeke were very cordial at first. The Ooni (traditional king) and his chiefs saw them as good allies in war and as good servants for agricultural work. Before this time, the Oyo people had provided military support to the Ife during the Owu War of 1825 and during the various invasions in Ijesha (a neighboring town of Ile-Ife). This had encouraged the Ife Chiefs to open doors to the Oyo refugees. They were given land and many of them worked for the Ife farmers. The first crisis of the Ife-Modakeke took place from 1835 to 1849.

The historical account of the origin of the Ife-Modakeke crisis as stated by Albert[46], is that an Ife chief, called Okunade and generally known as Maye, who was the leader of the Yoruba warriors who settled in Ibadan (the capital city of Oyo State) in the early nineteenth century, although a brave warrior, was an autocrat. He exercised so much influence in the politics of Ibadan so that Ife began to see Ibadan as an extension city. In 1835, the autocracy of Okunade had been challenged by some citizens in Ibadan, which had led to his expulsion from the city. He had tried to retake the city during the

---

44 Albert, I. 1999. Ife – Modakeke crisis. In Otite, O. and Albert, I. S; Community conflict in Nigeria: Management, Resolution and Transformation. Ibadan: Spectrum Books, p.143.
45 Akinjogbin, I. A. 1992. "Ife: The years of Travail 1793-1893" in I. A. Akinjogbin (ed.) The cradle of race: Ife from beginning to 1980. Port Harcourt: Sunray Publications.
46 Albert ibid., p.144-145.

Gbanamu battle[47]. He was killed and therefore the Oyo took the political leadership of Ibadan in total exclusion of their Ife allies. The Ife finally expressed their anger against the Oyo refugees who had settled in Modakeke[48]. The refugees were therefore given ill-treatment and had been sold into slavery. Around this same year (1835), there were rumors that the Fulani jihadists were coming to invade parts of the Yoruba country. On grounds of protection, the refugees came to settle in Ile-Ife, the capital city of Ife. But Ooni Abeweila, who ascended the throne in 1839, had to return some of the refugees. In the same year, the Ooni had created a separate territory for refugees who had no homes. This territory was named Modakeke after the cry of a stork on a tall tree near the site[49].

To this day, there have been seven major wars between the Ife and Modakeke - 1835-1849, 1882-1909, 1946-1949, 1981, 1983, 1997-1998 and 2000. This conflict is described as a conflict between the Ife as "owners" and the Modakeke as "aliens" or "tenants". The recent crisis has caused the death of more than 2,000 people and several others wounded.

The causes of conflict between the Ife and the Modakeke are numerous and varied. They are related to cultural identity, economic and political issues, land ownership, and the creation of local government for the Modakeke and the location of the headquarters of this local government. Moreover, this crisis, since the post-colonial period, has been a real weapon in the hands of those who are interested in creating political tensions in Yoruba land.

---

[47] It was a war of aggression against Ibadan conducted by the Egbas, Ijebus, Owus and Erunmus. They fought to restore Maye, the king expelled from Ibadan. By forming an alliance with the cities of Ife, Ikire, Ipetumodu, Apomu and other nearby towns, they managed to raise a very important army against Ibadan. This battlefield was later called "Gbanamu" which means "Gripping Fire."

[48] See Akintoye S. A. (1970). Cited in Albert, I. 1999. Ife – Modakeke crisis. In Otite, O. and Albert, I. S; Community conflict in Nigeria: Management, Resolution and Transformation. Ibadan: Spectrum Books, and Ajayi J.F.A. and Akintoye S.A. (1980). Cited in Albert, I. 1999. Ife – Modakeke crisis. In Otite, O. and Albert, I. S; Community conflict in Nigeria: Management, Resolution and Transformation. Ibadan: Spectrum Books.

[49] For the history of the Modakeke, see Johnson S. (1973). The history of the Yorubas, C.M.S., and Akinjogbin, I. A. 1992. "Ife: The years of Travail 1793-1893" in I. A. Akinjogbin (ed.) The cradle of race: Ife from beginning to 1980. Port Harcourt: Sunray Publications.

HISTORICAL MANIFESTATIONS OF ETHNO-RELIGIOUS CONFLICTS IN NIGERIA

Violent Clashes between the Yoruba and the Hausa in Shagamu, Ogun State

In the above contexts, it means that for a long time, many regions of Nigeria have become theaters of war, characterized by an increasing number of ethnic and religious crises. The wave of ethno-religious conflicts in Nigeria, however, increased with the birth of the Fourth Republic in 1999 which restored democracy in this country. The first phase of ethnic and religious riots in Nigeria in recent years was in July 1999, when some members of the Oro traditional cult in Sagamu, Ogun State had accused a Hausa woman of coming out in the night when the members of the cult were outside in ritual procession.

The area in which these ethnic clashes had taken place is completely a Yoruba area. Sagamu, about 50km from Lagos, is a typical Yoruba town and a busy commercial center. The Yoruba have a reputation for cultural festivals. The Yoruba can today be practicing Christians or Muslims, but there are still shrines of the gods in the countryside as well as traditional festivals - such as the Oro festival of worship that triggered the violent clashes - which are still celebrated and always taken very seriously.

During the religious festival of Oro, it is forbidden for women and strangers to watch masked figures. The problem had started in Sagamu when a Northern Hausa woman was killed to have seen these masked people during a night procession.

Although Sagamu is far from northern Nigeria, a Hausa community resides there. All the major cities usually have a separate area where the Hausa people live, speak their own language and dress in their own style, run their own stores and markets, and attend their own mosques in which almost all are Muslim.

The murder of this Hausa woman from the North caused some clashes resulting in a deep crisis. Many people, especially from the Hausa and Yoruba tribes lost their lives. The infamy was, however, temporarily controlled only when a curfew was imposed on the sleepy town of Sagamu. Unfortunately, when the infamy was controlled in Sagamu, killings caused by retaliation were committed in Kano (a major Hausa city) in northern Nigeria. As a result, many people were killed and properties were destroyed. Residents of Kano of Southwestern origin, who had lived their entire lives there, had to return to their homeland to count their losses. When the city of Kano was in the process of calming down, violence erupted in the city of Lagos (Nigerian Economic Capital, located in the south-west and predominantly Yoruba), obviously as a mark of revenge for the massacres of the people of the Yoruba ethnic group in Kano. This time, the O'dua People Congress was mobilized against the Hausa-Fulani traders in a market known as the "Mile 12 market", and after two days, the area was turned into a battle field.

CLASHES BETWEEN THE IJAW PEOPLE AND THE ILAJE IN ONDO STATE

Another conflict that broke out in the Yoruba region is the one that caused the war between the Ilaje people, who speak the Yoruba language, and the Arogbo-Ijaw, an Ijaw ethnic group living in western Nigeria forming part of the largest ethnic group in the Niger Delta. The two groups, who live as neighbors in the delta region of Ondo State, east of Lagos, had been in violent conflict over a land believed to be rich in oil and located near the area held by Chevron Company. The rivalry broke out on September 19, 1998, when hundreds of people were killed and thousands had become homeless in a series of battles. Both parties claimed to be the true owners of the region. At the end of July 1999, the Ilaje people launched a series of raids against the Ijaw in order to re-capture the villages held by the Ijaw since the troubles of 1998. The Spokesperson for the Ilaje people claimed to have taken over 51 of the 68 villages and towns which they had lost earlier against the Ijaws[50].

The Ijaw leaders in the region accused the Oodua Peoples Congress (OPC) to have participated in the attacks carried out against them by the Ilaje, which they claimed to correspond to an attempted genocide of the the Ijaw people by the Yorubas[51]. However, an influential voice for the Ilaje, Chief Adewole Dimehin, who was a member of the Ilaje

---

50   The Vanguard [Lagos], Dayo Johnson and Victor Ahiuma-Young, "Bloodletting Continues", 10 August 1999
51   Ibid.

Development Committee, said that his people were ready to fight to the end in order to return to their homes of origin. "We have suffered enough as refugees"[52], he affirmed.

The then governor of Ondo State, Adebayo Adefarati announced on August 17, 1999 that both parties were forced to maintain a cease-fire and were waiting for the arrival of the marine troops to maintain peace[53]. He had asked the federal government to declare the region a disaster area.

IDI-ARABA / OKO-OBA CRISIS IN LAGOS STATE AND THE REPRISALS IN KANO

In October 2000 another ethno-religious conflict occurred. This was the violent clashes in Lagos (in Idi-Araba / Oko-Oba communities) and in Kano. The cause is related to a misunderstanding between the Hausa residents and the Yoruba in Idi-Araba in Lagos State over the use of a toilet by a Hausa resident. Because of this misunderstanding, many Yoruba residents in the area were killed with bows, arrows and machetes. In retaliation, the Oodua Peoples Congress (OPC), a Yoruba militia, entered the scene and the situation deteriorated. Later, Oko-Oba, another Lagos suburb with a large population of Hausa / Fulani, joined the fray of madness. Violence was then extended to Kano and as expected, the southerners were the main victims.

Ethnic Conflicts in the Southeast

For the ethnic conflicts in the southeastern Nigeria, we examine two instances of conflicts: the Nigeria – Biafra war and the conflict between Aguleri and Umuleri.

THE NIGERIA – BIAFRA CIVIL WAR

The civil war in Nigeria, also known as the Nigeria - Biafra war, lasted almost three years. It was a bloody conflict with a very high number of deaths of more than a million people. Seven years after Nigeria's independence from Great Britain, the war began because of the attempted secession of the southeastern Nigeria on May 30, 1967,

52 Ibid.
53 The Vanguard, Julius Alabi, "Ijaw, Ilaje Communities Embrace Truce", 18 August 1999

FROM CULTURAL JUSTICE TO INTER-ETHNIC MEDIATION

when it declared itself the independent Republic of Biafra. The battles that followed and which largely revealed human suffering aroused the indignation and the intervention of the international community.

This war occurred not only as a culmination of previous conflicts between different ethnic groups, but also as a form of response to the massacres of the Igbo people in northern Nigeria by the Hausas. Between 1966 and 1967, the Federal Military Government of Nigeria led by Major General Yakubu "Jack" Gowon[54] asked to convene a constituent assembly for constitutional review that could allow a rapid return to civilian rule. Nevertheless, violence increased in intensity. In September 1966, attacks against the Igbo in northern Nigeria had been renewed with unprecedented ferocity. The army was sharply divided along ethnic and regional lines. According to a rumor that was circulating, military troops of the northern region had participated in mutilations. The estimated number of deaths was more than 30,000. More than one million Igbo were returned to the eastern region. In retaliation, some people from the North were massacred in some cities in the Eastern Region of Nigeria and a repatriation of the non-Igbo people was initiated.

The military governor of the Eastern Region, Lieutenant Colonel Chukwuemeka Odumegwu Ojukwu, was under the pressure of the Igbo officers to assert greater independence. Indeed, the Government of the Eastern Region and its military refused to recognize the legitimacy of Major General Yakubu «Jack» Gowon, saying he was not the highest officer in the chain of command. Some colleagues of Ojukwu wondered whether the country could be reunited amicably

---

54   Yakubu Gowon, also known as Jack Gowon   (born October 19, 1934, Pankshin, Nigeria), Nigerian military leader, who served as head of state (1966–75). From Plateau state in the middle belt of Nigeria, Gowon's father was an early convert to Christianity. Gowon was educated in Zaria and later became a career army officer. He was trained in Ghana and in England at Sandhurst and twice served in the Congo region as part of Nigeria's peacekeeping force there in the early 1960s. After the coup of January 1966, he was appointed chief of staff by Major General Johnson Aguiyi-Ironsi, the new leader. Northern officers staged a countercoup in July 1966, during which the former Commander in Chief, Major General Johnson Aguiyi Ironsi and many other Igbo officers were killed. Gowon emerged as the compromise head of the new government. For detailed information on Gowon, read Yakubu Gowon, article from the Encyclopædia Britannica available at: http://www.britannica.com/EBchecked/topic/240299/Yakubu-Gowon.

after the outrages committed against the Igbo people in the northern region. Ironically, many Eastern leaders who had advocated a unitary Nigerian State became critical and launched an appeal to loosen the links with the other regions.

The military officers and governors, including Ojukwu, met in Lagos to explore possible solutions to regional conflicts. But they failed to reach an agreement despite the concessions offered by the Northern officers, because it was impossible to guarantee the security of the Igbo people outside the Eastern Region. Concerned about his safety, Ojukwu refused invitations to attend subsequent meetings in Lagos.

In January 1967, military leaders and senior police officers met in Aburi, Ghana at the invitation of the military government of Ghana. At this time, the Eastern Region was threatening to secede. In a last minute effort to maintain the unity of Nigeria, the military reached an agreement which provided for a confederation of the regions. However, the federal public service was firmly opposed to the Aburi Agreement. Awolowo[55], regrouping his supporters, demanded the withdrawal of all Hausa troops working in the Western Region and warned that if the Eastern Region leaves the Federation, the Western Region would follow. The Federal Military Government approved the withdrawal of troops.

In May, Gowon published an implementation decree of the Aburi Agreement. Even the leaders of Northern Region, who were the first to threaten to secede, were now favorable to the formation of a

---

55 Jeremiah Obafemi Awolowo (March 6, 1909 - May 9, 1987) was a Nigerian politician, trade unionist and a statesman. A Yoruba and a native of Ikenne in Ogun State of Nigeria, he began his career as a regional political leader like most of his contemporaries before independence and was largely responsible for the progressive and social legislation which made Nigeria a modern nation. He founded many organizations, including Egbe Omo Oduduwa, the Trade Union Congress of Nigeria and the political party, Action Group. He was an active journalist and trade unionist as a young man. After earning a Bachelor of Commerce in Nigeria, he went to the United Kingdom where he obtained a degree in law. He was the first indigenous Premier of the Western Region under Nigeria's parliamentary system from 1954 to 1960. For more information on Awolowo, see Historical Dictionary of the British Empire, Volume 1, Edited by James Stuart Olson and Robert Shadle, article written by James Coleman, Nigeria: Background to Nationalism, 1971; Who's Who in Africa, The Political, Military, and Business Leaders of Africa, 1973; West Africa, May 18 and June 1, 1987, pages 89 and 90.

multistate federation. Meanwhile, the military governor of the Mid-West region announced that his region should be considered neutral in the event of civil war.

The Ojukwu government rejected the reconciliation plan and made known his intention to freeze all income received in the Eastern Region in compensation for the cost of resettling Igbo refugees. The leaders of the East had reached the point of rupture in their relations with Lagos and the rest of Nigeria. Despite the proposals made by the Federal Military Government, the Consultative Assembly of the Eastern Region voted on May 26, 1967 in favor of secession from Nigeria. In Lagos, Gowon proclaimed a state of emergency and unveiled plans for the abolition of regions in order to further divide the country into twelve states. This provision had caused a disintegration of the northern region, and had reduced the possibility of the continued domination of the North, and also offered a major concession to the Eastern Region. It was also a strategic decision, which had won the support of the minorities of the Eastern Region and deprived the Igbo rebels of the control over the oil producing areas.

On May 30, 1967, Ojukwu responded to the federal decree with the proclamation of the independent Republic of Biafra, named after the Bight of Biafra. He cited as the main cause of this action, the inability of the Nigerian government to protect the lives of the Easterners. According to Ojukwu, the Nigerian government was guilty of genocide. And so, secession was for him the ultimate decision to be taken after all efforts to protect the Igbo people in the other regions had failed.

Initially, the Federal Military Government had launched "police measures" to restore the authority of Lagos in the Eastern Region. The army units tried to advance into secessionist territory in July 1967, but the rebel forces easily stopped them. The Biafrans fought back with surprised thrust in the Midwest region, where they seized strategic points. However, the effective control of the delta region remained under federal control, despite attempts by the rebels to take several non-Igbo areas. The federal government began to mobilize large numbers of recruits to complete its army to 10,000 members.

At the end of 1967, the federal forces had regained the Midwest region and secured the delta region, which was reorganized as Rivers State and Southeastern States, cutting off Biafra from direct access to the sea.

An impasse occurred because the federal government's attacks against major cities had been weakened in the face of the stubborn resistance of Biafra. Poorly equipped and hurriedly trained, the rebel troops nonetheless had the advantage of having a well organized, strong and determined leadership and a wonderful morale. Biafran attacks against its opponent across the River Niger succeeded in wedging large concentrations of federal troops on the western shore.

In September 1968, Owerri was captured by federal troops coming from the south, and in early 1969 the federal army had expanded to 250,000 men, and opened up three fronts nicknamed by Gowon as the "final attack." Although the federal forces flanked the rebels while trying to cross the River Niger at Onitsha, they failed to break through. The Biafrans subsequently regained Owerri in fierce fighting and threatened to push on to Port Harcourt until there was a new federal attack in the south. This attack tightened the noose around the rebel enclave without being stifled into submission.

Biafran propaganda, which stressed the threat of genocide to the Igbo people, was extremely effective abroad in winning sympathy for the secessionist movement. Food and medical supplies were scarce in Biafra. Humanitarian aid, as well as arms and ammunition arrived in the area besieged by international relief organizations and private and religious groups from the United States and Western Europe through the nocturnal air transportation in the war zone. The majority of Biafra's military supplies were purchased from the international arms market with official assistance provided by France through its former West African colonies.

The independence of Biafra was recognized by Tanzania, Zambia, Gabon and Ivory Coast, but was undermined in the eyes of most African states led by South Africa, Southern Rhodesia (present day Republic of Zimbabwe), and other foreign countries like Portugal.

FROM CULTURAL JUSTICE TO INTER-ETHNIC MEDIATION

Great Britain extended diplomatic support and military assistance to the federal government. The Soviet Union became an important source of military equipment to Nigeria. Modern combat planes built in the Soviet Union, and piloted by Egyptian and British pilots, banned supply flights and inflicted heavy casualties during raids on Biafran urban centers. In line with its policy of noninvolvement, the United States banned the sale of military goods to either side while continuing to recognize the Federal Military Government.

In October 1969, Ojukwu sent an appeal to the United Nations (UN) for mediation and possibly for a cease-fire as a prelude to peace negotiations. But the federal government insisted on the surrender of Biafra. And Gowon observed that "rebel leaders clearly stated that it was a fight to the finish and that no concession will satisfy them." In December, the federal forces launched an attack in four areas, involving 120,000 soldiers, who had cut Biafra in half. When Owerri fell into the hands of the Federal Military on January 6, 1970, Biafran resistance collapsed. Ojukwu was fled to Ivory Coast leaving behind his chief of staff, Philip Effiong as an "officer in charge of the government." On January 12, Effiong requested an immediate and unconditional cease-fire, and subsequently surrendered to the authority of the federal government during a ceremony in Lagos.

Estimates of the number of deaths in the former Eastern Region because of the war, disease and starvation during the civil war of thirty months were between one million and three million. The end of fighting had caused more than 3 million Igbo refugees packed into an enclave of 2,500 square kilometers. The prospects for the survival of many of them and the future of the region were dim. There were severe shortages of food, medicines, clothing and housing. The economy of the region was completely poor. The cities were in ruins, schools, hospitals, utilities, and means of transport were destroyed or inoperative. Foreign groups established important emergency relief assistance, but the Federal Military Government insisted on the management of all operations of assistance and recovery, and thus suspended certain organizations that provided assistance to Biafra.

Because reports of genocide had fueled international sympathy for Biafra, the Federal Military Government authorized a team of international experts to observe the cessation of war and to look for proofs. Subsequently, the observers said they had found no evidence of genocide or systematic destruction of property, although there were considerable evidence of famine and death as a result of the war. In addition, under the close supervision of Gowon, the federal government ensured that Igbo civilians were not treated as defeated enemies. A program was launched to reintegrate the Biafran rebels in Nigeria in a unified state entity. A number of officials who had "actively advised, assisted, or encouraged the secession" were dismissed, but a clear distinction was made between them and those who had simply carried out their duties. The Igbo personnel were re-enrolled in the Federal Armed Forces. Ojukwu, in exile, was the scapegoat, but efforts to obtain his extradition failed.

An Igbo official, Ukapi "Tony" Asika, was appointed administrator of the new East Central State, including the Igbo core cities. Asika had remained faithful to the federal government during the civil war, but as a further act of conciliation, his cabinet comprised of the people who had served under the secessionist regime. Asika was unpopular to many Igbo people, who considered him as a traitor, and his administration had been described as incompetent and corrupt. In three years under his leadership, however, the state government realized the rehabilitation of 70 percent of industries paralyzed during the war. The federal government provided funds to cover the operational expenses of the state during the transitional period and most of the war damages were repaired. Social services and public services were gradually restored, but not to the level before the war.

Aguleri – Umuleri Conflict

In order to present the conflict between the Aguleri and Umuleri, we want to show how this conflict can be explained with reference to the pre-colonial, colonial and postcolonial era, its nature, intensity and intervention strategies that have been used.

FROM CULTURAL JUSTICE TO INTER-ETHNIC MEDIATION

The people of Aguleri and the people of Umuleri are of the same ethnic extraction of the Igbo region. They are both predominantly Christians. Both communities are located in the southeastern part of Nigeria, particularly in Anambra State near the city of Onitsha, which is located close to the Niger River. In the southeastern part of Nigeria, they are considered among the most educated following their first contact with missionaries. The question "who owns the land?" is the cause of intercommunity clashes in many instances across the country. The same question also explains the bloody battles between the communities of Aguleri and Umuleri. The crisis dates back to the beginnings of recorded history of each community as it focuses on the question of who is the first community to settle in this territory and to whom belongs the area known by the name Otuocha. To understand the source of the conflict, however, a historical overview of the dynamics of land conflict between the Aguleri and Umuleri is required.

The importance of land to the people of Nigeria during the pre-colonial period, especially those occupying the equatorial forests, cannot be doubted. They were mainly farmers and outside its direct economic importance, land was also used for the payment of dowry, compensation for murders and other serious crimes, and also as a medium of exchange. Therefore, land became a symbol of wealth and social status in these societies. Land was also a major cause of war.

The colonial state exacerbated the contradictions that already existed in these societies by supporting some communities more than others. Records show that Captain O'Connor, head of the Regional District in 1930 partly compounded the problem by encouraging the Umuleri to make claims to the whole of the land of Otuocha, and promised to support them in this war[56]. This apparently increased the bitterness in the region and had bottled it for the future. Policies of this type had led to a substantial loss of faith in the colonial legal system. It is this lack of faith, partly induced by the colonial state, which explains the failure of the postcolonial state to solve the problem. Land acquisition by European traders and the colonial government

---
56 Chinwuba R. Legal essay on the Otuocha Land Case, Enugu Star Printing and Publishing Company, 1981, p.1

for various purposes provided the land needed for commercial and residential reasons, for missionaries, churches, schools and farms, Government residential quarters and administrative infrastructures. The study initiated by Ibeanu and Matthew[57] shows that these lands are generally located in the border areas. It was these granted or seized lands that became the source of the most famous conflict between the neighboring communities. This conflict was exacerbated by the competition among the European communities, especially among the different churches. In some areas, neighboring communities were divided between two missions. A land granted to one mission meant a refusal of land to the other. Once the disputed territory was involved, a spiral conflict immediately triggered. The land dispute over Otuocha between the communities of Aguleri and Umuleri clearly illustrates the role of Europeans in the creation and intensification of land disputes. This is a case of land donation and refusal of land donation, sale of land and the fight against such sales to the Europeans (lands that have historically been used in common by the two communities without any problems).

The post-colonial period has seen an escalation of the conflict between the Aguleri and Umuleri. There is no doubt that to a large extent, these differences were carried over from the colonial era. Land became a rallying point for the villages, communities and cities. Ibeanu and Matthew conclude that these conflicts are difficult to resolve because they tend to become a vehicle for the expression of community sentiments[58]. The dispute between the Aguleri and Umuleri over the land of Otuocha reached alarming proportions after the Civil War[59]. The terrible economic condition of post-colonial

---

57 For detailed understanding of the study of Ibeanu and Matthew, refer to Ibeanu O. and Matthew, The Refugee Situation in Nigeria - Paper presented at the conference of the African Studies Association of the United Kingdom (ASAUK), Cambridge University, September 14-16, 1988; Also, see Ibeanu O., The State and Population in Displacement in Nigeria; Politics, Social Stress and Displacement in Rural Anambra State. Ph.D. Dissertation, University of Nigeria, 1992, quoted and analyzed by Raphael Chima Ekeh in Nigeria: Aguleri-Umuleri Conflict - The Theatre of Fratricidal War, (Searching for Peace publications), 1999, available at: http://www.conflict prevention.net/page.php?id=40&formid=73&action=show&surveyid=50.
58 Ibid.
59 Chinwuba, op cit, p.25.

FROM CULTURAL JUSTICE TO INTER-ETHNIC MEDIATION

Nigeria fueled the tensions already latent in the situation. However, the claims of the two communities for the land of Otuocha and the land of Agu-Akor had even reached the Supreme Court. In 1993, the Umuleri sued the Aguleri people but lost the case because they had already sold the land in question at the time to Royal Niger Company Ltd in 1935, and in 1950 they also lost their appeals in West African Court of Appeal and at the London Privy Council. In 1964, the amendment of the act which made Otuocha the headquarters of Old Anambra local government area, changing the name to "Otuocha Aguleri" provoked another reaction from the Umuleri, which was, however, overtaken by civil war. However, the Government of the Eastern Central State restored the name, "Otuocha." In the judgment delivered in 1984, the Supreme Court ruled that "neither Aguleri nor Umuleri were able to establish that they are the exclusive owners of the land Otuocha"[60]. After 1984, the community of Aguleri took a belligerent and provocative position and began to claim Otuocha as its exclusive property.

Despite their historical ties, the people of Aguleri and the community of Umuleri were at loggerheads for centuries. The two communities have lived and farmed side by side for decades, but with suspicion and hostility. In September 1995, the situation exploded. This year, public property including schools, banks, post offices, city halls and churches were destroyed, even to the ground. In addition, approximately 200 private homes were destroyed and countless people killed. The clashes in April 1999 broke-out as a result of the death of Mr. Mike Edozie, a native of Aguleri, who was also the chairman of the local government during the 1995 crisis. During his funeral, some young men identified as the youth of Umuleri beat the mourners. There was pandemonium as the youth of Umuleri dispersed the mourners, beating some of them in the process. The exact number of victims is disputed, but more than one hundred people were killed. Such is the intensity of the conflict between the

---

60 Raphael Chima Ekeh, Nigeria: Aguleri-Umuleri Conflict - The Theatre of Fratricidal War, (Searching for Peace publications), 1999, available at: http://www.conflict prevention.net/page.php?id=40&formid=73&action=show&surveyid=50.

Aguleri and the Umuleri to the extent that both communities were deserted except for those who had actually continued the war. Most of the indigenes of the communities in conflict took refuge in nearby villages; while hospitals in Onitsha and its environs were full of victims of community confrontations.

Apart from the Red Cross emergency aid to refugees and displaced persons, there was hardly any Non Governmental Organization initiative in the region[61]. This is regarded as a reactive measure rather than a proactive step towards conflict transformation. In terms of the official intervention of the government, the Nigerian state took three main types of action in order to control violent clashes between the people of Aguleri and the people of Umuleri. These types of preventive action include peacemaking, the acquisition of disputed areas, and legal actions on disputed land. The government intervention essentially took the form of legal action on the disputed land. The government also established a number of commissions of inquiry to investigate the causes of conflict, identify stakeholders and make recommendations. As a result of the disturbance and killings in 1995, a commission of inquiry was established to investigate the circumstances and determine the role played by the different parties in the conflict. Although the government issued a white paper on February 1997 with wide-ranging recommendations, nothing was done to defuse the situation until the final conflagration of 1999. The apparent failure of the Nigerian state to fight against this conflict is due to a lack of faith or confidence in the ability of the state. Thus, state intervention in land disputes is viewed with suspicion. Even the judicial system failed to build confidence in the peoples of Aguleri and Umuleri. Despite many lawyers and access to external legal advice, both communities interpreted the statements of various courts at their convenience and these misinterpretations have been responsible for most of the animosities between the two communities.

---

61 Ibid.

◄ FROM CULTURAL JUSTICE TO INTER-ETHNIC MEDIATION

Ethnic Conflicts in the Niger Delta Region

The Niger Delta covers an area of about 70,000 square kilometers and accounts for 7.5% of the total mass of land in Nigeria, which range from Apoi in Bakassi and from the Mashin creek, the Gulf of Benin. It covers a coastline of 560 km, about two-thirds of the entire coastline of Nigeria[62]. The Niger Delta comprises nine of the 36 states that make up the Federal Republic of Nigeria. These states are Abia, Akwa-Ibom, Bayelsa, Cross River, Delta, Edo, Imo, Ondo and Rivers. The people of the Niger Delta are the largest group among the minority groups in the south-south geopolitical zone. The estimated population of this region is about 30 million. Since 1975 until now the oil resources of the Niger Delta accounts for 90% of export earnings of the country. Yet the area remains the least developed region of the country in terms of the environmental and socio-economic situation.

The current violent conflicts in the Niger Delta were noted in the early 1990s during tensions between the foreign oil companies and a number of ethnic minority groups in the Niger Delta who felt exploited, particularly the Ogoni and the Ijaw . Ethnic and political unrest continued throughout the 1990s and until 2007, despite the transition to democracy in 1999.

The recurrent crisis in the Niger Delta region is the product of deep sense of marginalization and neglect by the government and oil companies to support human development, infrastructure, and provision of basic social services. Although the area of the Niger Delta is home to the oil resources that have made Nigeria and the oil companies rich, it is largely underdeveloped compared to the rest of the country. Indeed, it is a paradox of poverty amidst plenty, which causes violent clashes. There is also a high rate of youth unemployment, while a large number of people are not literate. In addition, health indicators are low and they lag far behind the national average. As has been observed, the pollution generated by oil companies has created risks for health and fishing, and has also made

---

62 See Emeka Nkoro, Conflict In the Niger Delta: the Way Forward, an article published by Searchwarp on October 11, 2005, retrievable from http://searchwarp.com/swa20447.htm

other agricultural activities almost impossible. There is a high rate of fatality from waterborne diseases, malnutrition and poor hygiene. The quantity and quality of housing infrastructure are less than in most of the regions. Only few people have access to safe drinking water. Transportation is often difficult and expensive.

Competition for oil wealth has fueled violence between ethnic groups, causing the militarization of nearly the entire region by ethnic militia and the Nigerian military and the police forces. Crime victims are afraid to seek justice for crimes committed against them because of "the impunity of those responsible for grave violations of human rights, which created a devastating cycle of conflicts and violence"[63].

Being essentially a conflict related to oil, the conflict in the Niger Delta is manifested at different levels of relationships. At one level, it is the confrontation between local communities and oil companies. At a corresponding level, you have a confrontation between local communities, including young militants and the Nigerian federal state authorities. And ironically, at the third level, there are widespread hostilities among some ethnic groups or local communities themselves.

An important observation to make at this stage is that in all these three levels of conflict, the main instruments of violence have been the marginalized youths and the alienated groups in the region. The activities of the aggrieved youths in the form of pipeline vandalism, oil theft, piracy, hostage taking and intercommunity hostilities, have often caused the massive and devastating intervention of security forces, such as that which took place in Odi in Bayelsa State, which led to the complete ransacking of the city and the loss of many lives and properties worth billions of Naira[64]. Since a detailed analysis of all these forms of conflict in the Niger Delta is difficult, we will focus only on the following three conflicts: the Ogoni crisis, the Ijaw unrest and the Ijaw-Itsekiri conflict.

---

63 See "Background Briefing" at: http://www.hrw.org/legacy/backgrounder/africa/nigeria0205/1.htm

64 Thomas A. Imobighe, Conflict in Niger Delta: A Unique Case or a 'Model' for Future Conflicts in Other Oil-Producing Countries? Publié par FRIEDRICH-EBERT-STIFTUNG à http://library.fes.de/pdf-files/iez/02115/imobighe.pdf

◂ FROM CULTURAL JUSTICE TO INTER-ETHNIC MEDIATION

OGONI CRISIS

A practical case study is that of the Ogoni ethnic group in the Niger Delta, Rivers State whose claims are led by the Movement for the Survival of Ogoni People (MOSOP) with the deceased rights activist, Ken Saro-Wiwa, as leader.

The Ogoni people are among the indigenous peoples of Rivers State. They share with the people of Ijaw and the other groups of the Niger Delta, an environmental problem caused by oil operations. They constitute about 1.5 million people and live in an area of 1,050 km2. This territory is located in Rivers State, on the coast of the Gulf of Guinea to the east of the city of Port Harcourt. It includes four Local Government areas, namely Khana, Gokana, Tai and Eleme. Traditionally, the Ogoni are divided into six kingdoms of Babbe, Eleme, Gokana, Ken-Khana, Nyo-Khana, and Tai. Among the languages spoken by the Ogoni are Khana, Gokana, Tai (TEE), Eleme and Ban Ogoi[65], constituting therefore part of the linguistic wealth of the Niger Delta.

The Ogoni people have pointed out, like other communities in the region of the Niger Delta, that their lands have been devastated and degraded, their atmosphere has been polluted, water contaminated, the trees are poisoned and their fauna and flora have almost disappeared, because of the activities of the oil companies in the region. To intensify this negative situation, there is no developed infrastructure in the locality, such as electricity, portable water and access roads. Thus, on 26 August 1990, the Ogoni People published a bill emphasizing the importance of giving them their fundamental human rights which was sent to the federal government of Nigeria, demanding political freedom that guarantees political control of Ogoni affairs by the Ogoni people, the right to control and use of Ogoni economic resources for Ogoni development, adequate and direct representation as a right in all Nigerian institutions and the right to protect the Ogoni environment and ecology from further degradation. However, their request was rejected, which resulted in

---
65   See Ethnologue Languages of the World, sous Language Family Trees, publié à http://www.ethnologue.com/show_family.asp?subid=2050-16

the delegation of MOSOP by the Ogoni people on August 26, 1991 to file a complaint with the United Nations Commission on Human Rights and also to the European Community, alleging that the Nigerian government refused their request. MOSOP was also tasked to alert these organizations that the Federal Republic of Nigeria has refused to pay royalties for oil and petroleum extracted from the Ogoni land for more than three decades.

From December 1992, the conflict between the Ogoni and the oil companies led to a grave level. Both sides started to carry out acts of violence, and MOSOP issued an ultimatum to the oil companies (Shell, Chevron and the Nigerian National Petroleum Corporation) requesting $ 10 billion in royalties accumulated from damages and interests, and "the immediate end of the environmental degradation, and negotiations for an agreement on all future drilling[66].

The Ogoni threatened to embark on mass action to disrupt their operation if oil companies did not respond. By this act, the Ogoni diverted the attention of their actions from a federal government that was not responding, in order to target oil companies engaged in their own region. The rationale for this decision was based on the responsibility and the benefits gained by the oil companies that exploit the natural resources of the Ogoni homeland, and the neglect of the federal government to repair the damage caused to Ogoni people.

The government responded by banning public gatherings, saying that the disruptions of oil production were acts of treason.

In 1990, the Mobile Police Force (MPF) shot the Ogoni people who were demonstrating against Shell in the village of Umuechem, killing 80 people and destroying 495 homes. In 1993, following protests that were organized to prevent the installation of new pipelines, the Police Mobile Force raided the region to quell the unrest. In the chaos that followed, it was alleged that 27 villages were attacked resulting in the death of about 2,000 Ogoni people and the displacement

---

[66] See The Report of Oputa Panel, vol. 2, retrievable from: http://www.nigerianmuse.com/nigeriawatch/oputa/OputaVolumeTwo.pdf

of about 80,000 people[67]. On May 21, 1994, soldiers and mobile policemen came to most of the Ogoni villages. On that day, four Ogoni chiefs were brutally murdered. Ken Saro-Wiwa, leader of the opposing faction, had been forbidden to enter the Ogoni territory on the day of the massacre. Then he was arrested in connection with the killings. Amnesty International described it as a deliberate policy of terrorism. In mid-June, security forces razed 30 villages, arrested and detained 600 people and killed at least 40. This figure eventually reached 2,000 deaths among civilians and some 100,000 internally displaced persons[68].

In May 1994, nine activists of the movement, among them Ken Saro-Wiwa, were arrested and charged with incitement to murder following the deaths of the four Ogoni chiefs. Saro-Wiwa and his colleagues denied the charges, but were imprisoned for over a year before being sentenced to death by a specially convened tribunal chosen by General Sani Abacha on November 10, 1995. These Ogoni activists were denied a fair trial and were executed by hanging by the Nigerian state[69].

Their executions were condemned by the international community. The trial was widely criticized by the Human Rights Organizations and the governments of other states, who condemned the action of the Nigerian military government. But despite all these, the conflict remains unresolved.

The Ogoni are not alone in the demands to change the status quo. The Ogbia communities of Rivers State had complained of similar problems. Others include the communities of Ikot Abasi, who had already demonstrated their problem to the public in 1987 by protests and consequently 38 houses were destroyed due to the intervention of

---

67 Magne Oven Varsi, World Marks 15th Anniversary of Nigeria's Writer and Human Rights Activist's Murder, article modified on 12.11.2010 by GALDU Resource Centre for the Rights of the Indigenous Peoples, found on their website at: http://www.galdu.org/web/index.php?odas=4908&giella1=eng
68 Tobias HALLER et al.(2000):Fossile Ressourcen, Erdölkonzerne und indigene Völker, Giessen : Focus Verlag, P.105
69 Nick Mathiason, Shell in court over alleged role in Nigeria executions, article published by The Observer, Sunday 5 April 2009 found at: http://www.guardian.co.uk/business/2009/apr/05/shell-saro-wiwa-execution-charges

security forces of the state. The Itshekiri, the Ijaw and the Urhobo are also among the marginalized minority groups we examine in this book.

IJAW UNREST

The Ijaw (an anglicized term of Ijo or Ejo and a variation of Ujo or Ojo) is an ethnic nation of more than fourteen million people in the region of the Niger Delta. They are the most populous indigenous inhabitants of the Niger Delta, representing the fourth largest ethnic group in Nigeria[70]. They are spread mostly in forest areas of the states of Bayelsa, Delta and Rivers in the Niger Delta. Some are from the states of Akwa-Ibom, Edo and Ondo. They have lived for a long time in many places near the sea trading routes, and they were well connected to other regions through trade. The current president of Nigeria, Goodluck Jonathan, is an Ijaw.

The Ijaw ethnic group consists of 40 tribes. These tribes are based on the lines of kinship and share the same culture and tradition. The Ijaw consider themselves as belonging to a unique and coherent nation, bound together by ties of language and culture. This tendency has been encouraged in large part by what is considered as the environmental degradation that accompanied the exploitation of oil in the Niger Delta region.

This link or the ethnic unity of the Ijaw tribes is visible in the formation of the Youth Council and their demands for ethnic rights. In December 1998, the Conference of all the youths revived the struggle for the control of oil resources with the formation of the Ijaw Youth Council (IYC) and the Kaiama Declaration[71]. In this declaration, the concerns of the Ijaw about losing control of their homeland and their lives to the benefit of oil companies were joined by a commitment to direct action. In a statement and in a letter addressed to the Oil Companies, the Ijaw demanded for their fundamental human rights and asked that oil

---

70 See Benaebi Benatari, "Ijaw History" publié par IJAW FOUNDATION, sur leur site web à http://www.ijawfoundation.org/people.htm
71 For more details on the Kaiama Declaration and the activities of the Ijaw Youth Council "IYC" visit the website of the Ijaw People's Association (IPA) at: http://www.ijawland.com/kiama-declaration.html

FROM CULTURAL JUSTICE TO INTER-ETHNIC MEDIATION

companies suspend operations and withdraw from the Ijaw territory[72]. The Ijaw Youth Council (IYC), committed to "a peaceful struggle for freedom, self-determination and ecological justice"[73], launched a campaign for celebration, prayer and outreach, named Operation for climate change at the beginning of December 1998.

In December 1998, two warships and nearly 15,000 troops of the Nigerian security forces intervened in the states of Bayelsa and Delta at the moment when the Ijaw Youth Council (IYC) was mobilized for the operation for climate change. The soldiers entered Yenagoa, the capital of Bayelsa State and announced that they had come to attack the youths who were in the process of protesting and disrupting the activities of oil companies. In the morning of December 30, 1998, two thousand young people, dressed in black, gathered for a protest in Yenagoa singing and dancing. The soldiers opened fire with rifles, machine guns and tear gas, killing at least three demonstrators and arrested more than twenty five. During a walk to request for the release of these detainees, three other demonstrators were shot by the soldiers[74]. The army declared a state of emergency throughout Bayelsa State banning public meetings. At military checkpoints, residents were severely beaten or arrested. At night, soldiers invaded private homes, terrorizing the inhabitants with blows, and women and girls with attempts of rape[75].

On January 4, 1999, about a hundred soldiers of the military encamped near the Chevron Corporation attacked Opia and Ikiyan, two Ijaw communities in Delta State. Bright Pablogba, a traditional chief of Ikiyan, who came to the river to negotiate with the soldiers, was attacked with possibly tens of others[76]. Of the approximately

---

72 Ijaw Youth Movement, letter to "All Managing Directors and Chief Executives of transnational oil companies operating in Ijawland," December 18, 1998.
73 For the violent clashes between the Ijaw and the security forces, as well as more information on Kaiama Declaration and the activities of the Ijaw Youth Council "IYC", see Human Rights Watch, Nigeria: Crackdown In The Niger Delta, 1 May 1999, available at: http://www.unhcr.org/refworld/docid/3ae6a7f74.html [accessed 11 January 2012]
74 Ibid.
75 Ibid.
76 For the massacres of Opia and Ikiyan, also read Human Rights Watch Nigeria, « Crackdown in Niger Delta op cit. Also consult Victoria Aluyor, Massacre in another Delta Community, CHEVRON'S NEW YEAR GIFT: THE OPIA AND IKIYAN MASSACRE DESPATCH LINE:

1,000 people living in the two villages, four people were found dead and sixty-two were missing the month after the attack. The same soldiers burned the villages, destroyed canoes and fishing equipment, killing livestock and destroying churches and religious shrines.

However, the Operation for Climate Change continued and disrupted Petroleum Production Operations for a large part of 1999 by turning off pipes through the Ijaw territory. Within the context of the high conflict between the Ijaw and the Federal Government of Nigeria (and its police and army), the army carried out the massacre of Odi[77], killing dozens if not hundreds of Ijaw. Subsequent actions by the Ijaw against the oil industry included both a renewed effort to nonviolent action and attacks against oil installations and the foreign workers of the petroleum industries.

Ijaw-Itsekiri Conflict

Before the Ijaw unrest of 1998 and 1999, there were violent clashes between the Ijaw militants and the militants of Itsekiri origin. Estimated at over 450,000[78], the Itsekiri are among the five distinct ethnic groups in Delta State with an economic and commercial center known as Warri. "The Itsekiri inhabit the northeastern end of the Niger Delta. Their neighbors are the Edo from Binin in the north;

OPIA & IKIYAN 1999, retrievable at: http://www.mail-archive.com/ctrl@listserv.aol.com/msg03287.html

77 The Odi massacre was an attack carried out on November 20, 1999, by the Nigerian army in the town of Odi, predominantly Ijaw in Bayelsa State. The attack occurred in the context of an ongoing conflict in the Niger Delta on indigenous rights to oil resources and environmental protection. Before the massacre, twelve members of the Nigerian police were murdered by a gang near Odi, on November 4 and the rest in the following days. (See "The Destruction of Odi and Rape in Choba" published by Human Rights Watch on 12 December 1999 http://www.hrw.org/press/1999/dec/nibg1299.htm). On the other hand, the military invaded, exchanged fire, and then indiscriminately attacked civilians and buildings of the city. Every building in town except the bank, the Anglican Church and the health center was burned (ibid.). A wide range of estimates were given for the number of civilians killed. Human Rights Watch concluded that "soldiers could certainly have killed dozens of unarmed civilians and that the numbers of several hundred dead are entirely plausible." (ibid .) Nnimmo Bassey, executive director of the Environmental Rights Action, says nearly 2,500 civilians were killed. (see Bassey, Nnimmo (June 2006). "Trade and Human Rights in the Niger Delta of Nigeria, published by Pambazuka News at: http://www.pambazuka.org/en/category/comment/34801)

78 Read Who are the Itsekiri?, an article published on the website of the Association of the Itsekiri in the United States at: http://www.itsekiri.org/files/history/history_itsekiri.php

in the south are located the Ijaw, the Urhobo in the east and the Yoruba of Ondo in the northwest "[79].

The promotion of economic activity was a major concern of the Itsekiri monarch of the 16th century. The fact that there was a kingdom was important in the decision of the Europeans to do business with the Itsekiri. Europeans had a tendency to go into areas that had a political system to ensure peaceful commerce. The first contacts of the Itsekiri with medieval Europe, particularly Portugal, helped to promote a conservative Christian education and the Itsekiri civilization; and the people remain proud of this historic occasion.

The coastal situation of the kingdom and the navigable and accessible waterways as well as the rivers not only led to the first contact of the Itsekiri with medieval Europe, particularly Portugal, but it also led to its significant prosperity between the sixteenth and nineteenth centuries, when trade with the neighboring ethnic groups and Europeans had thrived[80].

However, unlike in the past when the prosperity of their homeland had propelled the Itsekiri people to glorious heights, the contemporary period has paradoxically seen their economy deteriorated. Not only did the exploitation of crude oil in the region weaken the ecosystem and destroy local economies from 1997 to 2003, the Itsekiri also experienced violent ethnic conflicts with some of its neighbors, of which a typical case is that of the 1997 conflict with the Ijaw people.

The violent conflict between the Ijaw and the Itsekiri militias over the last decade has killed thousands of people and destroyed towns and villages. The first outbreak of violence was in March 1997 in the city of Warri. The cause was ostensibly the decision of the military authorities to move the headquarters of the Warri South local government located in an Ijaw town called Ogbe-Ijaw to the Itsekiri community of Ogidigben. The relocation of the headquarters provoked the anger of the Ijaw who interpreted it as "a new proof

---

79   Obaro Ikime PhD, Merchant Prince of the Niger Delta, 1968, cited by the Association of the Itsekiri in the United States, ibid.
80   The Association of the Itsekiri in the United States: Who are the Itsekiri? Ibid.

HISTORICAL MANIFESTATIONS OF ETHNO-RELIGIOUS CONFLICTS IN NIGERIA

of their marginalization"[81]. A report by AFP says that more than 80 people died in the fighting and the army was ordered to intervene (on April 23, 1997)[82]. The conflict strained the relationship among the three ethnic groups: the Ijaw, the Urhobo and the Itsekiri. Six pumping stations belonging to Shell were seized by community groups and 127 staff members of Shell were taken in hostage. Later, in April, other young people seized the pumping stations in Ogidigben, causing another temporary suspension of production. A large number of military troops were then deployed to the west of the Niger Delta and a curfew was imposed in Warri.

According to a report of the Immigration and Refugee Board of Canada, the Ijaw and the Itsekiri communities resolved to put an end to the hostilities which "had lasted seven weeks." The agreement was concluded at a meeting of peace by the youths and the leaders from both ethnic groups at Effon, near Warri. The meeting was chaired by the administrator of the State, Colonel David Dungs, and the General Officer commanding the 82nd Division of the Nigerian Army, General Felix Mojapero. The ethnic groups also made a commitment to release all captured persons on both sides and return all seized property belonging to oil companies[83].

However, violence continued to erupt periodically. A violent conflict in May and June 1999, during the democratic transition to civilian government, left at least 200 people dead in the clashes between the Ijaw and the Itsekiri ethnic militias. In a report on the conflict, Human Rights Watch concluded that "the continued impunity for years of brutal violence" was a fundamental reason for this ongoing struggle[84].

---

81   See, Immigration and Refugee Board of Canada, Nigeria: The conflict between Itsekiri and Ijaw ethnic groups in Warri, Delta region (March 1997-September 1999) , 14 September 1999, NGA32676.E , available at: http://www.unhcr.org/refworld/docid/3ae6ad6864.html [accessed 17 March 2011]
82   Ibid.
83   For more information on this peace reunion, see Immigration and Refugee Board of Canada, Nigeria: The Ijaw-Itsekiri conflict in Delta State, including time period, causes, whether the authorities intervened, whether the police support the Ijaw or Itsekiri and the current situation, 1 April 1998, NGA29098.E, available at: http://www.unhcr.org/refworld/docid/3ae6abe720.html [accessed 17 March 2011]
84   "The Warri Crisis: Fueling Violence", Human Rights Watch, November 2003.

◄ FROM CULTURAL JUSTICE TO INTER-ETHNIC MEDIATION

The next outbreak of violence took place during the 2003 elections, when perceptions of favoritism by the oil companies and the unfulfilled promises have contributed to a serious outbreak of ethnic violence. The clashes involving the Ijaw, the Itsekiri, the Urhobo and the Nigerian security forces left hundreds of people dead, and thousands homeless[85]. About 40 percent of the country's oil industries were closed down for weeks.

Ethnic Conflicts in the North Central Zone

Regarding the ethnic conflicts in the central zone, we examine these three types: the Tiv--Jukun conflict in Wukari in Taraba State, the ethnic conflict between the Jukun / Chamba and the Kuteb in Taraba State (1998 / 1999), and the massacres of Jos in Plateau State.

TIV- JUKUN CONFLICTS IN WUKARI, TARABA STATE

Although the Yoruba in the southwest, the Igbo in the southeast and the Hausa / Fulani in the north dominate national politics, the "Middle Belt," which stretches from west to east between the north and the south, contains many small ethnic groups. These minority groups have been marginalized politically and economically. Probably, only few people in the other parts of the country know where Taraba State in general and the city of Wukari in particular are located. Wukari is not of strategic importance to the federal government, hence the neglect it has suffered.

What is the origin of this city? Anthropologists believe there was a great movement of people across Africa. Indeed, the Jukun, who are probably the first to settle in Wukari, say they originated from Yemen, as well as the Kanuri, who settled in the Chad Basin. The Jukun established a kingdom called Kwararafa, which reached its zenith in the seventeenth century. The Jukun say that they lived in peace with their neighbors until the Tiv migrated from Cameroon into the valley of Benue in the eighteenth century. The Tiv and the Jukun seem to have coexisted peacefully in the pre-colonial period for several reasons: the "Uka Aku" (the Jukun king) was the only

85 See Crisis Group Africa Briefing N°115, The Swamps of Insurgency: Nigeria's Delta Unrest", 3 August 2006.

supreme leader that everyone respected. There was plenty of land: the Tiv were mainly farmers in rural areas who did not interfere in the Jukun administration, and there was no politics of exclusion of the Tiv.

However, things began to change in the early twentieth century, as the Tiv population started to increase and agricultural land became more densely populated. In the 1940s, the Tiv were not only the largest ethnic group in the "Middle Belt region", but also three times more numerous than the Jukun in Wukari, a territory that the Jukun consider to be their land. The British colonialists were concerned about the influx of the Tiv farmers in the territory that they, themselves, also consider to be Jukun territory and tried to curb the phenomenon. An example is the creation of the Local Federal Council of Wukari, which included all other major ethnic groups, excluding the Tiv because they were regarded as immigrants. The agitation for the inclusion of the Tiv began in the 1940s and remains a source of conflict between the Jukun and the Tiv. Almost all the section of the Tiv and the Jukun trace the cause of their conflict to the introduction of the politics of exclusion in Nigeria. In the various elections since 1954, the Jukun and the Tiv have been in different political parties. Violent clashes such as the Tiv riots from 1959 to 1960, the crisis of 1964 during the First Republic of Nigeria, and the battles during the Second Republic from 1979 to 1983, stopped during the military periods from 1966 to 1979 and from 1983 to 1987. A conflict manifested itself with the local elections in 1987, when the Tiv gained positions of power at the local and national levels. Of course, this made the Jukun angry and put them in an uncomfortable condition. After the clash from 1990 to 1992 in which most of the Tiv were driven from Wukari, the elections held in 1996 and 1997 were peaceful mainly because the Tiv were not there to make their voices heard. However, the deep fear of political marginalization remains a major cause of the Tiv - Jukun conflict.

The political dimensions of the conflict are of two types: traditional and modern. While the first concerns the control of the Local Government Council, political appointments and other resources, the second is centered on the Jukun refusal to include the Tiv in the traditional Council of Wukari, where decisions that affect them are taken. Land is another factor that is often cited as a cause of conflict. Although it is often said that the Tiv encroach on agricultural land belonging to the Jukun, it turned out that the real problem is that the Tiv do not follow the traditional laws of land administration, which oblige them to obtain permission from the village chief, the district chief and follow the cardinal rule before starting to cultivate the land. Instead, the Tiv would not accept that they are settlers who came to settle in Wukari and do not recognize the Jukun as indigenous people.

Another factor in the conflict is the high population growth of the Tiv which, more and more, creates a need for agricultural land. Also, the Tiv were accused of inviting their relatives living in the neighboring state of Benue to settle with them in Wukari, which increases the demand for land, and strengthens the numerical strength of the Tiv. The Jukun therefore have the impression that their culture, of which they are very proud, is undermined by the influx of the Tiv and have embarked on a process of strengthening it. The various cited causes have led to an extremely violent confrontation between the Tiv and the Jukun from 1990 to 1992. No one including the government or the parties involved can give the exact figures of the victims. However, there was a massive burning of houses, commercial buildings, and schools, accompanied by looting of property. The methods used to kill people were extremely brutal and included beheading, setting fire on victims, the killing of pregnant women and children. The government failed to help victims rebuild their property and to this day, the destruction is still visible.

When an association called the "Academic Associates PeaceWorks" (AAPW) began to work on the Tiv-Jukun conflict in 1997, both groups were clearly separated, physically and psychologically. Most of the Tiv had been driven from Wukari, in effect only few number of the Tiv felt comfortable about the thought of spending the night in the city. In the workshop organized by the "Academic Associates PeaceWorks" for Wukari leaders in January 1998, the Tiv leaders refused to stay with the Jukun in the hotel, because they believed they would be an easy target for attack. The Jukun were quite happy with the situation, as they had undisputed control of the traditional and modern political power. However, the economy was down, as the Jukun had fewer customers for their goods and because of limited sources of food, which before were provided by the Tiv farmers.

In 1997, many Jukun were reluctant to follow a peace process because they did not want the Tiv to return to Wukari to reestablish their numerical strength. The Jukun were also reluctant to negotiate peace because they believed the government had betrayed them in previous negotiations. They thought that senior Tiv military officers could benefit from this negotiation to manipulate government decisions in their favor. Many of the Tiv were displaced from the lands they had lived for decades or even centuries, and had no place to go. The Jukun had sworn not to be surrounded by the Tiv farmlands, as was the case before 1990. As a result, the Tiv were forced to camp in remote places or unwanted areas. Schools, churches and healthcare facilities also remained closed for years. The army intervened to stop the fighting, but the underlying questions were not addressed. Most residents knew very little about conflict resolution mechanisms such as mediation and felt that only the government could find solutions to the conflict. Each party believed that the other party was extremely stubborn and difficult, and felt that the people themselves could never resolve their own problems.

In recent years, things have improved considerably. Some of the Tiv returned to Wukari town. Tensions have decreased, and both sides have resumed interaction. Of course, there are still tough people who would like to derail peace processes. But presently, a Wukari Peace Committee has been established with the aim of preventing future outbreaks of conflicts.

Ethnic Conflict between the Jukun / Chamba and the People of Kuteb in Taraba State

The conflict between the Jukun / Chamba and the Kuteb[86] like the one that occurred between the Tiv and the Jukun which we have

---

86 The People of Kuteb are the inhabitants of the South-West of Taraba State in Nigeria with a population of about 600.000 and West of Cameroon with a population of about 2,000. They have the Jukun, Ichen, Tiv, Chamba, Tigon, Ndoro and Bafum as neighbors. They speak the Yukuben-Kuteb language. For the history of the peoples of Kuteb, visit this website: http://kuteb.tripod.com/biography.html

just examined, has its roots in the pre-colonial period. The main cause of this conflict is linked to the question of land ownership: who owns the land of Takum which is the Headquarters of the Takum Local Government Area and inhabited by the Jukun, Chamba and the Kuteb? Because this problem was not resolved, it generated feelings of marginalization, misunderstandings on the demarcation of borders, and a violent confrontation occurring after the creation of a new Local Government Area.

According to historical accounts, the Kuteb, earlier known as "Ndetirikwen" or "Zompere", are believed to have emigrated from Egypt to the interior of Africa around 1000 BC under a chief called Kuteb. They moved to central Africa and eventually to West Africa through Cameroon. Then they settled on and around the hills of Takum. The name "Kuteb" eventually became the name of the tribe, and the names of his sons became the names of the clans. Their first capital was Ussa Hill named after one of the sons of Kuteb.

According to the Kuteb, the name "Takum" was a declension of the word "Teekum" which means "we go up." Historically, Takum was an important place for the Kuteb because they gathered there for religious, cultural, social and political reasons. The Kuteb were originally mountainous people, hence their claim that they were descending from the mountains to meet there for religious activities. But the Jukun and the Chamba reject this assertion.

Around the period of 1830, the Chamba, pursuant to heavy harassment of the Fulani, migrated from the region of Tibati in Cameroon towards the Takum zone. They settled around Jenuwa in Takum. However, Chamba accounts often claim that they conquered the Kuteb around Jenuwa, and this victory gave them a domination and power over the Kuteb.

During the pre-colonial period, Takum like some cities in northern Nigeria, were fenced up. The walls ensured the security of Chamba, as opposed to the hills which ensured the safety of Kuteb. However, in their attempts to occupy Takum during the First World

HISTORICAL MANIFESTATIONS OF ETHNO-RELIGIOUS CONFLICTS IN NIGERIA

War, the Germans destroyed part of the walls[87]. The cause of the conflict between the Jukun / Chamba alliance on one hand and the Kuteb on the other, comes primarily from the question: who actually owns Takum as a city and secondly, Takum as a Local Government Headquarters. This also constitutes the basis of border conflicts that followed the creation of Ussa local government from Takum.

The central point here is the belief that Takum developed to the point that each group wanted to have it as their ethnic headquarters, thus contributing to their psychological needs, their prestige, ego and control of the elites of all ethnic groups in Takum.

The colonial government responded by introducing an important political change in the political history of the Kuteb-Chamba relationship in 1912 by the creation of two districts: the district of Zumper for the Kuteb and a district called Takum / Tikani for the Chamba. "Each district was headed by a district chief, who ruled his ethnic group. The two leaders lived in Takum (...)"[88]. The creation of two districts as ethnic constituencies for the Kuteb and the Chamba in Takum ultimately failed in 1914. In order to respond directly to the existing threat and the state of insecurity, the colonial state had taken as a measure, the merger of two districts in one district of Takum in 1914. Similarly, the colonial state had dismissed and exiled the chief of Takum, Yamusa, a native of Chamba to Ibbi for slavery. Another measure taken to prevent the violence was the creation of a chiefdom of Takum for the two merged districts to form a single chiefdom. Ahmadu, a Kuteb was appointed as the head of this new chiefdom of Takum in 1914"[89]. The throne of the chiefdom has been occupied by the Kuteb since 1914, which has created a feeling of deprivation.

---

87 Rima Shawulu, 1988. A The Politics of the Ethnic and Religious Conflicts of Taraba state, in Festus Okoye (ed) Ethnic and Religious Rights in Nigeria, Human Rights Monitor Publications, Kaduna, p. 83.

88 Refer to Shedrack Gaya Best (DR): Communal Conflicts Management: The Jukun/Chamba-Kuteb Conflicts in Takum, Taraba State, A Research Report conducted under the auspices of Academic Associates Peace Works, Ikeja, Lagos. Funded by the British Council in Nigeria. December, 1998. pp. 2-10. Ces intervention d'Etat colonial étaient analysées par Rima Shawulu, 1988. The Politics of the Ethnic and Religious Conflicts of Taraba state, in Festus Okoye (ed) Ethnic and Religious Rights in Nigeria, Human Rights Monitor Publications, Kaduna, pp. 83-84.

89 Ibid., p.10

FROM CULTURAL JUSTICE TO INTER-ETHNIC MEDIATION

Chamba elites argued that the dethronement of the Chamba Chief, (Yamusa) in 1914 by the colonial state (British) was a punishment for a deeper conflict between the British colonial political office and the Chamba who had resisted the British occupation in Takum and alternatively invited the Germans to Takum. The Chamba argued that Yamusa was dismissed by the British for having dared to invite the Germans[90].

After the independence of Nigeria, there was an extensive consultation in 1963 involving all stakeholders in the regional government of northern Nigeria in order to vote for the ethnic group which should lead the chiefdom of Takum. According to the results of the vote, 19 members voted for the Kuteb, while six voted for the Chamba. As a result, the chiefdom of Takum was exclusively restricted to the Kuteb[91].

In 1967, the state of Benue / Plateau was created from the northern region, under the regime of Joseph Gomwalk. The regime had a large number of elites from Jukun in Wukari and Takum who transferred their grievances, petitions and opposition to the Gazette of 1963 to the new regime in the new state, which they did by increasing pressure for the Government to repeal the Gazette. Consequently, tension began to rise in the district of Takum because the Kuteb became restive because of these demands and pressures. Two and half years later, the military government of the state of Benue / Plateau radically changed its position on the question when it issued another Gazette in relation to the selection of the chief of Takum published in 1975. First, this government repealed the Gazette of 1963, and second, it made Chamba families or the clans of Tikari and Dinyi eligible for the throne of Takum for the first time since the creation of the chiefdom of Takum. The Gazette of 1975 caused disputes. The High Court in Jos and the Court of Appeal in Kaduna heard the case. The case was dismissed on the grounds that the Military Governor may revoke a previous order, and that the question of chiefdom was of an administrative nature and must be resolved administratively. The Chamba now use this Gazette as the basis for their claims for the

---
90   Ibid., p. 11
91   Ibid., p. 15

throne of Takum. The Chamba see this order as fair and equitable, while the Kuteb see it as an unjustified interference and unfounded. The Kuteb "fully attributed it to the large number of Jukun influential elites in the administration of Gomwalk working in various capacities. They believe that the relatives of the governor (Jukun elite) used their proximity to the administration to achieve a change of position"[92].

Since the repeal of the Order, the relationship between the Kuteb and the Jukun-Chamba continued to deteriorate and is manifested in hatred, suspicion, mutual distrust and ethnic rivalries. In 1976, there was a violent political confrontation in Takum, after the creation of the State of Gongola from the former State of Benue / Plateau, and after the elections. These clashes led to the destruction of lives and property.

The state government of Gongola responded to the disturbances in the normal way by the establishment of the Commission of Inquiry headed by Abubakar Girei to investigate the conflict. The group concluded and submitted its report to the government with the following recommendations: first that the conflict between the Jukun / Chamba alliance and the Kuteb is centered on the chiefdom of Takum. The Commission therefore recommended that the right to the throne be kept exclusively for the Kuteb, while all the major tribes of the region should become members of the council of King Makers. It added that the name of the monarch in the Kuteb language historically known as "Ukwe" has been a subject of dispute. The commission suggested that the title: "Chief of Takum" be chosen to reduce friction. Finally, the special commission of inquiry identified electoral abnormalities as a catalyst for disturbances[93].

The government was reluctant to communicate and implement the report. This has further exacerbated the tension. Although the Chamba had rejected the report of the Commission, the Kuteb on the other hand, were satisfied with the report but felt that the government's reluctance to act on the report was an act of dishonesty and refusal

---

92 For a detailed discussion on this issue, read The Garvey A. Yawe Committee Report Investigating the Kutebs/Jukuns-chamba Conflict. April-May, 1993, Office of the Governor, Taraba State, p. 19.
93 Ibid. p. 17

to pursue the truth and justice. The Kuteb attributed the government's reluctance to the continuing interference of the Jukun / Chamba elites in the State of Gongola[94].

In 1991, the former Gongola State was divided into two to create the states of Adamawa and Taraba. In 1993, the Government of Taraba State set up the Garvey A. Yawe Commission to investigate the disturbances of 1991 according to the verdict of the elections Tribunal. The Commission recommended that "from the previous decisions since 1912 and the colonial documents available, the throne of Takum should be left exclusively to the Kuteb. It recommended the repeal of the Gazette of 1975 and the revalidation of the1963 Gazette "[95]. However, the government did not act on the recommendations of the Committee. Therefore, the two communities continued on the path of hatred and mutual suspicion of each ethnic group led by the elites.

The Government of Taraba State also set up a Commission for Peace in 1998 led by the Chief Justice of Taraba State, Aliyu Adamu. The Commission negotiated temporary peace and the cessation of hostilities always appreciated by both ethnic groups. Before that, the military administrator of Taraba State, Amen Edore Oyakhire, sent in October 1997, a full report on the chiefdom of Takum in Taraba State to the Chief of Staff in Abuja. However, there was no response from the federal government to the recommendations of the commissions. In 1998, the federal government established a High Commission on the conflicts in Nigeria, with the primary objective to examine the various conflicts in the country, including the ethnic conflict between the Kuteb and the Chamba / Jukun. This explains the role played by the federal government in this conflict[96].

The federal government intervened in this conflict by creating a new local government. A circular to the Government of Taraba State ordered the creation of this new local government of Ussa on March 12, 1997. This happened three days before the local government

---

94 Ibid. p. 18
95 See, A Comprehensive Brief on the Chieftaincy Stool in Takum Chiefdom of Taraba State by the Military Administrator of Taraba state, 1st Oct. 1997. To the Chief of General Staff, General Staff Headquarters, State House, Abuja, p.11
96 Shedrack Gaya Best, Op. Cit,p. 2; see also, Military Administrators Brief, ibid p. 12.

elections scheduled on March 15, 1997. Surprisingly, the Kuteb won the elections in the local government of Takum and in the newly created Ussa local government[97]. The Chamba / Jukun elites protested against the election results. They argued that the newly created local government, three days before the elections, caused confusion with unclear boundaries and that many people in Takum were not aware that the new local government existed. The federal government published on 28 April 1997 another circular amending the boundaries between the two local governments in favor of the Chamba / Jukun. In response to this crisis and other similar circumstances, the federal government under the regime of General Sani Abacha, established the Danlami Rabiu Commission to modify the territorial boundaries. The Commission visited the areas where border changes created problems. However, before the Commission could visit Jalingo, the capital of Taraba State, the federal government ordered the cancellation of Takum and Ussa local governments' elections, which were moreover headed by the Kuteb leaders. And then, the federal government undertook the implementation of border modifications.

One of the major causes of the resurgence of conflicts between Jukum / Chamba alliance and the Kuteb could be attributed to the failure to implement the recommendations of the previous commissions[98] by the federal government on the one hand, and the state, on the other. This has become a major institutional failure on the part of the state or public institutions in addressing the problems associated with the conflict in Takum. Consequently, this situation increased frustration and occasionally leads to violent clashes.

---

97 Ibid.
98 Instances of these commissions are:
   i) The Abubakar Girei Commission of Inquiry of 1977, the State of Gongola;
   ii) The Gurin Suleiman Committee of 1985, the State of Gongola;
   iii) The Yawe Garvey Panel's report of 1993, Taraba State;
   iv) The Commission for Peace of Judge Adamu Aliyu in 1998, Taraba State;
   v) The Expert Group of the federal government on the creation of local governments headed by Arthur Mbanefo;
   vi) The Rabiu Danlami Commission created by the federal government for the modification of territorial boundaries in 1997;
   vii) The High Commission on the conflicts in Nigeria, created in 1998 by the federal government.

◄ FROM CULTURAL JUSTICE TO INTER-ETHNIC MEDIATION

THE MASSACRES OF JOS IN PLATEAU STATE

Jos is located in the center of Nigeria. The temperate climate of Jos makes it one of the coldest cities in Nigeria, and its plateau adds to its beauty which makes it a city of major tourist attraction. Plotnicov had once described Jos as "one of the safest places in West Africa"[99]. Founded at the dawn of the 20th century (about 1902) as a mining city of tin, Nigeria became the sixth world producer of tin with most of this production coming from the mine fields of Jos.

According to historians, indigenous people of Jos are the Berom, Anaguta and Afizere[100] who inhabited the area before the arrival of the Hausa-Fulani immigrants and others who came from other parts of Nigeria for commercial reasons, such as the Igbo, Yoruba, Urhobo, Ibibio and Edo.

Since the days of tin mines in Jos, the growth of the city of Jos has been phenomenal. The creation of Benue-Plateau State in 1967 with Jos as its social headquarters resulted in the influx of officials and other businessmen to the city. Today, the status of the Public Service of Jos has surpassed the mining activities of tin, which had characterized Jos in its formative years.

Since its inception, Jos has experienced the influence of heterogeneous population because of its strategic location and its role in mining. According to Plotnicov, "the problems of the administration of a heterogeneous community were recognized in 1962" and "the extreme heterogeneity of Jos reflects the diversity of the peoples of Nigeria, of whom almost all are represented"[101].

Other factors that have contributed to the growth of Jos are the strong presence of Christian mission entities, educational institutions and the peaceful atmosphere of the city. With the reintroduction of the legal system of Sharia in some northern states in 1999 and the crises that followed, Jos experienced a considerable influx of people coming from Kaduna, Kano, Bauchi, Zamfara and other northern states to seek refuge.

---

99 Leonard Plotnicov, Strangers in the City: Urban Man in Jos, Nigeria, University of Pittsburg Press, 1967, p. 33.
100 Anthony Dung Bingel. Jos: Origins and Growth of the Town 1900-1972, Department of Geography Publication, Jos, 1978, p. 2.
101 Leonard Plotnicov, op cit, pp. 44-66

HISTORICAL MANIFESTATIONS OF ETHNO-RELIGIOUS CONFLICTS IN NIGERIA

The cause of the incessant massacres of the Nigerian citizens in Jos, the capital of Plateau State, has remained the same for over a century. This is a case of ethnic groups, particularly the Berom, Anaguta and Afizere, and the Hausa-Fulani who claim supremacy over the others. The contention is to know who among these different ethnic groups are the "natives" or "immigrants" in Jos.

The Hausa-Fulani (also known as Jasawa) said that during the colonial period, specifically between 1902 and 1947, they were appointed leaders of Jos, with the title "Sarki Jos" as evidence. They also state that before Nigeria's independence in 1960, they represented Jos politically in the Northern Regional Assembly and in the Conference preceding the independence of Nigeria. They also affirmed that after independence, political appointments were always performed by them.

However, the people of Berom, Anaguta and Afizere, who claim joint ownership of Jos, argue that the name "Jos" derives from the Berom word, "Gwash" or "Jot", which means a source of water. They base their claims on the "Gazettes of the provinces of Northern Nigeria", as compiled by the British colonial masters between 1920 and 1932, which does not mention the Hausa-Fulani as the Indigenous Peoples of the Plateau Province. They also argue that the historical narratives explain how the Hausa-Fulani Jihadists who attempted an invasion of their territory in 1873 were defeated by them.

Amidst these arguments, the creation of the Jos North and Jos South Local Governments by the military ruler Ibrahim Babangida in 1991 has aggravated the malaise among the various ethnic groups. Although the majority of the Berom, Anaguta and Afizere are located in the South of Jos, the Hausa-Fulani Community had a numerical advantage in the North of Jos where the metropolitan city of Jos is located. This has worsened the tension as the recognized king in Jos, the " Gbom Gwom Jos ", was isolated among the Hausa-Fulani.

The accumulated years of animosity eventually degenerated into an open confrontation on April 12, 1994. This was due to the Hausa-Fulani protests against the cancellation ordered by the military government of Plateau State of the appointment of a Hausa-Fulani as the administrator of the Jos North Local Government, after the rejection by the Berom, Anaguta and Afizere.

The crisis had led to the loss of many lives, and property worth of millions of naira was destroyed. The government created a commission of inquiry on the crisis, with recommendations to prevent future events, as well as prosecute the perpetrators of the chaos. The recommendations provided by the commissions of inquiry have never been fully implemented.

The government's failure to learn lessons from the 1994 crisis had degenerated into the 2001 crisis that claimed over 1,000 lives, left many people displaced, and destroyed many properties. Between 1994 and 2011, there were at least 70 cases of violence in Jos and its environs. On October 1, 2010, there were bomb blasts in Abuja and Tuesday, January 11, 2011 there were killings of 13 innocent members of the Christian families from Wareng (a village near Jos) in Plateau State. Before this abominable massacre, there were four bomb blasts in and around Jos on December 24, 2010, that killed over 80 people with more than 120 injured. On January 17, 2010, the most violent clashes erupted in Kuru Karama, near Jos, killing over 150 people and wounded dozens of others. In early January 2011, some young Christian militants had laid ambush for a bus carrying Muslims and about eight people, including Christians, were killed. Again, Saturday, January 8, 2011, Christian traders in Dilinea / Terminus market in Jos were violently attacked by armed Muslim youths and dozens of people, including some Igbo traders, were killed. Since the beginning of violent conflicts in Jos in 2001, more than 3,500 people may have been killed. In 2010, more than 800 people may have also been killed. In September 2001, as many as 1,000 deaths were recorded. In May 2004, a violent conflict that swept the city of Yelwa in the south of Plateau State caused over 700 deaths. In November 2008, a massacre estimated at 700 deaths was reported in sectarian violence that rocked the city of Jos[102]. Violent conflicts in Jos

---

102 For more information on the Jos crises, read Emeka Umeagbalasi, Jos crisis: Saving Nigeria from the brinks, an article published by Vanguard, available at: http://www.vanguardngr.

are no longer between the natives and the Hausa-Fulani immigrants alone: at present, members of the other ethnic groups such as the Igbo from the southeast of Nigeria, the Yoruba from the southwest, the Christians and the Muslims alike are equally involved.

In order to resolve the conflicts in Jos as the death toll of innocent Nigerians rose after the attacks on Christmas Eve of 2010 and subsequent attacks and reprisals, the efforts made by past and present governments of Nigeria have been to institute commissions of inquiry and the use of coercive measures. At least seven of these "High Commissions" at all levels of government have been established in the past 17 years. Unfortunately, it is most likely that the recommendations from these commissions were not fully implemented. This casts doubt on the ability of the Nigerian government to resolve ethno-religious conflicts that threaten the unity, peace, stability and the development of the country.

Religious Conflicts in Nigeria

Noting that ethnic cleavages generally remained unresolved, religious bigotry has emerged as the most potentially explosive catalyst for social and political division. Islam and Christianity spread rapidly in the twentieth century to the detriment of indigenous religions. Almost half of the Nigerian population was Muslim in 1990, most of whom live in the north of the country. About 40 percent are Christians, living primarily in the south, particularly in the southeast. The two main religions are sometimes portrayed as rival entities confronting each other in battles. Since 1980, there are several instances of religious violence, causing thousands of deaths, injuries and arrests, mainly due to religious tensions. The causes of these conflicts are sometimes strictly religious, sometimes political, sometimes a combination of both as shown with the formal implementation of Sharia law, the legal code which also provided a spark of violent conflict. To get an overall idea of this problem, we will examine two forms of religious conflicts in Nigeria, namely, intra-religious and inter-religious conflicts.

---

com/2011/01/jos-crisis-saving-nigeria-from-the-brinks/

FROM CULTURAL JUSTICE TO INTER-ETHNIC MEDIATION

INTRA-RELIGIOUS CONFLICTS

Among many intra-religious conflicts in Nigeria, a careful selection of the case studies below has been made for the purpose of this research. These cases include: the Maitatsine crisis, the disturbances of the Yan Izala Movement, the Muslim extremists, and the fight against Western education by the Boko Haram movement.

Maitatsine Crisis (1980)

The first and most dramatic eruption of religious disturbances induced by the Maitatsine movement or Yan Tatsine was a degraded situation and a crisis of eleven days in Kano from December 18, 1980. The incidence that started in a football field at Shahuchi was then extended to Yan Awaki, Fagge, Koki, Kofar Wamba, etc. Led by Alhajji Muhammadu Marwa (also known as Tatsine or Maitatsine), the followers of this Islamic heretical sect ranging from 3,000 people and opposed to secular authorities were prepared to use violence and demanded absolute obedience to Marwa. This crisis is the result of differing interpretations of Islamic injunctions and religious practices by Maitatsine against the provisions of the orthodox sect[103]. Kano riots were suppressed by the army and the air force after the police failed to restore order. More than 4,000 people died, including Marwa the leader of the movement. The security forces arrested nearly 1,000 people including about 224 foreigners.

More and more riots caused by the Maitatsine supporters exploded in Maiduguri at the end of October 1982 and extended to Kaduna where thirty-nine members of the sect were killed by the vigilante group. The official death toll was 188 civilians and 18 police officers (mostly in Maiduguri), and 635 arrested, but the Commission of Inquiry concluded that the deaths probably exceeded 500. The sect was banned in November 1982, and its members were subjected to surveillance and arrests. However, in February 1984 members of the Maitatsine sect struck again, this time in the North-eastern Nigeria

---

103 Hussaini Abdu, Ethnic and Religious Crises in Northern Nigeria; Issues in Informer Repression, Department Of Political Science And Defence Studies Nigerian Defence Academy Kaduna, disponible sur son siteweb à http://hussainiabdu.info/My_Articles

and specifically in Yola, the capital of the State of Gongola. The army was again forced to intervene, using artillery to quell the unrest, but between 1980 and 1985, the army was poorly equipped with riot control equipment. As a result, more than 700 people died, 30,000 were left homeless, and many houses were destroyed. In April 1985, riots inspired by the Maitatsine adherents in Gombe caused more than 100 deaths and led to 146 arrests of suspected members of the sect.

Another violent incident occurred in November 1988 over the disputed succession of a new Sultan of Sokoto. Ten people died and fifty people were arrested.

The Disturbances of the Yan Izala Movement (1980)

There were other disturbances caused by the Muslim movement known as Yan Izala which started in Zaria and Kaduna in the 1960s. This group, which caused unrest in the early 1980s, protested against innovations in Islam and particularly opposed to the Sufi brotherhood movement[104].

Muslim Extremists (1981)

The repeated unrest in Kano in July 1981, which destroyed several state government buildings, was attributed to Muslim extremists who were opposed to the proposed withdrawal of the Emir of Kano.

The Fight against Western Education by the Boko Haram Movement (2009)

In Nigeria, an armed Islamist movement called Boko Haram[105], which is active in the northeastern Nigeria, has emerged in recent

---

104 Sufism is a movement of organized brotherhoods, which is grouped around a spiritual leader or Sheikh. There are no Muslim countries which see themselves as officially Sufi. Sufism is characterized by the veneration of local saints, and the brotherhoods practice their own rituals. The Sufis are organized into "orders" or groups, called Tariqas. These groups are led by a leader called Sheikh who is considered as the most spiritual man with the most Taqwa among them. For more details on "Sufism", consult "Sufi Islam" under the title "Military" available at: http://www.globalsecurity.org/military/intro/islam-sufi.htm

105 A name that comes from the Hausa dialect and means "Western education is a sin" whose ideology is based on the Taliban movement of Afghanistan

years to reject modernity with the objective of establishing Sharia law in the states of Nigeria. Boko Haram was founded in 2002 in Maiduguri, the capital of Borno State, by Ustaz Mohammed Yusuf. The name Boko Haram is translated as «Western education is religiously prohibited.» The group also claims that only an Islamic state can be legitimate. This ideology has justified their attacks against the representatives and institutions of the Nigerian government. Yusuf, its leader, being hostile to democracy and the system of secular and western education swore that «this war which has not yet started will continue for a long time» if the political and educational system is not changed[106]. The violence began when the members of the sect attacked a police station in Maiduguri. Afterwards, the clashes spread to neighboring cities.

On July 26, 2009, a series of violence exploded following a simultaneous attack by the Islamists in four northern states of Nigeria, known as Bauchi, Borno, Yobe and Kano. These combats were between government troops and members of Boko Haram movement in Maiduguri and lasted five days. On July 30, 2009, security forces inflicted a serious defeat to the fundamentalists and had them driven from the capital. The fighting resulted in over 700 dead, including at least 300 Islamist militants. Mohamed Yusuf, captured in Maiduguri, was said to have been executed by the security forces. But the police said that Mohammed Yusuf, the leader of Boko Haram movement died of gunshot injuries he sustained while trying to escape.

In recent months, the group reportedly claimed responsibility for many violent attacks and bombings in the northern part of Nigeria and at the Capital, Abuja. These attacks include the May 2011 bombing of several states after the inauguration of the newly elected Nigerian President; the June 2011 Police Headquarters bombing in Abuja; the late August 2011 attack on the United Nations building in Abuja that resulted in the deaths of 24 people; the bomb and gun attacks in the northeastern Nigerian town of Damaturu, the capital of Yobe State on November 4, 2011. At least 65 people were killed in Damaturu

---
106 See Deadly Nigeria clashes spread, Last Modified: 27 Jul 2009 19:47 GMT à http://english.aljazeera.net/news/africa/2009/07/2009727134953755877.html

and Potiskum, according to media reports, after Islamist insurgents bombed churches, mosques and police stations and fought hours of gun battles with the police[107]. The attacks followed a triple suicide bomb attack on a military headquarters in Maiduguri. The Boko Haram group is also reported to have claimed responsibility for the recent 2011 Christmas bombings at St Theresa's Catholic Church in Madala, a satellite town located at about 40 km (25 miles) from the centre of the capital Abuja, the Mountain of Fire and Miracles Church in Jos, a church in northern Yobe state at the town of Gadaka and at the police stations in Damaturu. About 41 people were said to have died as a result of these bombings while more than 50 people were seriously injured.

In his effort to prevent further bombing attacks and to arrest the perpetrators, President Goodluck Jonathan declared state of emergency on December 31, 2011 in some parts of Yobe, Plateau, Borno and Niger states, while international borders near the affected areas were ordered closed. As a response to the President's state of emergency decision, however, the purported spokesman for the Islamist group, Abul Qaqa issued on Sunday, January 1, 2012 a three-day ultimatum to Christians living in the northern part of Nigeria, ordering them to leave the northern region. The group also gave a three-day ultimatum to the southerners living in the northern part of Nigeria to move away. Qaqa also criticized President Jonathan for visiting the church, where more than forty people died as a result of bomb explosion. According to him, "The President had never visited any of the theatres were Muslims were massacred"[108] during post-election riots that occurred in April 2011.

A fresh wave of violent attacks perpetrated by Boko Haram was launched on Friday, January 6, 2012 against the southern and Christian

---

[107] "Ban and Security Council strongly condemn terrorist attacks in Nigeria". The Secretary-General Ban Ki-moon and the Security Council's statement after the Damaturu attack in Nigeria on November 5 2011, available at: http://www.un.org/apps/news/story.asp?News ID=40319&Cr=terrorist&Cr1=

[108] Tunde Sulaiman, Boko Haram Issues Three-day Ultimatum to Christians, Ready to Attack Soldiers, Article published by This Day, January 02, 2012, available at: http://www.thisdaylive.com/articles/boko-haram-issues-three-day-ultimatum-to-christians-ready-to-attack-soldiers/106286/

communities in Mubi, Adamawa State, resulting in the death of about 17 people and leaving at least 15 other people seriously injured[109]. Mubi, the second largest city in Adamawa State, is about 175 km south of the Borno State capital, Maiduguri, which had been the base of Boko Haram and the epicenter of its attacks[110]. The attack was launched against the Igbo traders gathered in a town hall for a meeting aimed at discussing how to transport the body of an Igbo man, who was shot dead by gunmen the previous evening, back to his hometown for burial. Witnesses said that the attackers were chanting "God is great" as they opened fire on them and carried out their assault. "We started hearing many gunshots through the windows," affirmed Okey Raymond, who attended the meeting in Mubi. "Everyone scampered for safety, but the gunmen chanted: 'God is great, God is great' while shooting at us". According to BBC report, the presumed Boko Haram spokesman, Abul Qaqa told the local media, "We are extending our frontiers to other places to show that the declaration of a state of emergency by the Nigerian government will not deter us. We can really go to wherever we want to go"[111].

These bombings and gun attacks in Nigeria have attracted the attention of the international community and religious organizations. The Secretary-General of the United Nations, Ban Ki-moon and Security Council strongly condemn deadly bombings in Nigeria. According to a statement issued by his spokesperson, "The Secretary-General calls once again for an end to all acts of sectarian violence in the country and reiterates his firm conviction that no objective sought can justify this resort to violence"[112]. While urging "all States to actively cooperate with the Nigerian authorities…" the Security Council stresses that "terrorism in all its forms and manifestations

---

109 "Nigeria Christians hit by fresh Islamist attacks", an article published by BBC NEWS AFRICA on January 7, 2012, also available at http://www.bbc.co.uk/news/world-africa-16442960
110 In the article posted by SaferNigeria on January 6, 2012 with the title, "20 Igbo traders killed by suspected Boko Haram gunmen in Mubi, Adamawa State », and available at: http://saferafricagroup.com/2012/01/06/20-igbo-traders-killed-by-suspected-boko-haram-gunmen-in-mubi-adamawa-state/
111 See BBC, "Nigeria Christians hit by fresh Islamist attacks", op cit.
112 The United Nations, "Ban condemns deadly bombings in Nigeria", a statement issued by his spokesperson of Secretary-General, 25 December 2011, available at: http://www.un.org/apps/news/story.asp?NewsID=40838

is criminal and unjustifiable, regardless of its motivation, wherever, whenever and by whomsoever committed, and should not be associated with any religion, nationality, civilization or ethnic group."[113] In a similar statement, Pope Benedict XVI "appealed for an end to violence in Nigeria, condemning the Christmas church bombings that led to the deaths of at least 39 people". Talking to visitors gathered in St. Peter's Square, the Pope affirmed, "Once again I want to repeat: Violence is a path that leads only to pain, destruction and death; respect, reconciliation and love are the paths to peace."[114] Similarly, the Organization of Islamic Cooperation (OIC), in a statement issued on January 4, 2012 also condemned the Boko Haram violent attacks in Nigeria. This condemnation was made known by the Secretary General of the organization, Prof Ekmeleddin Ihsanoglu who "appealed to all Nigerians including the authorities to continue to strive to preserve the peace, unity and stability of their nation"[115].

Looking at the past and recent attacks launched by Boko Haram, it could be concluded that, though Christians and southerners are mostly affected, some Muslims and northerners have also fallen victim of these violent attacks. Therefore, the fight against Western Education by the Boko Haram Movement could be regarded not only as an intra-religious confrontation, but also as an inter-religious conflict.

INTER-RELIGIOUS CONFLICTS

Many of the inter-ethnic conflicts examined in the previous sections could as well be said to have religious factors in them. However, there were many other violent conflicts in Nigeria that were strictly caused by religious differences and intolerance. Some of these

---

113 Ibid.
114 Cindy Wooden, Pope condemns Christmas bombings in Nigeria, article published by Catholic News Service on December 28, 2011 at: http://www.catholicnews.com/data/stories/cns/1105037.htm
115 Organization of Islamic Cooperation (OIC), "OIC Secretary General Calls For Peace And National Unity In Nigeria", a statement issued on January 4, 2012 by the Secretary General of the organization, Prof Ekmeleddin Ihsanoglu, available at: http://www.oic-oci.org/topic_detail.asp?t_id=6234

◄ FROM CULTURAL JUSTICE TO INTER-ETHNIC MEDIATION

conflicts include: the Fagge crisis, the violent clashes in Kafanchan, the demonstrations of the Christian Association of Nigeria in the eleven northern states, the crusade of Evangelist Reinhard Bonnke and the massacres in Kano, the beheading of an Igbo trader named Gideon Akaluka by Muslims, and conflict associated with the fight against terrorism.

The Fagge Crisis (1982)

Inter-religious violence was uncommon in Nigeria until the October 1982 crisis occurred in Kano. This crisis was triggered by the decision of the Anglican Church at Fagge to build a larger Church on its premises[116]. The predominant Muslim population in this district was against the decision. They felt that the premises of the Church was too close to the Central Mosque of Fagge. They did everything to ensure that the state government does not approve the construction. Despite this effort, the Christians began to rebuild the church. The failure of the state government to take a categorical decision on the issue provoked a violent reaction. As a result, three churches were burned in Sabon-Gari and several other churches were vandalized.

The Violent Clashes in Kafanchan (1987)

In 1987, religious conflicts took new and inauspicious dimensions when the unprecedented violence between members of the two religions in Nigeria, Christians and Muslims, occurred in the secondary schools and universities. Clashes between Muslim students and Christian students in March 1987 in the School of Education in Kafanchan, Kaduna State, left at least twelve dead and several churches burned or damaged. After a few days, riots spread to Zaria, Katsina and Kano. The police arrested 360 people in the city of Kaduna and about 400 in the university city of Zaria. The army troops intervened again, and the commander warned that the army will shoot anyone causing arson or murder. Bayero University in Kano was closed down after about twenty students were injured in the confrontations between

---
116 See Ibrahim, Jibrin (1987): The Politics of Religion In Nigeria: The Parameters of 1987 Crisis In Kaduna State, cité par Hussaini Abdu, op cit.

Muslims and Christians. At Zaria, Muslim students burned the chapel of the College of Advanced Studies and attacked Christian students. The riots were extended to the city, where more than fifty churches were burned. A curfew was imposed in Kaduna State, and beyond. Religious processions and preaching were banned in the states of Bauchi, Bendel, Benue, Borno, and Plateau. All schools in Kaduna and five in Bauchi State were closed. Babangida[117] denounced these violent clashes orchestrated according to him "by the wicked to overthrow the Federal Military Government." He also published a decree of civil strife proposing the creation of a special judicial tribunal to identify, arrest and prosecute those responsible for the clashes. He also banned preaching by religious organizations in all institutions of higher education. In June and July 1987, authorities in Kaduna State had twice closed one girls' secondary school, called "Queen Amina College Zaria" following the clashes between Muslim and Christian students.

The Demonstrations of the Christian Association of Nigeria in the Eleven Northern States (1990)

Religious groups started to experience a relative calm until January 1990, when thousands of Christians in the northern states of Plateau, Kaduna, Bauchi, and Gongola protested against the ministerial reshuffle of Babangida, which seems to affect Christian officers. Protesters of the Christian Association of Nigeria in all the eleven northern states and the District of Abuja Capital walked in Kaduna to protest against the perceived religious imbalance and to present a petition signed by the high Catholic clergy and the Archbishop of Kaduna.

The Crusade of Evangelist Reinhard Bonnke and the Massacres in Kano (1991)

In 1991, there was a violent reaction from Muslim youths against the government's decision to give permission to a protestant and

---
117 General Ibrahim Badamasi Babangida , born on August 17, 1941, popularly known as IBB, was a Nigerian army officer and military ruler of Nigeria. He began to rule Nigeria after the success of his coup d'etat against Muhammadu Buhari on August 27, 1985 until he left office on August 27, 1993 after canceling the democratic elections held on June 12, 1993.

charismatic church in Kano to organize a crusade animated by a German evangelist Reinhard Bunnke and his colleagues. This Muslim protest was influenced by the government's refusal to allow a Muslim preacher from South Africa to come and preach in Nigeria.

The coming of the evangelist was massively diffused. Thousands of flyers and posters were distributed. Announcements were made in print and electronic media. This publicity attracted the attention of Muslims who thought that the crusade should not be allowed to take place in Kano. They accused the government of double standards, since it did not grant permission to a Muslim preacher from South Africa, Sheikh Ahmed Deedat, who had wanted to come to Kano[118]. "This is injustice to allow a German Christian evangelist"[119], affirmed by a Muslim preacher. For the Muslims, it was not just seen as a provocation, but an attempt to Christianize the Islamic city or present it as a Christian city. Muslims expressed their anger against some of the messages in the media advertisements, for instance, the evangelist will make the deaf hear; open the eyes of the blind, make the lame walk, Jesus for all by the year 2000, etc.

To present their problem and make known their anger, the various Muslim groups first sent emissaries to the government to withdraw the authorization granted to the Christians to hold a crusade in Kano. On October 13, 1991, the day of the crusade, Muslims organized a peaceful demonstration in the palace of the Emir and later had an urgent prayer. Suddenly the charged atmosphere erupted into a violent crisis. Young people began to destroy churches, looting shops and setting fire on cars, hotels, taverns, night clubs, etc. The Igbo as usual seem to be the main targets. Their shops were looted and their houses destroyed. In retaliation, the Christians and the Igbo groups attacked Muslims and destroyed their houses, mosques and killed some Muslims in Sabon Gari. This led to the exodus of many foreigners in Kano. The people fleeing were members of the Igbo

---

[118] For more information on Evangelist Reinhard Bunnke's crusade and the massacres in Kano, read Abdu Hussaini (2000), "Religion and the challenges of Democratisation And National Integration in Nigeria. Equal Justice, Kaduna, HRM; also read, Albert, Olawale Isaac (1999), op cit.

[119] Ibid.

ethnic group, the Yoruba and other minority groups from the South, many of whom had spent years in Kano. For a whole week, trucks, trailers and buses were loaded with non-natives fleeing the city every day, mostly children and sad women. It was unofficially reported that more than 500 people were killed in places like Sabon Gari, Mata Kofar, Kofar Nassarawa, Ibrahim Taiwo Road, Konar Jaba, Gama Brigade, Rimin Kebe, Tudun Murtala, etc.[120]

The Beheading of an Igbo Trader Named Gideon Akaluka by Muslims (1994)

In December 1994, the Shiite Muslim fundamentalist group brutally beheaded one Gideon Akaluka, an Igbo trader who was accused of defaming the Holy Quran. Akaluka was accused of using a paper (torn) from the Koran to clean up after using the toilet. This caused the angry reaction of the Shiite group who declared that his "blood is lawful," meaning that he must be killed[121].

The police intervened by arresting Mr. Akaluka to keep him in custody. But the Muslims, who were not satisfied with the progress made by the court on the case, challenged all security arrangements, and then went into the prison at Goran Dutse. They brought Akaluka out, and then brutally beheaded him. They took the head and walked around the city chanting "Allah Akbar!" (Allah is great). Although there were no retaliations on the part of the Igbo or Christians, the incidence had led to several arrests, severe tensions and a stampede. Shops were closed down and children kept in the house. Many fled away from the city for security in anticipation for crisis or attacks on non-indigenous and Christian communities.

The government of Kano State, in return, arrested the members of the Shiite group. The government of Colonel Abdullahi Wase was accused to have secretly and extra judicially killed many of them. The group said that about a hundred of their members were killed[122].

---
120 Hussaini Abdu, Ethnic and Religious Crises in Northern Nigeria, op cit
121 Ya'u, Y.Z. (1998): "Participation of Shi'at and Almajirai In Religious Conflicts In Northern Nigeria". In Okoye F. (ed), (ed) Ethnic and Religious Rights in Nigeria. Kaduna, Human Monitor, p.157.
122 Hussaini Abdu, Ethnic and Religious Crises in Northern Nigeria, op cit

◄ FROM CULTURAL JUSTICE TO INTER-ETHNIC MEDIATION

Conflict Associated with the Fight against Terrorism (2001)

In October 2001, there was another chaos in Kano. It was, however, caused by an international event when some terrorists attacked the twin towers of the World Trade Center in the United States of America. Shortly after the U.S. launched an offensive against the Taliban government in Afghanistan, Kano erupted with another series of ethno-religious conflicts. In this case, some Islamic fundamentalists who felt that the United States of America had no reason to bomb Afghanistan decided to put the city of Kano on fire. Like previous crises in the city, the natives of the ethnic groups from the south of Nigeria, the Igbo and Yoruba were the main victims of these ethno-religious conflicts in Kano.

All the events discussed above and the crises that occurred before, during and after the independence of Nigeria in 1960, and also since the advent of democracy in 1999, remain instances which strongly remind us that ethno-religious conflicts in Nigeria are still steaming and ready to explode. Instances of ethno-religious conflicts that have invaded the country as indicated above are also a reminder that the seeds of conflicts in the country are numerous. This shows that ethno-religious conflicts are consistently tending toward repudiating all efforts for national unity[123].

From the various examples of ethno-religious conflicts mentioned above, we see that there is no clear distinction between ethnic conflicts and religious conflicts in Nigeria. What this means is that a conflict that began as an ethnic conflict may end as a religious conflict and vice versa. This explains why ethno-religious conflicts in Nigeria are always destructive in their effects. It is therefore important to seriously pay attention to the factors that cause these conflicts.

---

[123] Read Jega, A.M (2002), Tackling Ethno-Religious Conflicts in Nigeria, The Nigeria Social Scientist 5 (2) Pp. 35-39.

CHAPTER 7

Causes of Ethno-Religious Conflicts in Nigeria and Preventive Measures Already Taken

IN THE PRECEDING chapter, we made an exposition of the different cases of ethno-religious conflicts as they occurred in Nigeria between different ethnicities / communities and religions. In each of the cases studied, we equally presented in brief the causes of those conflicts and the conflict management strategies used by the government or other agencies in order to respond to the challenges posed by these conflicts. Nevertheless, an adequate analysis or a summary of the causes of ethno-religious conflicts and the preventive measures already taken by the government will enhance our understanding of the subject. That is the aim of this chapter.

Causes of Ethno-Religious Conflicts in Nigeria Re-examined

In examining the causes of ethno-religious conflicts in Nigeria, it is important to identify two factors that are often seen by many people as being at the center of the subject. These are the "religious" and "ethnic" factors. Often, some people fight in the name of religion and ethnicity even when the causes of their dispute are political and personal in nature. Most importantly, some politicians use religion or ethnicity for political benefits and actions. The above points mean that ethnicity and religion cannot in themselves instigate conflict. But members of ethnic or religious groups can be manipulated to use violence in order to fight for their ethnic or religious rights and benefits. For a broader analysis of these causes, which we have passively mentioned in the previous chapters, it is necessary to consider the following points.

Nigeria was formed in 1914 by the amalgamation of the North and the South. Before independence, the British colonial administration encouraged a sense of community among different ethnic groups. It seized every available opportunity to spread the myth and propaganda that the people are divided from one another by a great distance, by the difference in history and tradition, and the ethnic, religious and political barriers. The different ethnic groups in the country became exclusive and inbred with a serious level of egoism, animosity and hostility against one another. 'That is to say, in Nigeria, ethnic group per se has been transformed into an ethnic group for itself'. The basis for the emergence of a common consciousness among ethnic groups has been inter-ethnic competition for resources.

Some of the major causes of ethno-religious conflicts in Nigeria include accusations and allegations of neglect, oppression, domination, exploitation, victimization, discrimination, marginalization, nepotism[124] and fanaticism. The distribution of economic resources was often biased in favor of some groups, pushing marginalized groups to use their ethnicity to mobilize for equality. These are the seeds of conflict. In all countries, including Nigeria, there are always difficulties to reach a consensus on how wealth, power and status must be shared among individuals and groups. This also applies to how changes and the necessary reforms could be made. Indeed, the various groups and individuals have different interests in such cases; some groups have had their objectives met, while others have not. What this means is that ethno-religious conflicts usually occur when disadvantaged groups and people are trying to increase their share

---

124 B. Salawu, Ethno-Religious Conflicts in Nigeria: Causal Analysis and Proposals for New Management Strategies, op cit.

of power and wealth or to modify dominant values, norms, beliefs or ideology[125]. In Nigeria therefore, and from the various examples of ethno-religious conflicts mentioned in the preceding chapter, one notices a state of confusion regarding the roles of politics, ethnicity and religion. This often overshadows the idea of separation of the State and religion that makes Nigeria a secular country, leading to the escalation of various ethno-religious conflicts that occur all over the country, and which require effective preventive and resolution measures.

Another important factor that has contributed to the outbreak of conflicts in Nigeria is the failure of the Nigerian leaders to establish good, transparent and uncorrupt governance, to "forge national integration and promote what might be called real economic progress through deliberate and articulated policies"[126]. This attitude of negligence is evidenced by the existence of high rate of unemployment and poverty in Nigeria. It is always difficult for a country with high rate of unemployed and poor citizens to experience peace. Individuals will develop a "survival of the fittest"- kind of mentality, and easily give in to be used by those insatiable and egoistic leaders who pursue their personal goals in the name of ethnicity. Unemployment and poverty could make people susceptible to engage or participate in crimes or violent conflicts when such will yield some monetary rewards. Such a trend is equally reminiscent of wars in other countries of Africa, as evidenced in the Sudanese conflicts, Liberia, Ivory Coast, etc. These shortcomings, "evident in the economic, social, and political spheres have affected employment opportunities, education, political participation and the provision of social services to the people"[127]. The absence of these 'basic needs' always gives the elite the capacity to mobilize groups for intense competition, employing ethnocentrism to achieve their goals.

The long military intervention in Nigerian politics, as noted by B. Salawu, tends to encourage and legitimize the use of force and

---
125 Ibid.
126 Ibid.
127 Nnoli, Okwudiba (1980) Ethnic Politics In Nigeria. Fourth Dimension Press. Enugu. p. 87

violence as instruments of social change and the realization of set objectives and demands. Anarchy, competition, and insecurity led to the disappearance of the First Republic. Military intervention resulted in horrible ethnic war from 1967 to 1970 (as we saw above) when the Igbo people (Biafrans) of the south-eastern Nigeria threatened to secede from the federation. The grievances of the Igbos were caused by the denial of the rights of equality, citizenship benefits (such as security and protection), and freedom. Wherever these basic needs are denied, conflicts can appear as the aggrieved groups often use violent means to fight for their human rights. From this military practice, the use of coercion and force to resolve conflicts has become a tradition in the political body of Nigeria. This is strongly linked to the supply of uncontrolled arms which accelerate the outbreak of conflicts, and "encourage the belligerents to continue fighting rather than to find a peaceful resolution of their disputes"[128].

Since independence, the situation in Nigeria has been charged with ethnic politics and the elites of different ethnic groups conspire to attract as many federal resources as possible for their regions, neglecting the questions that have united the country.

Differential and unequal treatment of ethnic groups has been responsible for the intense competition in the Nigerian society. It has created disparities in educational performances and deepened political and economic inequalities between the North and South of Nigeria. Political events and the coup d'état of January 15, 1966 and the backlash (another coup d'état) in July 1966 have intensified ethno-religious tensions in Nigeria. The massacres and reprisals that followed the coups d'état have ethnic and religious colorations as the predominantly Muslim ethnic group in the North were against the predominantly Christian ethnic groups of the South.

The influence of foreign factor on ethno-religious conflicts in Nigeria became evident in 1983 when the Minister of Foreign Affairs of Nigeria attempted to link the crisis of development in Nigeria to the global political economy. It was the opinion of the Federal Government

---

128 B. Salawu, Ethno-Religious Conflicts in Nigeria: Causal Analysis and Proposals for New Management Strategies, op cit.

of Nigeria that most of the ethno-religious crises benefited foreign groups. As a result, deportation measures were initiated against some foreigners without valid papers. The main reason for this deportation order was that the presence of foreigners at that time threatened the economic and political security of Nigeria[129]. One case particularly used as a justification for government action, was the riots of 1980 in Maitatsine, led by Marwa, a person of Cameroonian nationality. Also, in 1985, Major-General Tunde Idiagbon emphasized the link with foreigners in the ethno-religious conflicts in Nigeria. In this regard he alerted Nigerians on the imminent crisis and support coming from abroad, which some religious fundamentalists were receiving[130].

The link with foreigners in the ethno-religious crises in Nigeria is equally manifested in the involvement of non-Nigerians in a number of urban uprisings. These foreigners were seen participating actively in ethnic conflicts in the country especially in the North between the hosts, Hausa-Fulani Muslims and the southerners predominantly Christians who reside in their environment. A fight which began between an Igbo trader and a Fulani security guard in Sabon Gari market Kano developed across the city into an ethno-religious conflict where many foreigners - coming from neighboring African states - were arrested in support of the Muslim Hausa-Fulanis[131].

In addition to the foregoing, foreign preachers often contribute to the uprising of ethno-religious crises in Nigeria. In 1991, as we saw in the foregoing chapter, the religious crisis in Kano has been attributed to the decision of the evangelist Reinhard Bonnke (of German nationality) to animate a crusade tagged "Kano for Jesus". Just because the government had already denied access to a Muslim cleric from South Africa to come and preach in the city of Kano, a severe crisis occurred between the Muslims and Christians.

The problem of land resources as causes of ethnic conflicts in Nigeria has increased since the 1970s, and especially from the 1990s when oil companies in the Niger Delta and in other petroleum states

---
129 See Albert, (2005), op cit
130 Ilori, 1987:25
131 Kano State, 1995:1617.

identified activities of oil exploration. The claims fiercely expressed based on descent or genealogy arguments and the symbols of kinship were made in certain territories concerning what compensation and royalties are requested and paid. This factor has been an open invitation to conflicts not only between communities or ethnic groups, but also, among ethnic groups or communities and oil companies as well as the government. This kind of conflict has become an everyday reality in the zones of oil production of the south-south and southeast of Nigeria, with special impacts and consequences for the rest of the country.

The causes of ethno-religious conflicts discussed so far can be summarized within the theoretical framework developed by Ted Gurr Rober[132]. Gurr's model has three stages.

- First, he is of the opinion that discrimination against an ethnic or religious minority may induce the minority to form grievances.
- Second, these grievances contribute to the mobilization of the ethnic or religious minority for political action.
- Third, the more a minority is mobilized, the more it becomes susceptible to engage in political action including protest and rebellion.

Despite all government efforts to prevent and resolve these problems, ethno-religious conflicts still remain alive in Nigeria. However, before reflecting on ethno-religious mediation as one of the methods that could be useful in resolving and preventing ethno-religious conflicts in Nigeria, it will be very useful to summarize the preventive measures already taken and their limitations.

Preventive Measures Already Taken and their Limitations

The various manifestations of ethno-religious conflicts in Nigeria examined and discussed in the preceding sections of this chapter are

---

[132] In order to have a global idea about this theoretical model, read Gurr, Ted and B. Harff (1994) Ethnic Conflict In World Politics. (Sanfrancisco: west View press.). See also, Gurr, Ted (1970). Why Men Rebel (Princeton)

indications to the fact that ethno-religious conflicts pose enormous challenges to the Nigerian government and the Nigerian people in general. They are actively paralyzing the activities of the government with disastrous impact on the socio-economic life of the country. In order to bring these conflicts under control, the government has developed conflict management strategies. However, these conflict management mechanisms have not yet yielded concrete results. Our objective in this section is therefore to examine some of the major strategies often used by the governments in Nigeria to manage ethno-religious conflicts. These strategies include, but not limited to, federalism and secularism, the creation of new states and the system of resource allocation, national reconciliation, the establishment of the Institute for Peace and Conflict Resolution (IPCR), coercive measures and finally, the judicial method.

Federalism and its Secular Character

In order to manage its ethno-religious conflicts, Nigeria has constitutionally opted for federalism and secularism. A declaration of human rights is included in the 1999 Constitution, which seeks to allay the fears of the ethnic minorities in the South. The idea of federalism is enshrined in the constitution of 1999 of which the introduction says:

> "We the people of the Federal Republic of Nigeria, Having firmly and solemnly resolved, to live in unity and harmony as one indivisible and indissoluble sovereign nation under God, dedicated to the promotion of inter-African solidarity, world peace, international co-operation and understanding, And to provide for a Constitution for the purpose of promoting the good government and welfare of all persons in our country, on the principles of freedom, equality and justice, and for the purpose of consolidating the unity of our people, Do hereby make, enact and give to ourselves the following Constitution: (…)"[133].

---
133 Constitution of the Federal Republic of Nigeria (1999) : Introduction, available at : http://www.nigeria-law.org/ConstitutionOfTheFederalRepublicOfNigeria.htm

◄ FROM CULTURAL JUSTICE TO INTER-ETHNIC MEDIATION

According to this introduction, the constitution of Nigeria aims among other things, the promotion of good governance, unity and harmony, as well as the well-being of all the people living in the country according to the fundamental principles of human rights. Unfortunately, a rereading of the cases of ethno-religious conflicts examined in this book show a serious failure on the part of the federal government and the peoples of Nigeria to implement the terms of this constitution.

CREATION OF NEW STATES AND THE RESOURCE ALLOCATION SYSTEM

The past Nigerian dictators, under tremendous pressure from minority groups were obliged to think about a more equitable distribution of power and resources. From 1967 to 1999, thirty-six states have been created in Nigeria, cutting across ethnic and religious groups. This development was intended to allay the fears of minority groups to be dominated by the three major ethnic and language groups, the Hausa-Fulani, the Igbo and the Yoruba.

However, the rationale for these new states is not clear, with the exception of the oil producing states in the South. Some of these states have recently become instruments for the personal enrichment of the elites to the detriment of the fight against poverty and the creation of employment opportunities for the rest of the population.

There have been reports of disparities in the distribution of oil resources in Nigeria for many years. This controversial question has fueled most of the recent ethnic conflicts in the country. Although the Constitution provides for a new system of resource allocation, ethnic groups from the oil production zones see the new system as insufficient, arguing that they do not receive enough money for their own regional development. These are the dynamics that underline the Ogoni crisis and the recent ethnic violence in the oil producing states of the Niger Delta. Unless this problem is resolved, not only through the judicial measures, but most especially by ethno-religious mediation, Nigeria will not be able to experience peace, stability and development, and the people will not completely enjoy the peace, unity and security they deserve as citizens of Nigeria.

National Reconciliation

It is interesting to note that Nigeria is driven by its political strategies to manage conflict through national reconciliation, consensus building and economic development. This strategy was used after the civil war between Biafra and Nigeria, and during the Third Republic to calm the violent clashes between the Tiv and the Jukun. The two civilian governors of Benue and Taraba in the Third Republic reported this conflict to the presidency. The Jukun leaders and those of the Tiv were called to Lagos where they met with the Vice President to discuss and reflect together on the possibility of resolving their dispute. However, the effort was not successful and no resolution was reached.

This process of national reconciliation and transformation could only be strengthened by a vibrant economy in which citizens' basic needs are taken care of. It also needs a state and a civil society with a sense of shared destiny, where ethnic identities are integrated in a positive way as a unifying force rather than a divisive factor or an obstacle to nation building. The Nigerian people should learn from the South African civil societies that play an important role in creating the link between the formal bureaucratic activities and the interests of the people. This kind of attitude that promotes national unity and harmony should replace what has emerged in Nigeria over the period of transformation and transition under the umbrella of ethnic associations, like the Afenifere, the Ohaneze Ndi Igbo, the Arewa Consultative Forum, the Oodua Peoples Congress, the Movement for the Actualization of the Sovereign State of Biafra, the Arewa People's Congress, etc. Unlike a genuine civil society, some of these organizations act like political and ethnic militants fighting for their ethnic and independent rights. We must therefore strengthen the capacity of the government, NGOs, and civil organizations to develop a genuine national reconciliation program and the unity of the different ethnic groups.

FROM CULTURAL JUSTICE TO INTER-ETHNIC MEDIATION

CREATION OF THE INSTITUTE FOR PEACE AND CONFLICT RESOLUTION (IPCR)

The Institute for Peace and Conflict Resolution "IPCR" was founded in February 2000 by the President, Commander in Chief of the Armed Forces of the Federal Republic of Nigeria, Olusegun Obasanjo. The Institute derives from the Ministry of Foreign Affairs. It is primarily a research center, a "think-tank" and an organization that works toward the strengthening of the capacity of Nigeria for the promotion of peace, conflict prevention, management and resolution. It is charged with the mandate to regularly provide relevant information and advice to policy makers, and engage in collaboration with other people involved in peace negotiations and conflict resolution[134].

Since its creation was initiated by President Olusegun Obasanjo rather than the civil society, the credibility of the Institute for Peace and Conflict Resolution is questioned by the public. In fact, since its establishment in 2000, Nigeria has experienced many cases of violent ethno-religious conflicts as discussed in the previous chapters. Consequently, this casts doubt on the capability, capacity and intent of the members of this institute to prevent and resolve ethno-religious conflicts in Nigeria.

COERCIVE METHOD

As the name implies, the coercive method is the deployment of military troops or the police in areas of conflict with the aim of controlling crises through the use of coercion or force. In Nigeria, this method of managing ethno-religious conflicts has taken many forms depending on the magnitude of the crisis in question. In summarizing the form of coercive intervention of the Nigerian state during ethno-religious conflicts, Etannibi Alemika notes the following steps:

1. The grievances expressed by ethno-religious groups that can lead to violent conflicts are ignored by the government and the security forces.

---

[134] For detailed information about the The Institute for Peace and Conflict Resolution "IPCR", visit their website at: http://www.ipcr.gov.ng/index.html

2. If the grievances are expressed in the course of time with publicity mediums, persistence and an ardent determination, the state and security forces will threaten those responsible. In some cases, some people may be arrested, detained and accused of sabotage. In general, these responses enrage the injured community and the government can be accused of partisanship.
3. Grievances may be expressed violently - resulting in violent conflict. The state sends the security forces to quell the conflicts or riots. Most of the time, excessive force is used.
4. The security forces will arrest and detain some people for allegedly having instigated conflict. These responses aggravate and cause more conflicts.
5. The government sets up a special committee to investigate the conflict, or a special military tribunal is established to try suspects, who, if convicted, will face a range of penalties, including a long-term imprisonment and death sentences.
6. This committee established by the government will submit a report, which can be accepted, modified, or rejected. Government decisions may or may not be made public, and may or may not be implemented. Meanwhile, the conflict which is temporarily calmed is expected to be resolved by the government.
7. The grievances, however, persist until another circle of violent expressions and the government is also there to repeat the same process[135].

According to this analysis, once ethno-religious crises have exploded, for example, the police are the first to be sent to crisis locations. But in a very serious ethno-religious conflict, the government may be forced to use a joint military force of the army, the navy and the air force. Because of the military nature of such interventions, however, the coercive method is usually associated with many problems such

---

[135] Read Etannibi E.O. Alemika, 2000; A Sociological Analysis of Ethnic and Religious Conflicts in the Middle Belt of Nigeria. In Ethnic and Religious Rights. A quarterly publication of Human Rights Monitor, Special Edition, edited by Festus Okoye, April 2000, Kaduna Nigeria, p. 10.

as beatings, fightings and, in some cases, gunshots that may affect innocent citizens[136]. Consequently, this method of intervention in ethno-religious conflicts has not been successful as a mechanism for conflict resolution. While highlighting the problem associated with the deployment of security forces to conflict areas, Oromareghake and Akpator state that "... the problem with the deployment of security forces that are not supported by intensive efforts of mediation is that it unnecessarily prolongs the stay of these security forces deployed in different parts of Nigeria. This is because the mobile police units or the army often deployed to calm unrest in Nigeria are not trained to act as facilitators of conflict resolution"[137]. This passage means that the deployment of troops to locations of crisis is not, in most cases, the only appropriate method to deal with the phenomenon of ethno-religious conflicts. Because these forces are not adequately trained in conflict resolution, they sometimes cause more problems than they are supposed to resolve. In other words, they become part of the problem that they were asked to resolve.

An example of the failure of the coercive method could be the military intervention in the Niger Delta or Tiv- Jukun conflicts, as well as in the other violent conflicts in Jos and Northern part of Nigeria. The Tiv- Jukun conflict in Wukari, for example, was one of the most violent conflicts since the Nigerian civil war, but there was no significant international intervention and virtually nothing was done by the government outside the use of state power and force to stop the violence, without successfully addressing the underlying problems.

JUDICIAL METHOD

The creation of the judicial commission or the commission of inquiry or peace committee remains the last conflict resolution strategy

---

136 Omorogbe, S.K. and 'Omohan M.E. (2005): Causes and Management of Ethno-Religious Conflicts: The Nigeria Experience in A.M. Yakubu,et al (eds) Crisis and Conflict Managementin Nigeria Since 1980. Vol. 2. P. 557. Baraka Press and Publishers Ltd; Kaduna, Nigeria. P.556

137 Oromareghake P. and Akpator J.D. (200S): Managing Inter-ethnic Conflicts in the Niger-Delta: The Case of Warri in A.M. Yakubu et al (eds) Crisis and Conflict Management in Nigeria Since 1980 Vol. 2. Baraka Press and Publishers Ltd; Kaduna, Nigeria. p. 601.

used by the Nigerian government to intervene in ethno-religious crises. This method involves the selection of people of diverse backgrounds to study the problems, submit a report to the Government according to the terms of the mandate given to the committee and ensure that those responsible for violent conflicts are prosecuted, judged and sentenced. This commission often functions by appealing to the memorandum, the organization of public hearing, visits to the zones of crises and the constitution. The purpose of these visits is to make an authentic assessment of the real nature of the crisis[138].

However, the judicial method has not yet succeeded in resolving ethno-religious conflicts in Nigeria. There are many reasons to this assertion. On the one hand, many Nigerians do not trust the Nigerian judicial system because of past instances of failure to promote justice in an impartial, unbiased and timely manner. On the other hand, since most judges and attorneys are not trained in ethno-religious conflict resolution or mediation, they are not capable of addressing the root causes of these conflicts. "Even when courts are involved—while they may address the legal question, since they are not focused on conflict resolution or mitigation—they may miss the underlying catalyst. At times, court judgments can escalate disputes"[139]. Also, the government is often reluctant to implement the recommendations submitted by the commissions of inquiry.

In addition to the preceding reasons for the failure of these methods of resolution or management of ethno-religious conflicts in Nigeria, Omorogbe Omohan said ". . . the main reasons for the poor performance of the mechanisms of conflict management that are often used are the poor logistics, delays in the deployment of troops to crisis locations, lack of cooperation by the parties in conflicts, the non-implementation of the recommendations submitted to the government by the Commissions of Inquiry etc"[140]. The conflict in

138 Ibid., p. 557
139 Ernest E. Uwazie, Alternative Dispute Resolution in Africa: Preventing Conflict and Enhancing Stability (Washington, DC: The Africa Security Briefs series of the Africa Center for Strategic Studies), November 2011, NO. 16. Dr. Ernest E. Uwazie is a Professor of Criminal Justice at California State University–Sacramento and the Executive Director of the Center for African Peace and Conflict Resolution.
140 Omorogbe, S.K. and 'Omohan M.E. (2005), P.577

◄ FROM CULTURAL JUSTICE TO INTER-ETHNIC MEDIATION

Wukari is a typical example of this form of conflict resolution. To resolve the conflict between the Tiv and the Jukun, the Wukari Local Government Council established a peace committee in 1990, which consisted of some Jukun leaders and those of the Tiv. The members of this committee tried to calm the situation, but their efforts ended after a very serious resurgence of violence linked to the election of 1991.

The reasons given above indicate that these conflict resolution strategies, which have constantly been used at different times of ethno-religious crisis in Nigeria, have not yet yielded positive and sufficient results. It is very apparent that this process of response to ethno-religious conflicts by the State and the security forces is useful in suppressing conflicts rather than in managing and resolving them.

The case studies developed in this book show that Nigeria is not yet a united country. There is suspicion and destructive rivalry among ethnic groups. The Nigerian government has taken bold measures to reduce ethno-religious tensions based on the strategies that we have just examined. But the persistence of these conflicts always raises questions about the effectiveness of these mechanisms. Ake Claude said that "if these problems are not quickly resolved when there is still a possibility ... we will all lose. Notwithstanding the persistent illusions, Nigeria can be united only by negotiated consensus and not by force"[141]. We therefore affirm that ethno-religious conflicts are more likely to be resolved not only in a country where there is reasonable economic growth, but most importantly, where there is an establishment of effective and efficient democratic institutions and processes that promote cultural justice. We call this negotiated consensus and these democratic processes that promote ethnic justice, inter-ethnic mediation.

---

[141] For a detailed study, consult Ake, C. "Our Problems not in Others But Ourselves." Keynote Address to the Inaugural Dialogue of the Obafemi Awolowo Foundation, in The Guardian Newspapers, December 1992.

PART III
INTER-ETHNIC MEDIATION

CHAPTER 8

Transition towards Inter-Ethnic Mediation

THE QUALITY OF relationships between rival ethnic groups and the preservation of ethnic peace depend on the type and effectiveness of the available mechanisms of ethno-religious mediation and the political choices of the government. In addition, the use of inter-ethnic mediation tools to resolve ethno-religious conflicts has the potential of creating lasting peace. This was the case in South Africa, where the government established the foundations of a civil society, accountability and transparency in government through mediation.

Failure to find solutions to the ethnic problems of Africa will have political, social, economic, developmental and humanitarian consequences on a continent that is almost worn out by conflicts, poverty and diseases, including HIV/AIDS. For this reason, we propose inter-ethnic mediation. Inter-ethnic mediation conceived as a process, consists of a constructive resolution of conflicts linked to ethnic or cultural differences. It is a non partisan process of discovering and resolving the underlying causes of conflicts, and inaugurating new avenues that ensure a sustainable peaceful collaboration and cohabitation. In mediation, the mediator, neutral and impartial in his approach assists the conflicting parties to rationally come to a solution to their conflicts. Inter-ethnic mediation is an art of conceiving appropriate institutions to direct inevitable conflicts towards peaceful resolution. The importance of conflict resolution through mediation cannot be overemphasized. As we have seen in this book, it is when the leaders and the states fail to address important questions and the basic needs of the citizens that violent conflicts explode. There is no other place where the management of conflicts, the peaceful resolution of conflicts and the prevention of ethno-religious conflicts through inter-ethnic mediation are more important than in Africa.

This part is therefore a contribution to the ongoing research for new ways to resolve ethno-religious conflicts in Nigeria, since the coercive method and the judicial measure or retributive justice employed by the Nigerian government prove to be ineffective for the prevention and resolution of ethno-religious conflicts.

While still focusing on the Nigerian case, we reflect on the possibility of inter-ethnic mediation in this country and we affirm that it is time to move from coercive and judicial methods or from retributive justice to inter-ethnic mediation as an alternative method that is more democratic and a form of restorative justice.

We therefore affirm that ethno-religious conflicts which occur in a frequent, incessant and violent manner in our contemporary societies require a shift at the level of research for peaceful resolution, a shift in two stages: first, from retributive justice to restorative justice, and second, from coercive method to ethno-religious mediation.

In this regard, we propose two approaches for resolving ethno-religious conflicts in Nigeria: first, a shift from the judicial method of resolving ethno-religious conflicts or from retributive justice to restorative justice, and second, a shift from the coercive method of resolving ethno-religious conflicts to inter-ethnic mediation.

The First Shift: From Retributive Justice to Restorative Justice

The first shift in the strategies for resolving ethno-religious conflicts in Nigeria that we propose is a shift from retributive justice to restorative justice. Unlike the retributive justice (or punitive, repressive) which aims to restore order through the imposition of sufferings, punishments, sanctions, revenge, proportionate reprisals, just as we clearly explained in the first part of this book, restorative justice (restorative, transformative) is concerned with (a) the restoration, reconstruction or refurbishment of the victims and (b) the reintegration of offenders into the community. This approach often brings offenders and victims together, so that offenders can better understand the effect of their crime on victims.

Restorative justice focuses on the damage caused while trying to repair it and / or to restore the broken equilibrium among the parties: society, offender and victim. The objective will be the restoration and strengthening of the link between the various parties involved in order to restore peace in the community. Inter-ethnic mediation between the author(s) (of crime) and the victim(s) is one of the possible applications of restorative justice. One of the most interesting cases of restorative justice is that of South Africa and its Commission of Truth and Reconciliation[1], responsible for identifying all violations of Human Rights since 1960 under the apartheid regime without imposing sanctions in order to create room for national reconciliation. Prosecutions or amnesties have been recommended (when the motivations of the perpetrators of crimes or offenses were essentially political), and others were set free.

Instead of satisfying the abstract legal principles or to punish offenders as is the case in retributive justice, restorative justice is an approach to justice that focuses on the needs of victims, offenders and society in general. Victims play an active role in the process, while the offenders are encouraged to take responsibility for their actions, and "to repair the damage they have caused - by apologizing, restitution or doing community service"[2]. It is based on a theory

---
1 South Africa Truth and Reconciliation Commission
2 Rebecca Webber, A New Kind of Criminal Justice October 25, 2009, an article published on the website of Parade available at: http://www.parade.com/news/intelligence-report/archive/091025-a-new-kind-of-criminal-justice.html

of justice which considers crime and wrongdoings as an offense against an individual or a community rather than against the state[3]. By promoting dialogue between victims and offenders, restorative justice will show the highest level of satisfaction of the victims and meaningful accountability of offenders.

Thus, restorative justice is defined as follows: "A broad term encompassing a social movement to institutionalize peaceful approaches to damages caused, to violations of human rights and laws and to conflict resolution. This ranges from civic organizations for the restoration of peace such as the South Africa Truth and Reconciliation Commission, to innovations in the criminal and juvenile justice systems, schools, social services and communities. Rather than focusing on the law, professionals and the state, restorative resolutions engage those who are harmed (victims), the perpetrators (offenders) and their affected communities (communities) in the search for solutions that foster healing, reconciliation and the rebuilding of relationships. Restorative justice seeks to build partnerships for the restoration of mutual responsibility for constructive responses to wrongdoings in our communities. Restorative justice seeks a balanced approach to the needs of victims, offenders and community through processes that preserve the safety and dignity of all"[4].

Restorative justice is very different from the legal process or retributive or criminal justice because it seeks to "broaden the questions that are beyond those that are legally relevant, especially by emphasizing relationships"[5]. According to Liebmann, "a way to see restorative justice is to think that it is a balance between a number of different tensions: a balance between therapeutic and retributive models of justice; a balance between the rights of offenders and the needs of victims, a balance between the need to rehabilitate offenders and the duty to protect the public"[6]. While retributive or criminal

3   Marty Price, J.D. "Personalizing Crime," Dispute Resolution Magazine. Fall 2001
4   Suffolk University, College of Arts & Sciences, Center for Restorative Justice, What is Restorative Justice?
5   Braithwaite, J. Restorative Justice & Responsive Regulation 2002, Oxford University Press, p. 249
6   Liebmann, M. Restorative Justice: How it Works, 2007, London: Jessica Kingsley Publishers, p. 33

justice seeks answers to these three questions: which laws were broken? Who broke them? What sanction do the offenders or guilty deserve? Restorative justice asks a different set of questions: Who was injured? What are their needs? Who will take up the responsibility?[7]

Restorative justice can take place in a confidential room or outside, in a community or organization. In the community, concerned individuals meet all the parties to evaluate the experience and impact of the crime. Offenders listen to victims' experiences, preferably until they arrive to empathy. And then, they talk about their experience: how they committed the offense. A plan is established for the prevention of future events, and to ensure that the perpetrators address the damage caused to the injured parties. They all agree. The community members hold the offenders accountable for the implementation of this plan.

Restorative justice brings together several peaceful and democratic forms of conflict resolution, namely, family group conferencing[8], restorative conference[9], restorative justice community board[10], restorative circle[11], circle sentencing[12], and finally, mediation

---

7   Zehr, H. The Little Book of Restorative Justice, Intercourse, PA: Good Books, 2002.
8   This is a large circle of people linked to the main parties, such as family, friends and professionals. It is often the most appropriate system for juvenile cases, because of the important role of family in the life of a juvenile perpetrator.
9   Restorative conference was also known as restorative justice conference, the family conference and the conference of responsibility to the community. It originated as a response to juvenile delinquency. A restorative conference is a voluntary process, a structured meeting of offenders, victims and families of both parties and their friends, in which they discuss the consequences and restitution. Restorative conference is explicitly focused on the victims. The facilitator of the conference organizes the meeting. In some cases, a written statement or a substitute replaces a victim who is not present.
10 A restorative community board also known as Community Justice Committee in Canada is generally composed of a small group, established by intensive training, who conducts public or face to face meetings. Judges may oblige offenders to participate. Victims meet the board and the offenders, or submit a written statement that is shared with the offender and the board. The Board members discuss the nature and impact of the offense with the offender. The discussion continues until they agree to a schedule and specific actions that the offender will be taking. Subsequently, the offender will document the progress in the implementation of the agreement. After the deadline passes, the commission shall submit a compliance report to the court or the police, which ends the involvement of the board.
11 Restorative circle allows prisoners to meet their families and friends in a group process to facilitate the transition into society. The meetings are specifically on the need for reconciliation with the victims of their crimes.
12 Circle sentencing, sometimes called Peacemaking Circle, uses the structure or a traditional ritual circle to involve all interested parties. It usually involves a procedure that includes:

between the victims and the perpetrators of crime (Victim-Offender Mediation "VOM").

However, in order to fully understand the second shift in the strategy for resolving ethno-religious conflicts that we propose in this book, we will focus, in the following chapter, on the last form of restorative justice, in other words, on mediation between the victims and the perpetrators of ethno-religious conflicts in Nigeria.

The Second Shift: From Coercive Method to Inter-Ethnic Mediation

Since the method of military intervention in ethno-religious conflicts or the coercive method used by the Nigerian state has not been successful in resolving inter-ethnic and inter-religious conflicts in Nigeria due to lack of adequate training of the troops in conflict resolution and other related problems, we therefore propose another shift in the strategy for resolving ethno-religious conflicts: a shift from coercive method to inter-ethnic mediation.

The precarious relationships (i.e., imbalanced order) associated with acceptance or recognition on the one hand, and rejection or neglect on the other hand, as we have seen in the second part of this book, should be "readjusted" by acts of equalization or compensation. Mediation can begin this process or dialogue of recognition by creating room for a so-called "settling of scores". The most important thing is that the parties take each other seriously as individual subjects (and not as objects) and guarantee everyone personal dignity. Inter-ethnic mediation, therefore, consists in developing links of sociability and areas of understanding among peoples of different ethnicities and cultures that are in conflict. It is regarded as a technique of democratization in the field of the resolution of ethno-religious conflicts and as an educational resource for learning rules in social interactions. In the field of conflict resolution, it lays down democratic and civic processes which enable the citizens to live "better" together and in unity. Inter-ethnic mediation is free from all prejudice, meaning, it must be characterized with an open mind and a willingness to learn.

(1) the offender's request, (2) a healing circle for the victim, (3) a healing circle for the offender, (4) a sentencing circle, and (5) a monitoring circle to track progress.

TRANSITION TOWARDS INTER-ETHNIC MEDIATION

INTER-ETHNIC MEDIATION AND THE REDUCTION OF SOCIAL DISTANCE

As we have seen in the preceding chapters, ethno-religious conflicts in Nigeria have increased social distance and feeling of marginalization, discrimination and exclusion. There is a loss of the feeling of "living together". Worse still, the public sector or government authorities have failed to find remedies to these conflicts through the organization of programs that will bring all the ethnic groups together. In this democratic era, therefore, the civil society must take responsibility to develop new inter-ethnic mediation programs that will not only bring the different ethnic groups together, but also, will develop at the same time the consciousness of "living together" in order to give the disadvantaged groups a chance to express their opinions, to become visible and actively participate in the process of civic communication.

Mediators in multiethnic societies have a special and permanent task of promoting dialogue and communication among different ethnic groups. Thus, it is necessary that all inter-ethnic mediators master the methods and techniques of inter-ethnic communication, dialogue and mediation. The goal of inter-ethnic mediation is to develop the preconditions for mutual understanding and exchange of information through objects or artifacts and joint projects capable of fostering unity in diversity as a special value.

In the context of Nigeria, this means to work together to overcome prejudices, lack of understanding of others, ignorance of their values, needs and aspirations, and to do everything to provide the conditions for cooperation among different ethnic groups. A successful Inter-ethnic mediation will further promote the development of collective projects. Instead of neglecting the cultural differences of ethnic groups, these projects will recreate and restore mutual relationships and tolerance among them.

Therefore, inter-ethnic mediation aims at inter-ethnic relationships in a country, organizations or in a multi-ethnic society. It also fosters the mediation of values and ideas that these groups want to promote in the society through socio-cultural activities, diagnosis of problems and the organization of dialogue in order to resolve conflicts. In addition, inter-ethnic mediation enriches the processes of public communication through education or awareness initiatives.

The foregoing gains of inter-ethnic mediation could be achieved through the creation of public platforms, "steering or piloting" actions, leadership trainings, coordination of government and social actions in order to find concrete solutions and establish appropriate procedures in the process of decision making at all levels, creation of the conditions to revitalize the discussions that transcend ethnic affiliations or ethnic identity by enabling a discussion on the meaning of being human, being a citizen and being part of the world, animation of the public space with positive civic discussions, promotion and coordination of the actions of the international community in the processes of inter-ethnic mediation, in particular, in establishing standards for decision making and communication processes.

Thus, inter-ethnic mediators foster the inclusion and cooperation of members of different ethnic groups in the activities that are important to the general public, without ethnic, cultural, social, religious, sexual, educational and generational discriminations.

To ensure that inter-ethnic mediation achieve its full effect, mediators must choose a central and neutral space for communication, a public, common, and confidential space as a platform where the meeting of the different ethnic groups can take place. This is particularly important in the first stage of their work when there is still suspicion among ethnic groups and public institutions are ethnically divided. Thus, the observed problems are not only studied during work meetings where the view points of all the groups are analyzed, but they are also publicly exposed. Having become visible, public authorities can no longer continue to ignore and neglect them. In this way, ethno-religious conflicts, which cause apathy, fatalism, helplessness and even fear, are brought into the public eye and through a mediation process in the civil sector, proposals and solutions are given, which can then be imposed on public authorities and the community in general.

Thus, the instruments and methods of inter-ethnic mediation are often street theaters, carnivals, installation projects, mural paintings and sculptures in public spaces as well as the media, debates, series of interviews, projects and programs in the educational domain etc. On the other hand, they are preceded or followed by numerous workshops - namely the forms of action that provide opportunities for direct contact, exchange of information and also for discovering conflicting views on common issues. In the process of inter-ethnic mediation, there is no single or one form of diffusion of culture, such as exhibitions, plays, movie productions, but they must be combined and complemented by workshops, platforms, discussions, promotional events, participatory theater, radio programs and marketing techniques, such as campaigns, advertising, etc. These methods can also be used during the training sections for the admission and acceptance of differences (Diversity Awareness Training), by which a community is progressively oriented from the rejection of others to a certain degree of intercultural communication, mutual dialogue and cooperation with others. Some of the approaches to the training for the awareness of diversity include:

- Social integration: inter-ethnic mediation allows people to integrate differences.
- Adaptation: inter-ethnic mediation arouses empathy from the members of the different ethnic groups. It also helps in strengthening the capacity to understand the views and values of others.
- Acceptance: through inter-ethnic mediation, citizens develop a competence to accept differences in behavior and to acquire differentiated values. Citizens will be able to accept the way of thinking and world view of others.
- Minimum reduction of differences: inter-ethnic mediation can also help in minimizing cultural differences by focusing on the similarities and common factors that unite the different ethnic and religious groups in a country[13].

---
13 Source: M. Bennett: The developmental approach to training of intercultural sensitivity, International journal of intercultural relations, n. 10, 1986, pp. 179 - 196

◄ FROM CULTURAL JUSTICE TO INTER-ETHNIC MEDIATION

A typical example of inter-ethnic mediation could be a form of radio or television show specifically and carefully formulated. To achieve its real effect, this program will be reproduced in the different languages in Nigeria. And then, it initiates debates, roundtable discussions and new initiatives through which ethnic conflicts are examined more closely. Inter-ethnic mediators, who will facilitate this program, can choose topics that will touch all the citizens. Afterwards, there will be many reactions on the part of the audience and readers of written materials such as newspapers or magazines. Many institutions and civil organizations will therefore raise these issues in workshops, and these questions which have become very present in the country, will eventually lead to a positive response from the authorities.

CHAPTER 9

Forms of Inter-Ethnic Mediation

UNTIL NOW, WE have presented inter-ethnic mediation through the theoretical perspectives with instances of practical implementations. In order to have a complete idea of this method of resolving ethno-religious conflicts, we must translate these theoretical elements into practical forms. For this reason, we examine ten practical forms of inter-ethnic mediation that could be applied in Nigeria and even in Africa. These forms include:

- mediation channeled towards the largest ethnic groups in the society;
- mediation directed toward the re-establishment of dialogue and cultural exchange at a time when ethnic ties are broken;
- mediation directed toward the dissipation of ethno-religious prejudice;
- the therapeutic aspect of inter-ethnic mediation;
- workshops and inter-ethnic confrontation;
- mediation channeled towards the minority groups with specific identities;
- mediation organized for ethno-religious groups geographically marginalized or isolated;
- mediation aimed at strengthening the capacity of communities in conflict to "live together";
- mediation oriented towards sustainable peace;

- access to the community and civic enrichment of students through peace education.

Mediation Channeled Towards the Largest Ethnic Groups in the Society

The purpose of this form of inter-ethnic mediation is to promote the ideas of intercultural, inter-ethnic, interreligious and social tolerance by frequently making use of the media which are present in public life, such as local and regional radios and television networks, billboards and artistic interventions in public spaces. To achieve this mediation, mediators can create a "meeting point" where people are offered the opportunity to give their views concerning life in Nigeria and the collective memory of its inhabitants. In this perspective, the participants belonging to different ethnic groups communicate with one another in this new public platform in order to recreate a new form of inter-ethnic relationship throughout the country.

Mediation Directed Toward the Re-establishment of Dialogue and Cultural Exchange at a Time when Ethnic Ties are Broken

The objective is to coordinate the activities of the NGOs, intellectuals and artists who are also bound by a common interest directed towards the overcoming of prejudice, hatred, isolation and all other barriers established over the years of violent conflicts and ethno-religious wars. This mediation process which permits to stimulate links is often carried out through the projects of experts, for example, by working with writers and other social actors who will ring out the importance of peace in society. An example of such an initiative could be the publication of books, magazines, newspapers, etc., that will bring together the various authors, artists and intellectuals from the different ethnic groups in Nigeria. In this sense, book fairs, films and theater festivals, workshops, seminars, etc., are all equally important. These publications are intended to provide a positive analysis of the processes that have marked the previous years and represent the positive intention of inter-ethnic mediation.

Mediation Directed Toward the Dissipation of Ethno-Religious Prejudice

Inter-ethnic violent conflicts have placed Nigeria at the center of global attention. These conflicts are sometimes due to the problems of ideological interpretations of real events. Inter-ethnic mediators are required, through their training and projects, to question and re-examine the prejudices rooted in the ideological, ethnic, religious and cultural conflicts. In addition, it will also be useful to review the ideological values and the assumptions on which Islam and Christianity are founded as well as their transformation over the years.

The Therapeutic Aspect of Inter-Ethnic Mediation

Therapeutic forms of inter-ethnic mediation are often directed towards people who have health, psychological, and emotional problems. Sometimes these are the difficult traumas and perturbations caused by external factors like war, broken families, material and social crises, different forms of physical, psychological, and sexual abuses. In this case, the different methods of individual and group work is used that often make use of forms of artistic expressions (e.g., painting, music, writing, role play) in order to restore the victims' senses of trust, acceptance, relaxation, and also to diagnose the degree and nature of the problems and develop the capacity of the individual, through creative expressions. Unfortunately, war and the destruction caused by wars have made this particular form of mediation relevant in some African countries, especially for children and victims of war, as well as brutally raped women, people who suffer from Posttraumatic Stress Disorder, refugees and displaced persons. Inter-ethnic mediation destined for such persons has often stressed the intercultural characteristics as it is directed toward the acceptance of permanent cohabitation of different ethnic groups and their members, who participated in conflict or were victims of war. It is also used to facilitate the ingenuity of individuals in the environments where they live and who have been ethnically and socially changed. This type of mediation may also include a music-therapy program.

By using this form of mediation, the hidden problems of the community, the frustrations of the group or the individual and the injured subjects are revealed and made known. At the same time, there is also an attempt to find practical solutions to certain social problems, usually through role-plays (or simulations), through which a sense of self-esteem of some social actors or all the groups should be awakened, as well as criticism and objectivity in the observation, consideration and resolution of these problems.

Workshops and Inter-Ethnic Confrontation

Inter-ethnic Workshop or "Cultural Confrontation" is a long term project that will bring together cultural, ethnic, religious, political, legal and civic actors. The project objective is to introduce structural and practical changes in public and religious institutions. The workshop participants may include, but is not limited to, the various actors mentioned above, as well as other volunteers, professionals, students of different ages belonging to the different ethnic, sexual and religious groups. After several days of preparation in collaboration with theater professionals, such as actors, directors and project managers, intellectuals, peace advocates etc., this workshop will focus on the topics and role plays (or spectacles) related to the injustices and ethno-religious conflicts occurring mainly in Nigeria.

In this kind of social performance, the public is transformed into active participants in the event, by selecting and featuring the traumatic events that they find most painful in the ethno-religious conflicts in the contemporary Nigerian society. The audience learns the methods and techniques of the resolution of interethnic, interreligious and interpersonal conflicts. Therefore, trauma is confronted, discussed and often transformed into an experience of healing. The public debate on collective problems also includes interdisciplinary collaboration within the groups of participants and the audience of the role plays or spectacles. Everyone is invited and welcomed to join the workshops, regardless of gender, class, ethnicity or religion.

Mediation Channeled Towards the Minority Groups with Specific Identities

Inter-ethnic mediation channeled towards the minority groups with specific identities aims to educate the public authorities and the public as a whole, that there are minority groups that are not known and that are (actively or passively) denied the rights to any form of support system and affirmation and, therefore, are deprived of cultural rights as well as the fundamental human rights. The groups in question are the members of some communities and ethnic groups that are extremely small in number, or to which a positive strong social marginalization is directed.

Mediation Organized for Ethno-Religious Groups Geographically Marginalized or Isolated

Inter-ethnic mediation organized for ethno-religious groups geographically marginalized or isolated aims to include socially endangered groups of citizens in the social and cultural life of the entire community. This is usually done by art projects in the community, or through socio-cultural program activities. It is mostly regarded as "Arts for Social change".

Inter-ethnic mediators will go to the suburbs, to the refugee camps, disadvantaged neighborhoods, and urban spaces to interact directly with the people, while creating projects that will restore dignity to the environment and to the people who live there. In addition to the willingness and initiative of the mediators, such projects require excellent communication skills. This is why mediation requires a long-term engagement, leading to a real social and urban reconstruction in the region with the aim of uniting the entire people with the local communities.

Through plays often organized, art and music workshops, residents are encouraged to actively participate in training for future actions, or to reach their own decisions about what should be done, and the method of intervention to be used. They will decide whether a neglected space should be transformed into something better, like a park, a playground for children or a meeting point where some projects could be created.

Mediation Aimed at Strengthening the Capacity of Communities in Conflict to "Live Together"

Land disputes in general cause a serious threat to national security. The resilience of these disputes calls for a formulation of ways of strengthening global security. However, government interventions are temporary, instead of providing durable solutions. Indeed, in many cases, these strategies have only deepened and intensified conflict. An effective response to an inter-communal conflict, such as the Aguleri- Umuleri conflict, thus requires an integrated and holistic strategy of transformation by a third party. This third person or group will have the function of strengthening the capacity of the people of the community towards reconciliation and "living together". This could be achieved by bringing together all parties in conflict to a problem-solving workshop that will create the psychological space needed to talk about their needs and fears. In this way, they will be able to take their destiny in hand, working together for the resolution of their conflict and for sustainable peace.

Mediation Oriented Towards Sustainable Peace

Ethno-religious mediation oriented towards sustainable peace aims to achieve six main objectives:
- the expansion of public support for the peace process and the strengthening of national capacities on the plans for the future of the country and the positive relationships among competing groups;
- the identification of root causes of conflicts and violence in order to enable people from local communities to address them;
- the improvement of the prospects for the success of peace agreement by increasing the inclusion of the principal groups in conflict in the negotiation process;

FORMS OF INTER-ETHNIC MEDIATION

- the creation and development of solid methods for the inclusion of civil society organizations and democratic mechanisms in the public dialogue;
- the increase of government accountability for its actions and the expansion of citizen participation in the process of government decision;
- the establishment of the mechanisms that will enable local groups to recognize and respond quickly and effectively to ethno-religious conflicts.

An example of ethno-religious mediation oriented towards sustainable peace could be the type that settled the Ife - Modakeke crises in Osun State of Nigeria. As we explained in this book, the conflict between the Ife and the Modakeke lasted over 150 years. Past attempts by the police, the state committees, and even the presidential commissions to resolve this conflict have had little or no success. In February 2000, the Office of Transition Initiatives (OTI) of the United States Agency for International Development (USAID) made a significant commitment to help these two communities to manage their conflicts without the use of violence. In a nutshell, the program began with a grant to the Modakeke Progressive Union, a community association, which since 1948 has carried out development and community mobilization projects. The objective of this grant was to: create an awareness of the resolutions and management of community conflicts, identify the root causes and consequences of intercommunity conflicts, form a body or group of conflict mediators, acquire the skills of conflict resolution and transmit them to the vital stakeholders in the conflict, and to strengthen peace and development in Osun State.

The first activity of the OTI was a five-day visit aimed at introducing the training program of key actors in the Modakeke Community, including public leaders and market leaders, leaders of road transport workers, youth leaders, and village heads. Following this visit, a three day training program on the techniques and the alternative methods of resolving ethno-religious conflicts took place. Two hundred participants attended, including representatives of youth groups, professionals, artisans, villages and community leaders. A parallel effort was accomplished through a grant to the Ife Development Board, a community association of Ife, which had the same objectives and activities as those of the Modakeke Progressive Union.

Through these two grant activities, the joint workshops between the Ife and the Modakeke on "forgiveness, reconciliation, and transformative leadership" took place. These workshops involved 15 representatives of the four major groups of both communities. The workshops highlighted the alternative methods of conflict resolution, and most importantly, provided opportunities for each group of 30 participants from Ife and Modakeke to identify the key issues embedded in the conflicts between them and to offer joint solutions. Also, during the workshops, a proposal was made and accepted to form an "Inter-Community Peace Advocacy Committee" that would put into practice the resolutions and the benefits of these workshops. Since then, fighting between the two communities has stopped and the former adversaries are now working together as members of the Inter-Community Peace Advocacy Committee[14].

Access to the Community and Civic Enrichment of Students through Peace Education

Peace education is a constructive and non-controversial way to enter into the community, to gain cooperation and to help students, teachers, school principals, directors or headmasters, and the parents of the students to begin reflecting on the possibility of peace in their communities. Inter-ethnic mediators should therefore create and establish a program that could bridge the gap and engage the new generation of Nigeria in inter-ethnic dialogue and in the resolution of conflicts. This program could be organized for Muslim and Christian

---

14 For more information on the results of this mediation program conducted by the Office of Transition Initiatives "OTI", refer to the article titled: "OTI Special Focus Areas: Conflict Management and Peace Initiatives", available at: http://pdf.usaid.gov/pdf_docs/PDACH993.pdf

students, teachers, school principals, directors or headmasters, parents, and leaders of the different ethnic groups. The program's objective consists in transferring knowledge and developing strategies with the participants on ways to strengthen inter-ethnic and interreligious cooperation and the forms of conflict resolution. Based on the examples of the civil society and diversity experiences in other multi-ethnic and democratic countries and through the understanding of the broader regional context in which contemporary conflicts exist in Nigeria, participants will gain new perspectives to support future efforts for the construction of closer cooperation and understanding among different cultures, religions, ethnic and political groups.

The program should focus on a teaching module that will place emphasis on the ethnic, religious, and historical dimensions of the conflicts and the ethics of similarity and difference that underlie the relationships between ethno-religious groups in Nigeria. Workshops on the following topics would be very useful.

Workshop on Attachment

Attachment describes the dynamics of long-term relationships between humans. It could also mean a long-term connection to places, families, people, groups, ideas, values, ethnicities, religions, cultures, schools, books, games, objects, etc. From a cultural and religious perspective, individuals, especially children and young people become, consciously or unconsciously, attached to the people, belief system and ways of life of their respective ethnic and religious groups. These attachment figures or symbols are seen as a "secure base" from where individuals mirror or interpret their actions and interactions with others, leading to internal working models which will guide perceptions, emotions, thoughts, and expectations in later relationships[15]. The bond or tie resulting from attachment to one's ethnicity or religion is said to be based on the individual's need for development, survival, security and protection.

---

15 Bretherton I, Munholland KA (1999). "Internal Working Models in Attachment Relationships: A Construct Revisited". In Cassidy J, Shaver PR. Handbook of Attachment: Theory, Research and Clinical Applications. New York: Guilford Press. pp. 89–114.

FROM CULTURAL JUSTICE TO INTER-ETHNIC MEDIATION

A workshop on attachment, therefore, is primarily aimed at exploring the various reasons why people are attached to their respective ethnic and religious groups. Apart from discussing one's attachment to ethnicity and religion, the workshop's primary objective is to inspire a discussion on a different level of attachment – which is an attachment to Nigeria as a country. Such a discussion could help in the participants' development of mutual bond or tie with Nigeria as their country, thereby strengthening mutual responsibility and love, patriotism and the real meaning of citizenship.

From a methodological perspective, participants will be asked to present the reasons why they are attached to their respective ethnic and religious groups. While one participant is presenting, others will be listening in order to appreciate, accept, and understand what appears to be important in that person's life. At the end of the presentations, participants will be asked to summarize and reflect on those points that are common to all. With those common elements, a reflection on attachment to Nigeria (the participants' country) will be initiated. This time, the participants will be asked to discuss why they are attached or not attached to Nigeria. In a parallel scenario, an exposition of the level of attachments shown by the citizens of other countries (for example, the Americans, French, Canadians, Germans, South Africans, etc.) to their respective countries will be made. By making such an exposition, the participants will be introduced to the notion of civic rights and responsibilities.

This workshop will give the participants the opportunity to express themselves, understand what is important for others and discover why others behave in certain ways. In brief, it will not only be an avenue to develop and nurture attachment to Nigeria, but a workshop on attachment will be a good opportunity for the citizens of Nigeria to discuss their proximity to one another and to their country, as well as their fears, anxiety, disappointments, frustrations, anger, loneliness, abandonment and dissatisfaction. Also, the Nigerian leaders are required, by virtue of their electoral mandate, to strengthen their commitment and attachment to Nigeria and to the Nigerian people.

In accordance with the principles of democracy, the Nigerian people should be their priority in the execution of their mandate as noted by the Constitution of the Federal Republic of Nigeria in chapter II, article 14 (1) and (2):

> "(1) The Federal Republic of Nigeria shall be a State based on the principles of democracy and social justice.
> (2) It is hereby, accordingly, declared that: (a) sovereignty belongs to the people of Nigeria from whom government through this Constitution derives all its powers and authority; (b) the security and welfare of the people shall be the primary purpose of government: and (c) the participation by the people in their government shall be ensured in accordance with the provisions of this Constitution".

The role of the mediator in this workshop is, therefore, to help the participants develop and strengthen an "organism of attachments":
- attachment to one's ethnicity and religion;
- mutual bond or tie with one another as citizens of Nigeria;
- attachment to Nigeria (as an independent country and the participants' country of origin);
- attachment to Nigeria's Founding Fathers, documents, Constitution and values.

CREATIVE PATRIOTISM WORKSHOP

Peace education program workshop in Nigeria will not be complete without a creative program on patriotism. The idea of patriotism should not be restricted to the military alone, just because they see it as a moral obligation that motivates them to fight in order to defend their country, rather than yield to enemy attacks. All Nigerians are required, by virtue of their citizenship, shared values and history, to showcase love and pride for Nigeria through patriotic attitudes, actions, and creativity.

◄ FROM CULTURAL JUSTICE TO INTER-ETHNIC MEDIATION

In his definition of patriotism, Stephen Nathanson[16] identifies four important elements. Patriotism involves:
- Special affection for one's own country
- A sense of personal identification with the country
- Special concern for the well-being of the country
- Willingness to sacrifice to promote the country's good

Patriotism can therefore be defined as love of one's country, identification with it, and special concern for its well-being and that of compatriots[17]. It is a shared sense of belonging to the same country or fatherland (πατρίς – patris), feeling that reinforces its unity on the basis of shared common values. It helps to spark-up love and pride for one's country. The patriots are willing to devote themselves or fight to defend the interests of their country.

But how can a citizen become a good patriot if that person does not know his or her country's history, founding fathers, constitution and national symbols? In Nigeria, one finds three categories of citizens. First, those who, either through their education or personal readings, have acquired excellent knowledge of Nigerian history, founding fathers, constitution and national symbols; second, there are some Nigerians who have only little knowledge of the country's history, either because of the kind of schools they attended or because they do not show interest in acquiring more knowledge about their country; third, there are some people who have no knowledge of Nigerian history, founding fathers, constitution and national symbols, either because they are uneducated or they simply chose not to learn.

Since civic education is generally introduced in schools where children are taught how to become good citizens, the question that arises is: what should be done so that those children or adults, who had no opportunity to go to school, can, at least, learn essential things

---

16 For detailed reading on Patriotism, see Nathanson, Stephen (1989), "In Defense of 'Moderate Patriotism'," Ethics, 99: 535–552. Reprinted in Primoratz (ed.) (2002). Also read Nathanson, Stephen (1993), Patriotism, Morality, and Peace, Lanham: Rowman & Littlefield.

17 See Primoratz, Igor, "Patriotism", The Stanford Encyclopedia of Philosophy (Summer 2009 Edition), Edward N. Zalta (ed.), URL = <http://plato.stanford.edu/archives/sum2009/entries/patriotism/>.

about Nigeria? Or what kind of help should be given to those children who, because of their geographical location and poverty, go to schools in the rural areas where teachers are not even equipped with adequate tools to teach Nigerian history, founding fathers, constitution and national symbols. As it is often said that knowledge is power, an individual can only be proud of somebody he or she knows. In the same way, a Nigerian citizen can be patriotic and proud of Nigeria, if and only if that person really knows Nigeria, its history and heritage. Shared knowledge of this type can foster unity, peace and harmony. But in its absence, ethnic and religious conflicts may take over.

The Creative Patriotism Workshop is organized to address this kind of situation. Its ultimate goal is to help participants become knowledgeable of the Nigerian history, founding fathers, constitution and national symbols. This workshop is not only organized to discuss these elements that make Nigeria unique, distinguish it from other countries, and inspire a sense of unity among its citizens, it also offers the participants an opportunity to be engaged in a creative and innovative discussion on shared values and heritage. Many Nigerians think they are patriots, but how many are indeed creative patriots? It is the goal of the Creative Patriotism Workshop to inspire, nurture and strengthen the desire to become creative patriots; who will, in the end, initiate, develop and carry out original and innovative patriotic projects.

In order to achieve the goal of this workshop, participants will be divided in smaller groups comprising people of different ethnicities and religions. They will be given many exercises to do. The first task will be to study, discuss, and present aspects of the life, work, and vision of one of the Nigerian founding fathers. In other words, each group will be asked to present the contributions made by a founding father of their choice to national unity, peace and development. The founding fathers to be presented and discussed include, but not limited to:
- (Sir) Herbert Macauley (1864-1946)
- Dr. Alvan Ikoku (1900-1971)
- Dr. Nnamdi Azikiwe (1904-1996)

◄ FROM CULTURAL JUSTICE TO INTER-ETHNIC MEDIATION

- Chief Obafemi Awolowo (1909-1987)
- Alhaji (Sir) Ahmadu Bello (1909-1966)
- Alhaji (Sir) Abubakar Tafawa Balewa (1912-1966)
- Chief Dennis Osadebay (1911-1994)

In the end, an assessment of the present situation of Nigeria will be made in order to see if the vision of the founding fathers is upheld. If not, in what ways have the present leaders driven away from the path of freedom, peace and unity? How can we inspire our fellow Nigerians through the lives and works of these founding fathers?

The second task consists of a group discussion on and a presentation of one of the Nigerian national symbols. The symbols to be discussed are:
- National Flag of Nigeria
- Emblem: Coat of Arms
- National Flower
- National Anthem
- National Pledge
- National Motto

NATIONAL FLAG OF NIGERIA

The Nigerian National Flag is made up of a white vertical stripe sandwiched between two green stripes of equal dimensions. White stripe denotes peace and unity and is also symbolic of the Niger River bisecting the countryside. The green stripes represent agriculture. The flag was designed in the twilight of colonial rule in 1960 by Mr. Michael Taiwo Akinkunmi, then a student in London. His design was adjudged the best out of 2,000 entries for the National Flag Design Competition. It earned him a cash prize of 100 pounds, paid to him through the then Nigeria High Commissioner to the United Kingdom, M.A. Martins[18].

---

18 The Guardian, 1996 and 1999, quoted in The Nigerian National Flag, Nigeria's 50th Independence: Celebrating Greatness website, ibid.

FORMS OF INTER-ETHNIC MEDIATION

EMBLEM: COAT OF ARMS

The Nigerian coat-of-arms feature an eagle mounted on a black shield, which is tri-sected, by two wavy silver bands. Two white chargers support the shield, and at its base is a wreath (coctus spectabilis flowers), cast in the national colors of white and green. The black shield represents the fertile soil while the silvery bands denote the Niger and Benue rivers which form the main inland waterways in the country. The coctus spectabilis is a colorful flower which grows wild in Nigeria. The eagle stands for strength and the chargers symbolize dignity. The national motto originally, "Peace, Unity, Freedom" was changed to "Unity and Faith, Peace and Progress" in 1978.

NATIONAL FLOWER

The Nigerian national flower is the Coctus Spectabilis. It is a very common sight in the Guinea Savanna, which is the most extensive vegetation belt in Nigeria, occupying nearly half of the country's land area.

NATIONAL ANTHEM

Before Nigeria's independence, the British National anthem was used at festivals and official ceremonies, and not surprisingly, it prayed for the British Monarch. The National Anthem of Nigeria adopted at independence in 1960, titled "Nigeria, we hail thee" was written by a Briton, Miss Williams. This was then again changed in 1978 by a new anthem. The National Publicity Committee organized a competition for a new national anthem. The final lyrics (listed below) were formed from the entries of the best five candidates: John A Ilechukwu, Eme Etim Akpan, B A Ogunnaike, Sota Omoigui and P. O. Aderibigbe. The music was composed by Nigerian Police Band, headed by Ben Odiase[19].

The Lyrics are as follows:

Arise, O compatriots,
Nigeria's call obey
To serve our fatherland

---

19   Information available at: http://www.motherlandnigeria.com/patriotic.html

With love and strength and faith
The labor of our heroes past
Shall never be in vain
To serve with heart and might
One nation bound in freedom,
Peace and unity.

Oh God of creation,
Direct our noble cause
Guide our leaders right
Help our youths the truth to know
In love and honesty to grow
And living just and true
Great lofty heights attain
To build a nation where peace
And justice shall reign.

NATIONAL PLEDGE

I pledge to Nigeria, my country
To be faithful, loyal and honest,
To serve Nigeria with all my strength,
To defend her unity and uphold
Her honor and glory.
So help me God.

NATIONAL MOTTO

The National Motto of Nigeria is: "Unity and Faith, Peace and Progress".

Apart from encouraging a discussion on the Nigerian history, founding fathers and national symbols, the Creative Patriotism Workshop will also foster better awareness of and promote other creative patriotic initiatives such as:

- Patriotic articles and essays with informative and inspiring words about Nigerian heroes, patriots, troops, etc;

- Patriotic music or songs performed by talented fellow Nigerian patriots, stirring the listener's pride and love of Nigeria;
- Patriotic poems with heartfelt and inspiring words, expressing love, and pride of Nigeria;
- Patriotic videos which include presentations dedicated to the Nigerian military, founding fathers, heroes, memorable events, etc.
- Other forms of arts creativity that foster love, unity, peace and progress in Nigeria will be encouraged through this workshop.

The Voice of the Soul Workshop

One of the major factors that often fuel ethno-religious conflicts in Nigeria may be attributed to the deadly phenomenon of mass-mindedness, blind belief and obedience. In Nigeria, some people have the pre-conceived idea that members of some ethnic or religious groups are enemies. They think that nothing good will ever come out from them. These are the results of long accumulated grievances and prejudices. As we have seen in this book, such grievances always manifest in the form of distrust, stout intolerance and hatred between some southerners and some people from the north. Also, there are Christians who, for no reason, do not want to associate with Muslims. On the other hand, there are Muslims who would not like to live, seat down or even shake hands with Christians. If those people are asked to explain why they behave that way, they may not have concrete reasons or explanation. They will simply tell you: "that is what we were taught"; "the media talks about it every day"; "they are different from us"; "we do not have the same belief system"; "they speak a different language and have a different culture". Each time I listen to those comments, I feel completely disappointed. In them, one sees how the individual is subjected and doomed to the destructive influence of the society in which he or she lives. Instead of subscribing to such beliefs, each person should look inwardly and ask: if my immediate society tells me that the other person is evil, inferior, or an enemy, what do I who am a rational being think? If people say negative things against others, on what grounds should I base my own judgments? Am I carried away by what people say, or do I accept and respect others as human beings like me, irrespective of their religion or ethnicity?

In his book titled, The Undiscovered Self: The Dilemma of the Individual in Modern Society, Carl Jung[20] asserts that "much of the individual life of people in society has been subjugated by the cultural trend towards mass-mindedness and collectivism". Jung defines mass-mindedness as "the reduction of individuals to anonymous, like-thinking units of humanity, to be manipulated by propaganda and advertising into fulfilling whatever function is required of them by those in power". The spirit of mass-mindedness can devalue and minimize the individual, 'making him or her feel worthless even as humanity as a whole makes progress.' A mass-man lacks self-reflection, is infantile in his behavior, "unreasonable, irresponsible, emotional, erratic and unreliable". In the mass, the individual loses his or her value and becomes the victim of "-isms." Showing no sense of responsibility for his actions, a mass-man finds it easy to commit appalling crimes without thinking, and grows increasingly dependent on society. This kind of attitude could lead to disastrous consequences like "psychic abnormality" and conflicts.

Why is mass-mindedness a catalyst for ethno-religious conflicts in Nigeria? This is because the society in which we live, the media, and the ethnic and religious groups present us with only one point-of-view, one way of thinking, and do not encourage serious questioning and open discussion. Other ways of thinking—or interpretation—are ignored or denigrated. Reason and evidence tend to be dismissed and blind belief and obedience encouraged. Thus, the art of questioning, which is central to the development of the critical faculty, is stunted. Other opinions, belief systems or ways of life that are contrary to

20 Carl Gustav Jung, a Swiss psychiatrist and the founder of analytical psychology, considered individuation, a psychological process of integrating the opposites including the conscious with the unconscious while still maintaining their relative autonomy, necessary for a person to become whole. For a detailed reading on the theory of Mass-mindedness, see Jung, Carl (2006). The Undiscovered Self: The Problem of the Individual in Modern Society. New American Library. pp. 15–16 ; also read Jung, C. G. (1989a). Memories, Dreams, Reflections (Rev. ed., C. Winston & R. Winston, Trans.) (A. Jaffe, Ed.). New York: Random House, Inc.

what a group believes are aggressively and stoutly rejected. This kind of mentality is evident in Nigeria and has caused misunderstandings between different ethnic and religious groups. The attitude of massmindedness needs to be replaced with the disposition of the mind to question, revise and understand why some beliefs need to be held or abandoned. Individuals need to be actively involved and not passively following and keeping rules. They need to contribute or give for the general good, and not just consuming and expecting to be given more.

In order to change this kind of mentality, there is need to enlighten every mind. As Socrates will say, "the unexamined life is not worth living for a human being", individuals need to re-examine themselves, listen to their inner voice, and be courageous enough to use their reason before they speak or act. According to Immanuel Kant, "Enlightenment is man's emergence from his self-imposed immaturity. Immaturity is the inability to use one's understanding without guidance from another. This immaturity is self-imposed when its cause lies not in lack of understanding, but in lack of resolve and courage to use it without guidance from another. Sapere Aude! [dare to know] "Have courage to use your own understanding!" - that is the motto of enlightenment"[21]. Resisting this mass mentality can only be done effectively by the person who understands his own individuality, says Carl Jung. He encourages an exploration of the 'microcosm - a reflection of the great cosmos in miniature'. We need to clean up our own house, put it in order before we can go ahead to put others and the rest of the world in order, because "Nemo dat quod non habet", "no one gives what he or she has not".

The Voice of the Soul Workshop is a golden opportunity designed to help participants make a transition from the attitude of mass-mindedness to reflective individuality, from passivity to activity, from discipleship to leadership, and from the attitude of receiving to that of giving. The goal is to help participants discover their potentials, the wealth of solutions and capabilities embedded within, which are

---

21 Immanuel Kant, An Answer to the Question: What is Enlightenment? Konigsberg in Prussia, 30 September 1784

◀ FROM CULTURAL JUSTICE TO INTER-ETHNIC MEDIATION

needed for the resolution of ethno-religious conflicts and development in Nigeria. It is aimed at bringing the participants to change their focus from the "externals"— what is out there— to the "internals"—what is going on inside them. At the end of the workshop, the participants are expected to achieve metanoia, a spontaneous attempt of the psyche to heal itself of unbearable conflict by melting down and then being reborn in a more adaptive form[22].

In the midst of so many distractions and allurements, accusations and blames, poverty, suffering, vice, crime and violent conflicts in Nigeria, the Voice of the Soul Workshop will offer the participants the opportunity to discover the beauties and positive realities of nature that each person carries within him or her, and the power of the "soul-life" that gently speaks to us in silence. The moderator of this workshop will ask the participants to "retire into the inner sanctuary of their own being, away from all the rush and so-called allurements of the outer life, and in the silence to listen to the voice of the soul, to hear its pleadings, to know its power"[23]. "If the mind is filled with high incentives, beautiful principles, royal, splendid, and uplifting efforts, the voice of the soul speaks and the evil and weaknesses born of the undeveloped and selfish side of our human nature cannot come in, so they will die out"[24].

Reflecting on the consequences of ethno-religious violent conflicts in Nigeria, each participant will be asked to present what contribution he or she (the participant himself or herself as a citizen of Nigeria with rights, responsibilities and obligations, and not the government, ethnic or religious leaders or others who hold public offices) will make or the roles he or she will play in order to restore peace and harmony among the different ethnic and religious groups in Nigeria. These unbiased resolutions will be collected. From this pool

---

22 From the Greek μετάνοια, metanoia is a change of mind or heart. Read Carl Jung's psychology, op cit.
23 Katherine Tingley, The Splendor of the Soul (Pasadena, California: Theosophical University Press), 1996, quotation taken from chapter one of the book, titled: "The Voice of the Soul", available at: http://www.theosociety.org/pasadena/splendor/spl-1a.htm. Katherine Tingley was leader of the Theosophical Society (then named the Universal Brotherhood and Theosophical Society) from 1896 to 1929, and is remembered particularly for her educational and social reform work centered at the Society's international headquarters at Point Loma, California.
24 Ibid.

of solutions, an action plan will be drafted and distributed at the end of the workshop. Such an inward exploration and group discussion will motivate participants to begin to appreciate one another as they are, without prejudices and erroneous preconceptions. It will spark-up an ardent and unreserved desire to collaborate actively in the processes of peace-building and peace-making.

The Voice of the Soul Workshop is an important exercise through which individuals are brought to the knowledge of their inner richness, capabilities, talents, strength, purposes, longings and visions. Instead of waiting for the government to restore peace and unity, the citizens are inspired and mobilized through this workshop to begin to take the bull by its horns in order to work for forgiveness, reconciliation, peace and unity. In the end, they are expected to learn to be responsible, courageous, and active, and spend less time talking about other people's weaknesses. As Katherine Tingley puts it, « think for a moment of the creations of men of genius. If they had stopped and turned back in doubt at the time when the divine impulse touched them, we should have no grand music, no beautiful paintings, no inspired art, and no marvelous inventions. These splendid, uplifting, creative forces originally come from man's divine nature. If we all lived in the consciousness and the conviction of our own great possibilities, we should realize that we are souls and that we too have divine privileges far beyond anything that we know of or even think of. Yet we throw these aside because they are not acceptable to our limited, personal selves. They do not fit in with our preconceived ideas. So we forget that we are a part of the divine scheme of life, that the meaning of life is sacred and holy, and we allow ourselves to drift back into the vortex of misunderstanding, misconception, doubt, unhappiness, and despair"[25].

The Voice of the Soul Workshop will help us go beyond misunderstandings, accusations, blames, fighting, ethno-religious differences and wars, and courageously stand up for forgiveness, reconciliation, peace, harmony, unity and development of our country Nigeria.

---

25   Ibid.

◀ FROM CULTURAL JUSTICE TO INTER-ETHNIC MEDIATION

THE SIGNS OF THE TIME WORKSHOP

In chapter seven of this book, causes of ethno-religious conflicts in Nigeria and some of the preventive measures already taken are summarized. We also identified seven steps through which ethno-religious conflicts are managed in Nigeria. These steps explain that:

1. The grievances expressed by ethno-religious groups that can lead to violent conflicts are ignored by the government and the security forces.
2. If the grievances are expressed in the course of time with publicity mediums, persistence and an ardent determination, the state and security forces will threaten those responsible. In some cases, some people may be arrested, detained and accused of sabotage. In general, these responses enrage the injured community and the government can be accused of partisanship.
3. Grievances may be expressed violently - resulting in violent conflict. The state sends the security forces to quell the conflicts or riots. Most of the time, excessive force is used.
4. The security forces will arrest and detain some people for allegedly having instigated conflict. These responses aggravate and cause more conflicts.
5. The government sets up a special committee to investigate the conflict, or a special military tribunal is established to try suspects, who, if convicted, will face a range of penalties, including a long-term imprisonment and death sentences.
6. This committee established by the government will submit a report, which can be accepted, modified, or rejected. Government decisions may or may not be made public, and may or may not be implemented. Meanwhile, the conflict which is temporarily calmed is expected to be resolved by the government.
7. The grievances, however, persist until another circle of violent expressions, and the government is also there to repeat the same process[26].

---
26 Read Etannibi E.O. Alemika, 2000; A Sociological Analysis of Ethnic and Religious Conflicts in the Middle Belt of Nigeria. In Ethnic and Religious Rights. A quarterly

FORMS OF INTER-ETHNIC MEDIATION

A careful analysis of these seven steps will explain why ethno-religious violent conflicts have proven to be unmanageable in Nigeria. Logically speaking, if adequate and careful attention is given to step one, then step three will be prevented. In other words, there is step three because step one has been ignored. Whenever grievances susceptible to violent conflicts are expressed by ethnic or religious groups, the principles of peace require that a proactive and responsible preventive measure should immediately be applied. Such a preventive response should be carried out, not only from the perspective of the "need" of the time, but following the idea of "urgency".

However, the major reason why these grievances are ignored, and early, urgent and adequate preventive measures are not taken may not be because of the attitude of negligence that is often noticed in the country, but because of the ignorance of their existence at the early stage and at the local levels. This ignorance is due to the lack of adequate and functioning Conflict Early Warning Systems (CEWS), or Conflict Early Warning and Response Mechanism (CEWARM) or Conflict Monitoring Networks (CMN) at the local levels. Conflict Early Warning Systems professionals are carefully trained with special competencies and skills that enable them listen attentively and become alert to the signs of the time.

The Signs of the Time Workshop is, therefore, aimed at training participants in Early Warning Systems (CEWS) or in conflict monitoring mechanisms. The primary objective of this workshop is to train participants in the different levels of ethno-religious conflict monitoring activities: identification of potential and imminent ethno-religious conflicts, conflict and data analysis, risk assessment or advocacy, reporting, identification of Quick Impact Projects (QIPs)[27]

---

publication of Human Rights Monitor, Special Edition, edited by Festus Okoye, April 2000, Kaduna Nigeria, p. 10.

27 Quick Impact Projects are small-scale, rapidly-implementable projects, of benefit to the population. These projects are used by UN peacekeeping operations to establish and build confidence in the mission, its mandate, and the peace process, thereby improving the environment for effective mandate implementation. For further reading, see United Nations Department of Peacekeeping Operations (DPKO) Policy Directive on Quick Impact Projects (QIPs), 12 February 2007.

and response mechanisms enabling urgent and immediate action that will avert the conflict or reduce the risk of escalation. The objective of conflict early warning and crisis prevention initiatives in this sense is to prevent the use of violence or to transform the violent conflict into a constructive dialogue[28]. Conflict early warning systems are designed to provide information on potential conflicts and threats to peace and security in a timely manner. The information is then processed to develop scenarios, anticipate most likely developments and to propose appropriate response options designed to prevent violent conflicts. An effective conflict early warning system should help to:
- identify the causes of conflict;
- anticipate possible directions in the escalation of conflict[29], and, most importantly;
- help in the mediation of that conflict by providing strategic advice to stakeholders and decision-makers.

At the end of the Signs of the Time Workshop, participants are expected to acquire skills in:
- monitoring and identification of potential and imminent ethno-religious conflicts;
- mediation and diplomacy, helping to serve as confidential and unbiased sources of information;
- analysis of any given situation to define and detect trends for future development;
- risk assessment;
- identification of Quick Impact Projects;
- response mechanisms enabling urgent and immediate action that will avert the conflict or reduce the risk of escalation.

WORKSHOP ON DIVERSITY AND THE CORE VALUES OF FAITH

[28] Niels von Keyserlingk and Simone Kopfmüller, Conflict Early Warning Systems, Lessons Learned from Establishing a Conflict Early Warning and Response Mechanism (CEWARN) in the Horn of Africa, available at: http://www.gtz.de/en/dokumente/en-igad-Conflict-Early-Warning-Systems-Lessons-Learned.pdf
[29] Ibid.

A workshop on diversity and the core values of faith will enable participants to be able to identify the fundamental values of these religions: Islam, Christianity, and African Traditional Religions (ATR). During this workshop, the mediators and trainers will pay maximum attention to and place strong emphasis on the unity of religions and on the interreligious fundamental values. Such an approach will help participants identify the fundamental values common to all religions (Islam, Christianity, African Traditional Religions), etc.

The Magnetic Force of Attraction Workshop

The magnetic force of attraction workshop aims at bringing the participants to reflect on the various common elements in the country that unite all the Nigerian citizens together. Instead of paying attention to what separates Nigerians, a maximum effort will be made to identify, appreciate, discuss, and strengthen those common elements that unite the citizens together. One of the symbolic elements that the participants will be asked to work on is the Nigerian National Flag, which is a symbol of fertility, national peace and unity. According to Agiri Chris, Director General of the Flag Foundation of Nigeria, "the importance of the national flag of Nigeria lies in the fact that each color represents the rich cultural heritage of the country. The green color represents the fertile land and agricultural diversity of the land and the white stands for peace and unity (…). Thus, the national flag of Nigeria truly reflects the Nigerian nationalistic fervor and sentiments."[30]

The "I am" Workshop

The "I am" workshop aims to teach participants the importance of accepting their fellow citizens the way they are irrespective of their ethnic, cultural and religious affiliations. It places emphasis on the three major methods of recognition, namely, "look at me", "listen to me", "I am who I am". This workshop will enable participants to be able to:

---

30 Agiri Chris, "Nigeria: Our History, Our Flag…" : A Brief Historical Background of the National Flag of Nigeria, article published at the website of the Flag Foundation of Nigeria (FFN), available at: http://flagfoundation.net/nigeria.php

- Present their own cultures to the other participants;
- Listen and learn something from the other cultures;
- Appreciate the cultures of each person.

At the end of this program, participants will be in a position to develop a simple but concrete action plan aimed at promoting tolerance, mutual understanding, cooperation, conflict resolution and peace, as well as the elimination of all forms of discrimination and intolerance. Participants will design and prepare both individual and group action plans that they will implement when they go back to their respective communities.

These resolutions or action plans stemming from the Peace Education Program constitute the anticipated results of ethno-religious mediation as discussed in this book. Among many anticipated concrete results, we examine only the following seven that participants are susceptible to initiating at the end of the ethno-religious mediation project. These action plans or resolutions include:

1. Networks of peace advocates;
2. Effective and efficient peacemakers through self-improvement;
3. Multiplying effect of the peace education program;
4. Inter-ethnic mediation through writing and music;
5. Spreading of ethno-religious mediation gains through creative activities;
6. Formation of organizations that promote inter-ethnic and inter-religious dialogues;
7. Community volunteering program or community service.

Network of Peace Advocates

After the peace education program, students or participants will create a database for social networking. They will feel the need to collect and develop a database of all participants who completed the peace education program. From this database, a network of peace advocates will be created. Through the development of this structure, young

FORMS OF INTER-ETHNIC MEDIATION

people who share the same culture of peace will be engaged in social relationships that will help promote peace in Nigeria and in Africa.

EFFECTIVE AND EFFICIENT PEACEMAKERS THROUGH SELF-IMPROVEMENT

After undergoing personal transformations through the peace education program and workshops, participants will see the need to continue to work on themselves (self-improvement) on their road to perfection in order to become effective and efficient peacemakers in their respective societies.

MULTIPLYING EFFECT OF THE PEACE EDUCATION PROGRAM

Given the effective nature of this program through the participatory learning of the students, some participants may take personal or group initiatives to conduct training workshops or seminars for others in their societies so that what they have learned (i.e., alternative methods of ethno-religious conflict resolution) will have a multiplying effect in the Nigerian societies.

INTER-ETHNIC MEDIATION THROUGH WRITING AND MUSIC

Many participants actively engage in journalism, poetry, music or in other forms of arts and literature in their schools. For this reason, some of them will develop an interest to spread inter-ethnic mediation through the power of writing and music. They can thus contribute to the establishment of peace by writing on the positive effects of inter-ethnic mediation and subsequently submit them for publication.

SPREADING ETHNO-RELIGIOUS MEDIATION GAINS THROUGH CREATIVE ACTIVITIES

There are so many creative, talented and skilled young people who are likely to participate in the Peace Education Program. Some of them may think of spreading the peace message through some form of interactive and entertaining activities with the aim of reaching out to people from diverse ethnic and religious backgrounds. These activities may include, among others, sports, arts and crafts, community projects, workshops and theater presentations, peace concerts, intercultural and interreligious festivals, music festivals, dance, and peace walk.

Formation of Organizations that Promote Inter-Ethnic and Inter-Religious Dialogues

For there to be continuity and sustainability in the ethno-religious mediation projects, the participants in the Peace Education Program will have to join or form their own organizations that will help promote inter-ethnic and interreligious dialogues. In this way, even after leaving their schools or communities, the members of these organizations could continue to develop and carry out projects related to inter-ethnic and inter-religious dialogues. In addition to this structural context of ethno-religious mediation, people with similar interests can share resources as well as support communications and relationships that enhance "confidence building". This will not only help to stop or prevent conflicts, but will also encourage the promotion of social harmony.

Community Volunteering Program or Community Service

At the end of the Peace Education Program, participants are encouraged to be involved in community service activities in their respective communities by doing something concrete such as working for the poor or the marginalized groups of the society. They can volunteer, participate in awareness programs, provide relief assistance, and organize fundraisers.

CHAPTER **10**

Ethno-Religious Mediation as a Device for Building Democracy in Africa

THIS BOOK HAS taught us the importance and relevance of ethno-religious mediation in Africa, and particularly in Nigeria. Since each ethnic group has a unique culture that distinguishes it from others, it was necessary to begin this study by understanding cultural justice, with an emphasis on the different types of minority rights.

As we have seen, ethno-religious conflicts in Africa are, in most cases, caused by injustice which in turn has many consequences. No country can therefore afford to allow these conflicts or ignore them. As a contribution to the ongoing research for new ways to resolve ethno-religious conflicts in Nigeria, we have proposed ethno-religious mediation.

We affirmed that ethno-religious conflicts which occur in a frequent, incessant and violent manner in our contemporary societies require a shift at the level of research for peaceful resolution, a shift in two stages: first, from retributive justice to restorative justice, and second, from coercive method to ethno-religious mediation.

Faced with cultural diversity and religious affiliations in some African countries like Nigeria, ethno-religious mediation could

FROM CULTURAL JUSTICE TO INTER-ETHNIC MEDIATION

prove to be a unique means for the consolidation of peace, mutual understanding, dialogue, mutual recognition, development and unity in democracy. In addition, ethno-religious mediation can create an opportunity for civic education organized by and for the citizens, since it is intended to shake up long held positions and enable the birth of a mutual recognition and consensus building.

In this respect, the different ethnic or religious groups in Africa can resolve their conflicts and reach a consensus through discussion and confrontation of arguments in a free space of mediation while respecting the rules of mediation and the opinions and personal views of all concerned[31]. This mediation process encourages inter-subjectivity, the birth of a community of free men and women, and above all, it promotes democracy.

Therefore, we conclude by re-affirming that ethno-religious mediation can be a very important and valuable device for building democracy in Africa.

---

31 To discover the notion of consensus through discussion and confrontation of arguments, see Jürgen Habermas, De l'éthique de la discussion (Paris, « champs », Flammarion, 1992)

Acknowledgements

I WOULD LIKE to extend my heartfelt thanks to those who have given me their support and who, in one way or another, contributed to the realization of this book.

I wish to thank Dr. Corine Pelluchon, Director of Professional Masters in Mediation at the Université de Poitiers, France.

My gratitude also goes to Prof. Jean-Claude Bourdin, Founder and former Director of Professional Masters: Mediation in Organizations for his generosity and support despite his academic and professional activities.

I express my deep gratitude to Prof. Ernest Uwazie, Director of the "Center for African Peace and Conflict Resolution," California State University, Sacramento, United States, who inspired this research during my stay in his center as an International Research Scholar.

I cannot forget the Schoenstatt Fathers Community, especially Reverend Father Alfred Kistler and Very Reverend Father Edwin Germann, for their financial support, and without whom this book would not have been written.

I wish to express my gratitude to Mr. Modem Lawson-Betum, West African Team Leader in Africa 2 Division, Department of Political Affairs, United Nations Headquarters New York, who was kind to proofread and correct the first manuscript. Similarly, many thanks go to Mr. Joseph C. Kunav and Mr. Michael Ashamu for their constructive and critical evaluation of the manuscript. Their corrections and suggestions added flavor to this book.

Finally, I extend my sincere thanks to all the members of my family, and to Diomaris Gonzalez-Ugorji, my beloved wife, who has always supported and encouraged me, especially during the realization of this project.

Thanks to all of you who are ready to read this book.

Basil UGORJI
Wednesday, January 18, 2012
Mount Vernon, New York, United States

Bibliography

ALABI, Julius, "Ijaw, Ilaje Communities Embrace Truce", The Vanguard, 18 August 1999.

ANDERSON, Benedict, Imagined Communities: Reflections on the Origin and Spread of Nationalism, London: Verso, 1983.

ARISTOTE, l'Ethique à Nicomaque, Mémoire V, §15, 20, trad. Richard Bodéüs, Flammarion, 2004.

---------- Ethica Nicomachea, Translated by W.D. Ross, in The Basic Works of Aristotle, Edited by Richard McKeon, New York: Random House.

ALBERT, I. O., "Ethnic and Religious conflicts in Kano", in Otite and Albert (eds): Community Conflicts In Nigeria, Ibadan: Spectrum Books, 1999.

---------- Ife – Modakeke crisis, 1999. In Otite, O. and Albert, I. S, Community conflict in Nigeria: Management, Resolution and Transformation, Ibadan: Spectrum Books, 2001.

---------- Inter-ethnic Relations in a Nigerian City: The Historical Perspective of the Hausa-Igbo Conflicts in Kano, 1953-1991, Ibadan: Institut Francais de recherche en Afrique, 1993.

------------ Building Peace, Advancing Democracy: Experience with Third-Party Interventions in Nigeria's Conflicts, Ibadan, John archers Ltd., 2001.

AKINTEYE, O., "Zangon-Kataf Crisis: A Case Study", (pp 222-245), in O. Otite and I. O. Albert (eds.), Communal Conflict in Nigeria, Management, Resolution and Transformation, Ibadan: Spectrum Books, 1999.

AGUDA, A. S., "The effect of communal conflict and violence on urban residential segregation" A paper presented at the International Conference on Security, Segregation and Social Networks in West African Cities 19th to 20th centuries Organized by the French Institute for Research in Africa (IFRA) and Institute of African studies and Centre for Urban and Regional Planning, University of Ibadan, Ibadan Nigeria, 29th to 31st October 2001.

AUGSBURGER, D. W., Conflict mediation across culture: pathway and pattern, Alouisville, Kentucky: Westminster john Knox Press, 1992.

ACHUZIA, J. O. G., Requiem Biafra, Enugu: Fourth Dimension Publishing Co., 1986.

AKINJOGBIN, I. A., "Ife: The years of Travail 1793-1893", in I. A. Akinjogbin (ed.), The cradle of race: Ife from beginning to 1980, Port Harcourt: Sunray Publications, 1992.

AFIGBO, A.E., "Federal Character: Its Meaning And History", in P.P Ekeh and E. Osaghae, (eds), Federal Character And Federalism In Nigeria, Ibadan: Heinemann, 1989.

ALEMIKA, Etannibi, A Sociological Analysis of Ethnic and Religious Conflicts in the Middle Belt of Nigeria, in Ethnic and

Religious Rights, A quarterly publication of Human Rights Monitor, Special Edition, edited by Festus Okoye, Kaduna Nigeria, 2000.

ALUYOR, Victoria, Massacre in another Delta Community, Chevron's New Year Gift: The Opia and Ikiyan Massacre Dispatch Line: Opia & Ikiyan 1999, [en ligne] http://www.mailarchive.com/ctrl@listserv.aol.com/msg03287.html

AZAR, Edwards, The Management Of Protracted Social Conflict: Theory And Cases, Dartmouth, Aldershot, 1990.

Association of Itsekiri people in the United States, Who are the Itsekiri? [en ligne] http://www.itsekiri.org/files/history/history_itsekiri.php

BALL, T., FARR J. & HANSON R.C. eds., "Citizenship" in Political Innovation and Conceptual Change, Cambridge: Cambridge University Press, 1989.

BINGEL, Anthony Dung, Jos: Origins and Growth of the Town 1900-1972, Jos: Department of Geography Publication, 1978.

BRAITHWAITE, J., Restorative Justice & Responsive Regulation, Oxford University Press, 2002.

BENATARI, Benaebi, "Ijaw History" published by the IJAW FOUNDATION [en ligne] http://www.ijawfoundation.org/people.htm

CARENS, Joseph, Equality, Moral Incentives and the Market, Chicago: Chicago University Press, 1981.

CICERO's De Legibus, 106 BC.

CAVADINO, M & DIGNAN, J., The Penal System: An Introduction (2nd ed.), London: Sage, 1997.

CRAWFORD, James and MARKS Susan, The global democratic deficit: An essay in international law and its limits, In Re-imagining political community: Studies in cosmopolitan democracy, ed. D. Archibugi, D. Held, and M. Kohler, Stanford: Stanford University Press, 1998.

COLEMAN, James, Nigeria: Background To Nationalism, Berkeley and Los Angeles, 1958.

COLEMAN, P. T., "Characteristics of Protracted, Intractable Conflict: Towards the Development of a Meta-Framework," – I, Peace and Conflict: Journal of Peace Psychology, 2003, 9(1), 1-37.

Constitution of the Federal Republic of Nigeria, 1999: Introduction, [en ligne] http://www.nigeria-law.org/ConstitutionOfTheFederalRepublicOfNigeria.htm

Crisis Group Africa Briefing N°115, The Swamps of Insurgency: Nigeria's Delta Unrest, 3 August 2006.

DAYO, Johnson and AHIUMA-YOUNG Victor, "Bloodletting Continues", Lagos: The Vanguard, 10 August 1999.

DWORKIN, Ronald, "What is Equality? Part 1: Equality of Resources", Philosophy and Public Affairs, 1981.

------------ "What is Equality? Part 2: Equality of Welfare", Philosophy and Public Affairs, 1981.

DINSMOR, Alastair, "Glasgow Police Pioneers": The Scotia News [en ligne] http://www.scotia-news.com/issue5/ISSUE05a.htm.

------------ "History", Marine Support Unit : Metropolitan Police [en ligne] http://web.archive.org/web/20070716200107/, http://www.met.police.uk/msu/history.htm

Deadly Nigeria clashes spread, Last Modified: 27 Jul 2009 [en ligne] http://english.aljazeera.net/news/africa/2009/07/2009727134953755877.html

DENT, M. "Ethnicity and Territorial Politics in Nigeria", in Graham Smith (ed.), Federalism: The Multi-Ethnic Challenge, London and New York: Longman, 1995.

DICK, James, "How to Justify a Distribution of Earnings", Philosophy and Public Affairs, 1975.

DYKE, V. van, "The Individual, the State, and Ethnic Communities in Political Theory" 29 World Pol. 1977.

DEUTSH, Morton, "Justice and Conflict", in The Handbook of Conflict Resolution: Theory and Practice, M. Deutsch and P. Coleman, eds. San Francisco: Jossey-Bass Publishers, 2000.

DEREK, Parfit, Reasons and Persons, Oxford: Oxford University Press, 1986.

Ethnologue Languages of the World: Language Family Trees, [en ligne] http://www.ethnologue.com/show_family.asp?subid=2050-16

FEINBERG, Joel, "Justice and Personal Desert", Doing and Deserving, Princeton, NJ, Princeton University Press, 1970.

FBI, THE FBI: A Centennial History, 1908-2008, Washington, D.C.: FBI, 2009.

GURR, Ted, Why Men Rebel, Princeton, 1970.

GURR, Ted and HARFF B., Ethnic Conflict In World Politics, San Francisco: West View Press, 1994.

GUTMANN, A., "The Challenge of Multiculturalism in Political Ethics", 22 Phil. & Pub. Affairs, 1993.

GLAZER, N., and MOYNIHAN D.P., eds, Ethnicity And Experience, Atlanta Georgia: Harvard University Press, 1975.

GARVEY, A. Yawe, Committee Report Investigating the Kutebs/Jukuns-chamba Conflict, Office of the Governor, Taraba State, April-May, 1993.

GARLAND, David, "Of Crimes and Criminals", in Maguire, Mike, Rod Morgan, Robert Reiner, The Oxford Handbook of Criminology, 3rd edition, Oxford University Press, 2002.

HABERMAS, Jürgen, De l'éthique de la discussion, Paris : « champs », Flammarion, 1992.

-------------- Morale et communication, Théorie de l'agir communicationnel, t.2, Paris: Fayard, 1987.

HAYEK, F. A., The Constitution of Liberty, Chicago, The University of Chicago Press, 1960.

HOULT, T. F., ed. Dictionary of Modern Sociology, 1969.

HUSSAINI, Abdu, "Religion and the challenges of Democratization And National Integration in Nigeria. Equal Justice, Kaduna: HRM, 2000.

----------- Ethnic and Religious Crises in Northern Nigeria; Issues in Informer Repression, Department Of Political Science And Defence Studies, Nigerian Defence Academy Kaduna, [en ligne] http://hussainiabdu.info/My_Articles

HOROWITZ, Donald, Ethnic Groups In Conflict, Berkeley: University of California press, 1985.

HANNUM, Hurst, Autonomy, sovereignty and self-determination: The accommodation of conflicting rights, Philadelphia, PA: The University of Pennsylvania Press, 1990.

Human Rights Watch Nigeria, « Crackdown in Niger Delta, May 1999, Vol. 11, No. 2 (A), [en ligne] http://www.legaloil.com/Documents/Library/HRW1999a.pdf

Human Rights Watch, "The Warri Crisis: Fueling Violence", November 2003.

History of the Kuteb people, [en ligne] http://kuteb.tripod.com/biography.html

HARPER, Douglas, "Police": Online Etymology Dictionary, [en ligne] http://www.etymonline.com/index.php?term=police

HALLER, Tobias, Fossile Ressourcen, Erdölkonzerne und indigene Völker, Giessen : Focus Verlag, 2000.

« Ijaw People », [en ligne] http://ijaw-people.co.tv/

IBRAHIM, Jibrin, The Politics of Religion In Nigeria: The Parameters of 1987 Crisis In Kaduna State, 1987.

IMOBIGHE, A. Thomas, Conflict in Niger Delta: A Unique Case or a 'Model' for Future Conflicts in Other Oil-Producing Countries?

FRIEDRICH-EBERT-STIFTUNG [en ligne] http://library.fes.de/pdf-files/iez/02115/imobighe.pdf

International Crisis Group, Fuelling the Niger Delta Crisis; Africa Report N°118 – 28 September 2006.

Immigration and Refugee Board of Canada, Nigeria: The conflict between Itsekiri and Ijaw ethnic groups in Warri, Delta region (March 1997-September 1999), 14 September 1999, NGA32676.E, [en ligne] http://www.unhcr.org/refworld/docid/3ae6ad6864.html [accessed 17 March 2011]

Immigration and Refugee Board of Canada, Nigeria: The Ijaw-Itsekiri conflict in Delta State, including time period, causes, whether the authorities intervened, whether the police support the Ijaw or Itsekiri and the current situation, April 1998, NGA29098.E, [en ligne] http://www.unhcr.org/refworld/docid/3ae6abe720.html [accessed 17 March 2011]

« International Foundation for Election Systems, Washington, DC 20005, Nigeria: Attitudes Toward Democracy And Markets in Nigeria, Report of a National Opinion Survey », 2000, [en ligne] http://www.ifes.org/~/media/Files/Publications/Survey/2004/248/Nigeria_00_PO.pdf.

JEGA, A.M., Tackling Ethno-Religious Conflicts in Nigeria: The Nigeria Social Scientist 5 (2), 2002.

JAMES, Rachels, The Elements of Moral Philosophy, 2007.

Jung, Carl (2006). The Undiscovered Self: The Problem of the Individual in Modern Society. New American Library.

Jung, C. G. (1989a). Memories, Dreams, Reflections (Rev. ed., C. Winston & R. Winston, Trans.) (A. Jaffe, Ed.). New York: Random House, Inc.

Jeune Afrique : «Somalie: un obus de mortier tue 14 personnes à Mogadiscio dans une mosquée, 10/05/2009, [en ligne] http://www.jeuneafrique.com/actu/20090510T152620Z20090510T141610Z/actualite-afriquesomalie-un-obus-de-mortier-tue-14-personnes-a-mogadiscio-dans-une-mosquee.html

Kant, Immanuel, An Answer to the Question: What is Enlightenment? Konigsberg in Prussia, 30 September 1784

KAZAH–TOURE T. Kazah-Toure, "Inter-Ethnic Relations, Conflicts and Nationalism in Zangon-Kataf Area of Northern Nigeria: Historical Origins and Contemporary Forms." Paper presented at the 8th CODESRIA General Assembly, Dakar, 1995.

KYMLICKA, Will and COHEN-ALMAGOR Raphael, Democracy and Multiculturalism, in R. Cohen-Almagor, Editor, Challenges to Democracy: Essays in Honour and Memory of Isaiah Berlin, London: Ashgate Publishing Ltd., 2000.

KYMLICKA, Will and NORMAN Wayne, Citizenship in culturally diverse societies: Issues, contexts, concepts, in Citizenship in diverse societies, ed. Will Kymlicka and Wayne Norman, 1-41. Oxford: Oxford University Press, 2000.

KYMLICKA, Will, Contemporary Political Philosophy, Oxford: Clarendon Press, 1990.

------------- Multicultural Citizenship: A Liberal Theory of Minority Rights, Oxford: Clarendon Press, 1995.

------------- Liberalism, Community and Culture, Oxford: Clarendon Press, 1989.

KONOW, James, "Which Is the Fairest One of All? A Positive Analysis of Justice Theories," Journal of Economic Literature 41, 2003.

LIEBMANN, M., Restorative Justice: How it Works, London: Jessica Kingsley Publishers, 2007.

LAKES, D. A. and ROTHSCHILD Donald, "Containing fear: The Origins and Management Of Ethnic Conflict," International Security, vol. 21, no. 2, 1996.

LAMONT, Julian, "Incentive Income, Deserved Income, and Economic Rents", Journal of Political Philosophy, 1997.

Lettre datée du 15 décembre 1999, adressée au Secrétaire général par les membres de la Commission indépendante d'enquête sur les actions de l'Organisation des Nations Unies lors du génocide de 1994 au Rwanda, [en ligne] http://www.un.org/french/documents/view_doc.asp?symbol=S/1999/1257

LODGE, Tom, Towards an Understanding of Contemporary Armed Conflicts in Africa: Monograph No 36: Whither Peacekeeping in Africa? April 1999, [en ligne] http://www.iss.co.za/pubs/monographs/No36/ArmedConflict.html

MADIEBO, A. A., The Nigerian Revolution and the Biafra War, Enugu: Fourth Dimension Publishing Co., 1980.

MARTY, Price, J.D. "Personalizing Crime," Dispute Resolution Magazine, Fall 2001.

MAGNE, Oven Varsi, World Marks 15th Anniversary of Nigeria's Writer and Human Rights Activist's Murder, article modifié le 12.11.2010 par GALDU Resource Centre for the Rights of the Indigenous Peoples, [en ligne] http://www.galdu.org/web/index.php?odas=4908&giella1=eng

McGREW, W.C., «Culture in Nonhuman Primates?" Annual Review of Anthropology 27, 1998.

--- Chimpanzee Material Culture: Implications for Human Evolution". Cambridge University Press, 1992

MONTY, G. Marshall and GURR Ted, Peace and Conflict: A Global Survey Of Armed Conflicts, Self Determination Movements and Democracy: Center For International Development and Conflict Management, University of Maryland, 2003.

MARTIN, Jacqueline, The English Legal System (4th ed.), London: Hodder Arnold, 2005.

MILLER, David, Social Justice, Oxford: Clarendon Press, 1976.

--- Market, State, and Community, Oxford: Clarendon Press, 1989.

MILNE, Heather, "Desert, effort and equality", Journal of Applied Philosophy, 1986.

MOHAMMED, H., Plateau Crises: The Press as the No.1. Culprit, Daily Trust, June 30, 2004.

MATHIASON, Nick, Shell in court over alleged role in Nigeria executions: The Observer, Sunday 5 April 2009, [en ligne] http://www.guardian.co.uk/business/2009/apr/05/shell-saro-wiwa-execution-charges

MUNHOLLAND, K.A., Bretherton I, (1999). "Internal Working Models in Attachment Relationships: A Construct Revisited". In Cassidy J, Shaver PR. Handbook of Attachment: Theory, Research and Clinical Applications. New York: Guilford Press

NATHANSO, Stephen (1989), "In Defense of 'Moderate Patriotism'," Ethics, 99: 535–552. Reprinted in Primoratz (ed.) (2002).

--- (1993), Patriotism, Morality, and Peace, Lanham: Rowman & Littlefield.

NIELS, von Keyserlingk and Simone Kopfmüller, Conflict Early Warning Systems, Lessons Learned from Establishing a Conflict Early Warning and Response Mechanism (CEWARN) in the Horn of Africa, available at: http://www.gtz.de/en/dokumente/en-igad-Conflict-Early-Warning-Systems-Lessons-Learned.pdf

NKORO, Emeka, Conflict In the Niger Delta: the Way Forward, article published by Searchwarp le 11 octobre 2005, [en ligne] http://searchwarp.com/swa20447.htm

NEOCLEOUS, Mark, Fabricating Social Order: A Critical History of Police Power, London: Pluto Press, 2004.

NOZICK, Robert, Anarchy, State and Utopia, New York: Basic Books, 1974.

NNOLI, Okwudiba, Ethnic Politics In Nigeria, Enugu: Fourth Dimension Press, 1980.

BIBLIOGRAPHY

NNIMMO, Bassey, "Trade and Human Rights in the Niger Delta of Nigeria, June 2006, publié par Pambazuka News, [en ligne] http://www.pambazuka.org/en/category/comment/34801

NGAYIMPENDA, Evariste, "Histoire du conflit politico-ethnique burundais: Les premières marches du calvaire 1960-1973, Bujumbura: Editions de la Renaissance, 2007.

« National Population Commission of Nigeria » au Journal officiel de la République fédérale du Nigéria, vol. 96, n ° 2 du 2 Février 2009, [en ligne] http://www.population.gov.ng/index.php?id=3

OKWUDIBA, Nnoli, Ethnic Politics In Nigeria, Enugu: Fourth Dimension Press, 1980.

OMOROGBE, S.K. and OMOHAN M.E., Causes and Management of Ethno-Religious Conflicts: The Nigeria Experience, in A.M. Yakubu, et al (eds) Crisis and Conflict Management in Nigeria Since 1980, Vol. 2. P. 557, Kaduna: Baraka Press and Publishers Ltd., 2005.

OROMAREGHAKE, P. and AKPOTOR J.D., Managing Inter-ethnic Conflicts in the Niger- Delta: The Case of Warri in A.M. Yakubu et al (eds) Crisis and Conflict Management in Nigeria Since 1980 Vol. 2, Kaduna: Baraka Press and Publishers Ltd., 2005.

OMOTAYO, Bukky, "Women and conflict in the new information age: Virtual Libraries to the rescue" A paper presented at the World Library and Information Congress: 71th IFLA General Conference and Council "Library - a voyage of discovery" Oslo, Norway, August 15th – 18th 2005.

Préfecture de Police au service des Parisiens, "La Lieutenance Générale de Police" : La Préfecture de Police fête ses 200 ans Juillet 1800 - Juillet 2000, [en ligne) http://www.prefecturepoliceparis. interieur.gouv.fr/documentation/bicentenaire/theme_expo1.htm.

President's Commission on Law Enforcement and Administration of Justice: The Challenge of Crime in a Free Society, U.S. Government Printing Office, 1967.

PLOTNICOV, Leonard, Strangers in the City: Urban Man in Jos, Nigeria, University of Pittsburg Press, 1967.

Primoratz, Igor, "Patriotism", The Stanford Encyclopedia of Philosophy (Summer 2009 Edition), Edward N. Zalta (ed.), URL = <http://plato.stanford.edu/archives/sum2009/entries/patriotism/>.

Q&A: Sudan's Darfur conflict, BBC News, Page last updated at 14:39 GMT, Tuesday, 23 February 2010 [en ligne] http://news.bbc.co.uk/2/hi/africa/3496731.stm

RAWLS, John, A Theory of Justice, Harvard, MA: Harvard University Press, 1971.

------------ A Theory of Justice, revised edition, Oxford: Oxford University Press, 1999.

---------- Political Liberalism, New York: Columbia University Press, 1993.

RICOEUR, Paul, Le conflit des interprétations, Editions du Seuil, Paris, 1969.

ROGGE, John R., Draft Report: "The Internal Displaced Population in Western, Nyanza and Rift Valley Provinces: A Needs Assessment and Rehabilitation Programme", April 28, 1993.

RILEY, Jonathan, "Justice Under Capitalism", Markets and Justice, ed. John W. Chapman, New York: New York University Press, 1989.

ROTHSCHILD, Donald, Managing Ethnic Conflict In Africa: Pressures And Incentives For Cooperation, Brookings Press, 1997.

Report of Oputa Panel, vol. 2, [en ligne] http://www.nigerianmuse.com/nigeriawatch/oputa/OputaVolumeTwo.pdf

SHAWULU, Rima, The Politics of the Ethnic and Religious Conflicts of Taraba state, in Festus Okoye (ed), Ethnic and Religious Rights in Nigeria, Kaduna: Human Rights Monitor Publications, 1988.

Scottish Executive Consultations, Criminal Justice - Aims and Objectives, [en ligne] http://www.cjsonline.gov.uk/the_cjs/aims_and_objectives/index.html

SCHMOLKA, Vicki, "Principles to Guide Criminal Law Reform", Department of Justice, Government of Canada, [en ligne] http://www.justice.gc.ca/en/cons/roundtable/nov102/appendixb.html.

STOCKING, G. W., Franz Boas Reader: Shaping of American Anthropology, 1883–1911 (1982); biography by M. J. Herskovits (1953, repr. 1973) in The Columbia Electronic Encyclopedia, 6th ed., Columbia University Press, 2007.

SHEDRACK, Gaya Best, Communal Conflicts Management: The Jukun/Chamba-Kuteb Conflicts in Takum, Taraba State, A Research Report conducted under the auspices of Academic Associates Peace Works, Ikeja, Lagos, Funded by the British Council in Nigeria. December, 1998.

SADURSKI, Wojciech, Giving Desert Its Due, Dordrecht, Holland: D. Reidel, 1985.

« Sufi Islam » sous le titre : « Military » [en ligne] http://www.globalsecurity.org/military/intro/islam-sufi.htm

TINGLEY, Katherine, The Splendor of the Soul (Pasadena, California: Theosophical University Press), 1996

UMEAGBALASI, Emeka, Jos crisis: Saving Nigeria from the brinks: Vanguard, [en ligne] http://www.vanguardngr.com/2011/01/jos-crisis-saving-nigeria-from-the-brinks/

UNESCO, Conférence mondiale sur les politiques culturelles, Mexico City, 26 juillet - 6 août 1982, [en ligne] http://portal.unesco.org/culture/fr/ev.php-URL_ID=34321&URL_DO=DO_TOPIC&URL_SECTION=201.html

--- Convention for the Safeguarding of the Intangible Cultural Heritage 2003, Paris, 17 October 2003

United Nations Department of Peacekeeping Operations (DPKO) Policy Directive on Quick Impact Projects (QIPs), 12 February 2007.

WALKER, Samuel, A Critical History of Police Reform: The Emergence of Professionalism, Lexington, MT: Lexington Books, 1977.

WALDRON, J., "Minority Cultures and the Cosmopolitan Alternative", 1992.

WEBSTER, Merriam, Encyclopedia Britannica Company, [en ligne] http://www.merriam-webster.com/dictionary/injustice

WEBBER, Rebecca, A New Kind of Criminal Justice, [en ligne] http://www.parade.com/news/intelligence-report/archive/091025-a-new-kind-of-criminal-justice.html

---------- "Can Communal Goods Be Human Rights?" in J. Waldron, Liberal Rights: Collected Papers 1981-199 1, Cambridge: Cambridge University Press, 1993.

YA'U Y.Z., "Participation of Shi'at and Almajirai In Religious Conflicts In Northern Nigeria", In Okoye F. (ed), Ethnic and Religious Rights in Nigeria, Kaduna: Human Monitor, 1998.

ZEHR, H. The Little Book of Restorative Justice, Intercourse, PA: Good Books, 2002.